DEMONS & DEPRESSION, MENTAL ILLNESS & POSSESSION

A. POSKITT

DEMONS & DEPRESSION,

MENTAL ILLNESS & POSSESSION

First Published 2018

2021 Revised Edition

© Copyright A. Poskitt.

All Rights Reserved

Some names, identifying details and terminology in this book have been adapted to protect the privacy of individuals, and safeguard freedom of thought.

Email:

alan.poskitt2@gmail.com

One of Satan's greatest tricks is convincing
the world he doesn't exist.

Hell can be inside your head.

"I started to focus and ponder on the minutiae of life, gazing at objects and textures where previously they'd been unexceptional and insignificant background items. The tiniest bubbles in the glaze of a vase or a previously unseen knot of woodgrain in a doorframe was momentous and a highly unwelcome magnet for my attention. I would see an eye or often an evil face staring back at me – that 'looking into my soul' sensation accompanied by the notion that the object had a baleful life force pulsing through it. A discarded tissue on a bedside table could take on the features of a wicked old crone, or a sofa cushion would have to be hurriedly re-plumped to smooth away the crumpled goblin eyes staring into me.

Flicking through a number of medical guides, I eventually found one that listed LSD in the index. Scanning quickly through I reached a page that sent a gradual, growing shockwave through me like that fright you get when a low flying jet flies suddenly overhead as you grit your teeth and stand motionless because your brain can't figure out fast enough what it is, or what to do about it.

Gulping, I gripped the reference book in both hands, fidgeting with the sensation I was going to wet my pants in panic as I re-read the terrifying conclusion:

"LSD and Mental Illness: A psychotic reaction from LSD can be a dangerous condition with symptoms related to schizophrenia. Some people never recover from an acid-induced psychosis."

CONTENTS

PREFACE – What You Need to Know About Mental Illness   7
Acknowledgements   10

Part One - *My Story*   11

INTRODUCTION – Penned by a Madman?   12
CHAPTER 1 – Childhood's End   19
CHAPTER 2 – The Event   22
CHAPTER 3 – Mushroom Tea   27
CHAPTER 4 – Dropping Acid   30
CHAPTER 5 – Bedroom   35
CHAPTER 6 – The New Planet   38
CHAPTER 7 – A Short Pause   41
CHAPTER 8 – Psychotic Reaction   43
CHAPTER 9 – Hallucinogen Phobia   46
CHAPTER 10 – Bleak House   50
CHAPTER 11 – Bed Tremors   53
CHAPTER 12 – Low Summer   57
CHAPTER 13 – A Dreary Outlook   60
CHAPTER 14 – Climate Change   66
CHAPTER 15 – Sunny Spells   69
CHAPTER 16 – Early, Perilous Spiritual Steps   72
CHAPTER 17 – Taming the Party Animal   75
CHAPTER 18 – The Door Openers   81
CHAPTER 19 – Nursery Rhymes, Tonsillitis and
         Fabric Conditioner   84
CHAPTER 20 – Spiritual Attack   91

Part Two – *Spiritual Truths*   97

CHAPTER 21 – More Questions than Answers   98
CHAPTER 22 – Spirit is Not Unscientific   102
CHAPTER 23 – Old Fashioned Truths Meet
         Modern Psychiatry   105
CHAPTER 24 – The Truth is Out of This World,
         or Perhaps Not   111
     - *Possess or Oppress?*   113
CHAPTER 25 – Why do Demons Possess People?   115
CHAPTER 26 – Symptoms of Demonic Possession   118
CHAPTER 27 – Who is Susceptible?   121
CHAPTER 28 – Environmental Factors   125

CHAPTER 29 – Measuring the Immeasurable   129
CHAPTER 30 – An Evil Elephant in the Room   132
CHAPTER 31 – Possession in the Bible   135
CHAPTER 32 – Common Causes of Possession Today   138
CHAPTER 33 – Causes of Possession: Occult and Witchcraft   141
    - *Ouija*   143
    - *Channelling*   145
    - *Divination: Fortune Telling and Tarot*   147
    - *Objects and Curios*   149
CHAPTER 34 – Causes of Possession: Drugs and Sorcery   151
    - *Modern Sorcery*   151
    - *Vaccines*   157
    - *Psychedelics and Hallucinogens,*
      DMT, Nootropics etc.   163
    - *Cannabis / Marijuana*   167
    - *Alcohol*   167
CHAPTER 35 – Causes of Possession: Sexual Perversion
    & Promiscuity   170
    - *Sodomy*   173
    - *Paedophilia and Other Paraphilia*   180
CHAPTER 36 – Causes of Possession: Religion and Spirituality   183
    - *Islam or Mohammedanism*   184
    - *Eastern Mysticism*   187
    - *Hinduism*   188
    - *Judaism*   189
    - *Pseudo-Christian Cults*   186
    - *Other Cults and Affiliations*   192
    - *Angel Worship*   200
CHAPTER 37 – Causes of Possession: Deliberate Invitation   204
    - *'Selling your Soul' and Generational Satanism*   204
CHAPTER 38 – Causes of Possession: Programming   206
    - *Self Harming Behaviours*   210
    - *Eating Disorders*   211
CHAPTER 39 – Causes of Possession: Trauma and Shock   213
CHAPTER 40 – Causes of Possession: Technology   215
    - *Electromagnetic and Microwave Radiation*   216
    - *Genetic Engineering*   221
    - *CERN*   221
CHAPTER 41 – Causes of Possession: The UFO
    and Alien Deception   225
    - *It's Just a Theory*   226
    - *Space Brothers?*   228
CHAPTER 42 – Concluding Thoughts   238

Part Three – *Salvation, Deliverance and Healing*   241

CHAPTER 43 – How to Be Saved   242
     - The Sinner's Prayer   248
CHAPTER 44 – Spiritual Refreshment   252
     - Deliverance   252
CHAPTER 45 – The Future is Bright   254
CHAPTER 46 – 15 Pieces of Advice for the Mentally Ill   256
CHAPTER 47 – Words of Wisdom for Recovery   266
     - Bible verses   266
     - Non-biblical quotes   267
REFERENCES   268

PREFACE

What You Need to Know About Mental Illness

This is my story about how mental illness invaded my teenage life and how it changed me, initially for the worse, but in retrospect, for the better.

Had I not experienced the trauma of it I would not be the person I am today: hopeful, happy, often joyful, and generally very content in spite of life's typical ups and downs. My family would beg to differ on occasions as I often rant at people on the TV and can be a bit of a moan, but really, the gist of it is I now have a deep spiritual peace that came indirectly as a result of mental suffering.

Psychosis, or more accurately 'depressive psychosis' changed my perception about so many things and it certainly changed my attitude about taking normal, everyday life for granted. It also convinced me that many types of mental illness can be caused and energised by demonic spiritual entities when certain factors come together to allow their influence to oppress and even possess an individual.

How I got my form of mental illness may not be a typical scenario, but it's certainly not unique. My illness was triggered by recreational drug use, but I know there are many other contributory factors from physiological changes such as puberty; menopause and andropause; genetic or hereditary influences as well as social facilitators including unstable home life; sexual or emotional abuse; relationship breakdowns; trauma; sudden shock; mid-life crises; bereavement; medication reactions, alcoholism and so on.

For most people, developing mental illness is a gradual process and the culmination of many factors including cultural ones. In my case, there was a gradual lead up to the major form of depressive psychosis that afflicted me, with a distinct detonating event that changed a general low mood in my late teens to a disposition of extreme anxiety, profound despair and even desire for death. The spark was LSD.

Thirty five years later I sit down to write this book. It is the right time to do so because if I had started earlier I would never have grasped some of the issues I needed to convey which have arisen through maturity and experience; especially that of spiritual discernment.

Whatever the unique components of your own or your loved one's psychosis and whatever medical classification you or your doctor prefer to apply to it; schizophrenia, delusions, anxiety with depression, bi-polar or a mixture of all of them, it's quite immaterial, because simply put, you already know you have one of the worst conditions you've ever experienced or ever likely to endure this side of eternity. Your story and my story, although the details will differ, will nevertheless share common ground with many symptoms and descriptions of anguish and despair remarkably alike between us.

The 25th November 1983 marked the opening volley of my mental illness. It was the lighting-the-fuse moment for my psychotic cannon so to speak, although the priming of it had been going on for years and the trajectory of my particular projectile (toward a mental breakdown) had started in early childhood, building impetus as the years progressed. Had the fuse not been lit that night I am sure it would have been kindled later by another event.

I am relieved I got my mental illness over and done with when my life was relatively uncomplicated, with few responsibilities, no children to nurture or significant bills to pay which required the holding down of a steady job, because I firmly doubt I could have coped. I expect that had I been married at this time, my struggle may have damaged, if not ended any relationship, whereas in 1983 I had the excuse of being a single, rather unconventional young man and the hellish hiatus that put my life on hold for around 18 months I remarkably managed to conceal from even close family members who deemed my moodiness and restlessness simply components of late teenage angst.

The decision to hide my distress from my loving mother, my family and doctors was in some respects a bad thing to do given my suicide ideation, but I don't think that mental health practitioners doling out experimental psychotropic drug cocktails in the 1980s would have improved my situation and may well have made it worse.

Such was my success in cloaking my illness it comes as no surprise when I hear that others have managed to pull it off too, as I listen to the reports of suicides in the news with clichéd expressions of 'disbelief' from family members, uttering statements like, "We had no idea he was even depressed", or "She seemed so happy and had so much to live for".

Such is the stigma of mental illness, those who often need help the most can be expert at hiding behind a mask of normality and even cheerfulness.

Consequently, if you're reading this it's possibly because you're in a state of mental anguish and bleak spiritual isolation, maybe with thoughts about suicide. The book synopsis may well have attracted you because it gave you some hope that your current situation is overcome-able. It is. Perhaps some of the chapter titles also struck a weirdly familiar chord in you.

If you are a concerned parent who has a child suffering from some sudden personality change and want to figure out what's behind it and what to do for the best, this book is for you. Perhaps you have a history of suicide in your family and want to recognise the signs of an impending catastrophe.

This book is both an overview of what happened to me as well as a non-academic and Christianity-based self-help guide to bring you or your loved one back to sanity without the long term use of mind-altering drugs. It is written from experience, from someone who really knows what it feels like to be temporarily insane and to give you hope that you or your own child's happiness can and will return. Hope is an emotion that goes AWOL during a mental breakdown and hopelessness is what makes mental illness so frightening and isolating.

This book will also help you understand your plight is not unique. My story attempts to describe in detail the abstract feelings associated with detachment and dissociation and will help sufferers better describe their emotional state to others as well as reassure them their condition is not permanent and has been experienced by many people before.

Understand this: a door can be shut permanently on mental illness with normal levels of happiness restored whatever form of mental illness you are suffering. I say normal levels of happiness because expecting happiness at all times is unrealistic, but so too is being locked into a permanent state of depressive misery. There is a big difference between commonplace sadness and depressive psychosis. The former is cyclical, temporary and self-adjusting, the latter almost certainly has a spiritual cause and a person must receive spiritual deliverance from it.

I am confident you will find this book a blessing, either for new knowledge or for taking direct spiritual action.

ACKNOWLEDGEMENTS

Thanks to the online resources of Dr Scott Johnson, whose website www.contendingfortruth.com and podcasts have inspired much background research into areas of spiritual deception, as well as natural remedies for health; also Henry Makow Ph.D. www.savethemales.ca, whose trilogy of books on The Illuminati have helped me understand how the world is structured, exposing many unfruitful works of darkness. Also Trey Smith http://godinanutshell.com for his inspiring resources on the precision universe, the created Earth and the digital genetic coding of life. Above all to God Almighty for his abounding love, grace, persistence and patience with me.

Part One - *My Story*

INTRODUCTION

Penned by a Madman?

The book is divided into three parts:

Part 1 - *My Story* explains how my mental illness started, what it felt like, and how it abruptly ended.

Part 2 - *Spiritual Truths* outlines my views on the spiritual side of psychosis.

Part 3 - *Salvation, Deliverance and Healing* provides information on Christian salvation and on overcoming a mental illness with a suspected spiritual cause.

In the following chapters, I unapologetically propose the existence of spiritual doorways through which evil spirits can enter, masquerading as a mental illness or psychiatric disorder. If that sounds too wacky, this book is not for you. However, if you are a sufferer, depending on the severity and classification of your mental illness, I am quite sure you already have suspicions that your affliction is more than just physiological despite what your doctor tells you.

The book has also been written from a Christian world-view perspective. Why? Because the crux of it is my conviction that my psychosis originated from an external spiritual force of evil entering into me through drug use, among other reasons.

The evil spirit or spirits, did their very best to destroy me through depressing my soul to such an extent that I was tempted to destroy my own life through suicide. My deliverance came when I reached out in desperation to another external spiritual power - namely Jesus Christ. God's Holy Spirit rapidly overpowered the entity or entities which had infiltrated me, and gave me my sanity back. Yes. That's what I really believe happened.

My argument for considering a spiritual possibility behind some mental illness and other common neuroses is supported by (in my case) inexplicable paranormal phenomena associated with the bleakest moments of my condition as well as the fact that I miraculously and rapidly reverted back to sound mind through prayer.

In western society this demonic and 'spooky' explanation of my once severe mental health problem would be rejected, especially my belief God cured me with His healing intervention.

I know that from a western perspective, many more 'backward' cultures, still believe that spirit possession is the cause of most mental illness. Having experienced it myself, I think their assessment is occasionally right and that witchcraft and demonic possession can be a force behind psychosis and a factor in some non-psychiatric conditions too; though I disagree entirely with how some cultures treat a mentally ill person, often using violent rituals or tribal exorcisms to remove the spirits, or persecuting the sufferers rather than helping them.

There are many cases reported in the UK today where migrant children and some adults from African, Asian and Middle Eastern nations have been maimed or killed because their cultural circumstances have labelled them as witches simply because they have autism or display some other neurological problem. That is profoundly dangerous. These victims need help, and although some may indeed have legitimate spiritual problems, the right diagnosis should be sought and social protection against witch doctor remedies applied.

That does not mean that secular remedies for mental illness are any better. Not all mental health problems have physiological causes. Throwing drugs at a spiritual problem via pharmaceutical drug protocols can be just as damaging as the more primitive extremes.

I will never convince a hardened atheist or sceptic of my position and I will not waste time attempting to. This book is written for those of you who are open to the very real possibility that some types of mental illness are more than conditions with purely biological causes. I believe there is a fine line between the psychiatric and the paranormal.

When I started writing I knew I'd get flak from mainstream psychiatric sources (if they ever bothered to read it). The fear of ridicule almost stopped me. I was aware I had little defence against accusations of ignorance from scholars who had studied psychiatry and diseases of the mind from a secular scientific basis. I would doubtless be accused of being delusional and in need of help or sectioning; I mean, demons, really? Surely I must still be suffering from depressive psychosis to believe in such nonsense. Certainly, in a culture where discussing ideals of good and evil from a spiritual basis is mocked or where people display hostility at the mere whisper of God, I was really going to come up against it.

But, there was no way around it. If I was to write the book I just had to accept the fact that the majority of people will deem me a crackpot for mentioning 'prehistoric ideas' about demons and spirits, anticipating the accusations:

"You're positively medieval! Those ideas went out with the ark!"

"You are totally irresponsible putting ridiculous notions like that into people's heads, especially those suffering from depression, it'll knock them over the edge!"

"What kind of training have you that gives you the right to promote such foolish theories?"

"Are you telling me thousands of psychiatrists in the world should be doing exorcisms?"

"I did psychology at university and mental illness is all to do with nature and nurture, not demons".

And so on…

I vacillated so much about my inadequacies, the book was nearly not written. More particularly, I knew that among my friends, family, and wider circle of acquaintances, there would be a polite, restrained, yet derisive humouring of me, declaring one to another with incredulous rolling of the eyes, "He's lost the plot" or condescendingly stating, "I know you mean well and you've obviously had a very difficult personal experience which has made a big impact on you, but really, demons?"

Then I thought, so what? Why should I feel embarrassed or intimidated? I have good reason to tell my story and I've been around long enough to realise that academia gets knocked off its perch from time to time with the newest or latest theory that overrides previous thinking. What's more, I felt a compulsion to write it, particularly for my young daughter's benefit, just in case she should have the misfortune of experiencing, perhaps by inherited weakness for foolish behaviour or other epigenetic factor, some degree of mental illness in later life.

I thought about that soberly; about the crushing misery I'd been through and how isolating it was. I couldn't bear the thought of my daughter experiencing the same horror in the future without at least being armed with the reassurance that it was temporary and overcome-able.

I therefore resolved the book must be written in spite of my insufficient academic grounding and scholarly shortcomings. I am not attempting to undermine or ridicule scientific thinking, but rather add to it. I believe a spiritual analysis on the cause of mental illness has a vital place in the discussion. Modern psychiatry generally views spirituality

14

as foolishness and someone writing from this viewpoint is seen an eccentric at best and a suitable case for treatment at worst.

Alluding to a spiritual cause in psychiatric conditions is the domain of the internet or previously within old church documents. I have only found very limited evidence to suggest that mainstream science references spiritual arguments at all when discussing mental health. These include Roy Clements' Cambridge Paper, 'Demons and the Mind', or 'Demon Possession' by John Montgomery, both of which provide a much more academic overview of the subject than I can muster.

I realise many people will disagree with my opinions and ideas presented in the following pages. I don't care. Conventional Psychiatry already has a huge podium and peddles its propaganda daily, heavily funded by the drug companies and the mass-media public relations teams behind the profiteering. It pushes its own *extremist* point of view, which is to assume that all cases of 'possession' are in fact psychological illness with a physiological cause, rejecting any spiritual origin. It's time other voices are heard.

The problem with many culturally mandated treatments for 'sanity management' (and throughout medicine generally), is that the temptation to manage an individual's illness for profit rather than finding a cure will always be the preferred procedure for drug manufacturers. The Pharmaceutical Industry thrives on a diagnosis of *chronic illness* where managing a medical condition without a permanent remedy is the most pragmatic approach for shareholder benefits.

Medical schools and many universities largely owe their existence to drug manufacturers' funding, which compromises unbiased research and deliberately leans students toward drug-focused treatments. The unscrupulous practice of prescribing-for-profit will keep mental illness sufferers and their equally befuddled family doctors both banging their heads against the proverbial (or in extreme cases literal) brick wall. That is not to say that drugs are of no benefit. Some drug treatments are essential in providing patients suffering from physiologically caused mental illness with a stable and functional existence.

I admire individuals in the mental health arena who are passionate about finding alternatives to drug treatment such as innovative behavioural therapies and compassionate counselling therapies. Mental health patients need approaching with the open-minded assumption that their problems are not necessarily going to be effectively managed by chemical intervention. While drugs may temporarily mask spiritual problems, if root cause goes unrecognised the spiritual disorder can worsen.

A caveat here: Many psychotropic drugs have clear short-term benefits for psychiatric conditions, particularly those which boost depleted levels of serotonin, and I believe that emergency medicine can be an important component of an initial treatment of severe, life threatening, suicidal psychosis, whatever the cause, but only to provide temporary, short term relief, prior to a more complete diagnosis and not for long-term management. Psychotropic drugs are poisons; swallow them all at once and you'll quickly discover that. You can't drug your mind or your body into good health*. (*I acknowledge Dr Scott Johnson for borrowing his phraseology here: see www.contendingfortruth.com.)

Psychiatrists are generally suspicious about spirituality, more than other doctors are, because they often see pathological symptoms of 'religious' patients, prejudicing them against a spiritual diagnosis.

Christian psychiatrists and those in other faiths who discern spiritual problems do exist, but most incline towards secular diagnosis for the sake of their careers, disregarding the immense spiritual common-denominator in many mental conditions. It is common for Christian doctors to 'de-mythologise' the gospel stories of demon possession in favour of epilepsy or schizophrenia, whereas I believe these conditions can often be symptomatic of spirit possession.

In summary, I have only limited knowledge about clinical psychology, psychotropic medicine and the complexities of the human brain, the endocrine and lymphatic system and diseases of the same; however, in contrast to most psychology professors and psychiatrists who haven't experienced psychedelic drug use or mental illness themselves, I can speak as an expert. I have direct and personal knowledge of the sensations of two powerful hallucinogenic drugs and their effects that a non-user can only guess at. Experience over textbook always wins.

The information in this book should not be viewed as medical advice and is not intended to diagnose, treat or cure a mental health condition or be a substitute for advice from your doctor; however, it is intended to support health and healing, and help to challenge conventional treatment which may be hindering healing, especially if prescription drugs are the long-term management protocol. Whether you choose conventional treatments or alternative remedies or a mixture of both, it is important you work closely with a healthcare professional to accurately diagnose and treat your condition and monitor your progress.

There are countless academic studies on the many classifications of mental illness available to read in libraries and online. I encourage you to do so. I accept that mental illness has a variety of causes; we are body, mind and spirit, all three interplay.

The human endocrine and hormone production system plays a major role in how we feel, think and operate on a daily basis. There are studies on the effects of ageing, disease and trauma in mental health covering the menopause, andropause and dementia; all common catalysts of some types of mental illness. Similarly, dramatic life events like bereavement and redundancy can trigger psychosis and 'nervous breakdown' which is an old fashioned blanket-term for a number of conditions, with nervousness certainly a key attribute of many of them.

I know that drug use from cannabis; MDMA (Ecstasy); 'legal-highs'; nootropic drugs; DMT; and a profuse range of other hallucinogens can be rapid facilitators of psychosis. What's more shocking is the problem of prescribed medications causing mental illness, ranging from anti-malarial drugs like Lariam®, to vaccines and inoculations, not to mention the various psychotropic medications handed out willy-nilly for the most commonplace of life problems from exam nerves or losing a job, to simply feeling 'a bit low'; often resulting in consequences significantly more desperate than the routine problem they were supposed to deal with. I am also aware that mental illness can suddenly descend on a person unexpectedly without ascribing any known trigger. Scary.

In my case LSD was the facilitator, and whether or not I would have experienced psychosis without it prompted by some other life event, I do not know, but I think it's likely I would through the interplay of other factors in my case. What is for sure, if someone had come to me with this book in the early days of my psychotic episode I would have been relieved. Why? Because I had wrongly assumed my experience was unique and no other individual in the history of the world had suffered my variety of mental distress before. This sense of the situation being distinctive and exceptional compounded my despair. The belief eventually led to the notion I had no other option than suicide to rid myself of the anguish, fear and inexpressible gloom which I felt was a permanent condition. A book like this would have provided hope when I needed it most.

Principally, I advocate prayer in the life of a sufferer. Having experienced the power of prayer in eradicating an extreme level of depressive psychosis so rapidly, I would also urge other sufferers and their families to open their hearts and minds to the possibility that healing for mental illness lies in the application of a living faith (perhaps even alongside more traditional treatments such as medication and therapy).

As Psalm 145 affirms, in verse 14:
"The Lord upholdeth all that fall, and raiseth up all those that be bowed down."

And Psalm 34:18 states,
"The Lord is near to the brokenhearted and saves the crushed in spirit." (ESV)

The loneliness of mental illness can only be truly understood by a sufferer and to some extent their close family members and carers. I assure you if you are suffering right now or supporting a mental health patient in your family, you are not alone. Mental illness is so common and you can be confident that the craziest and scariest of your thoughts are not unique and even the most bizarre delusions have a commonality and resemblance to someone else's - possibly mine. As you read further you will be reassured by many examples.

In common with all people I still experience periods of increased anxiety and low mood; however, these are short lived and do not contain the extreme torment, crushing suicidal inclinations and nightmarish fear that my original illness contained.

Knowing what I know now and having been through great anguish and coming out the other end intact has given me highly developed mental muscles that continue to be flexed daily.

Most importantly of all, my experience has led to a conviction in the existence of a dynamic spiritual world all around me, as well as a very gracious and loving God who was drawing me to reach out to Him. Conversely, I am also acutely aware of another presence - a dangerous spiritual enemy with dark and destructive intentions who operates with spiritual legions of cronies who desire to crush your spirit, remove your hope, and destroy your light and life. Why? Quite simply because misery loves company.

CHAPTER 1.

Childhood's End

I still look at the sequence of numbers 1-9-8-3 with unease. The year after the release of Duran Duran's *Rio* and ABC's *The Lexicon of Love* albums was the year everything changed. I was eighteen and three quarters and quite immature.

It would be unfair to taint the whole of 1983 with what happened at the end of it, because everything up to November 25th had been quite normal; school, holidays, nice mum and dad, fun brothers, great older sister, range of friends, revision, exams, TV, Top of the Pops, getting hair looking perfect with hair gel in front of the 1970s bathroom cabinet; and doing embarrassing teenage stuff like smuggling Playboy magazines into the house down the front of my school games' socks. I had also started smoking cigarettes and in spite of the health propaganda, thoroughly enjoyed this new pastime, spending time in the garden, local pubs and relaxing by the hearth late in the evening (after my widowed mum had gone to bed), puffing away up the chimney with my two brothers, watching reruns of The Outer Limits and Twilight Zone, breaking mum's house rules while ignoring her constant admonitions 'You'll waste all your money and end up with cancer' and 'What girl wants to kiss a smoker?' (The sort I preferred, I ruminated).

The summer of 1983 was pleasantly happy in a four-pack-swilling and cigarette-smoking kind of way. There was an atmosphere of light rebelliousness that was winked at rather than clamped-down on and a silent acknowledgement that my friends and I were experiencing various teenage rites of passage like cider in the park and French kissing.

I had enormous respect for my mother who did her best for us in spite of my father's death seven years earlier. She lived on a widow's pension as my dad had died without life insurance which was an unfortunate though common fact of life in 1970s Britain, as most families found it unaffordable, however we had managed to move to the more prosperous south east of England to Marlow, Buckinghamshire from

19

the slightly more impoverished Whitley Bay, Tyne and Wear some five years earlier.

The spring and summer in Marlow was always humid and occasionally sizzling compared to the foggy coastal chill of Northern England we had left, and in spite of moving into a small house, I was delighted to live in the south east.

When the Home Counties sun shone there was an affluence and confident expectation in the air. The mood was buzzing with the hubbub of busy pub gardens; the rumble of jets on the Heathrow flight path; the sweet smell of the Thames and boats on the river; gleaming sports cars wheeling into gravelled drives; pretty wisteria-draped homes with flint coursed walls overarched by magnolia and lilac in bushy gardens with verdant shrubbery. For a while life was gorgeous.

I was in that hopeful transition between school and university, spending much of the time post A-levels relaxing on a garden lounger with a cup of tea and reading various Romantic poetry books (a lifetime love of poetry engendered by excellent teachers at Sir William Borlase's School, Marlow).

Although I had failed to make the desired grades in my A-Levels to go to a good university to study English Literature, I had decided, rather than attend a polytechnic, that I should retake the A-levels in the local college at High Wycombe. Here there was the pleasant novelty of girls, having been in the restrictive and often brutal confines of an all-boy's grammar school for the previous five years.

I had no inkling what was going to happen to me as I sat in the happy garden that summer, pondering foxgloves, bees and clouds and being poetical and pensive. Even if someone had tried to warn me I would have looked at them incredulously and denied it was possible, particularly considering the many positive things that were happening.

Summer marched onward to cooler autumn and I had become happily accustomed to the new scene at High Wycombe College of Further Education and was having fun, usually raucous, occasionally riotous and always involving beer and cigarettes with the odd joint thrown in; surrounded by hordes of lovely girls; friends old and new and, in the background, the security of a cosy, stable home with hot food and a warm bed to fall into every evening.

Then came the 25th November 1983. It was a date that marked the end of a long and happy, relatively typical English childhood and the beginning of something viciously grown-up.

20

Like the teenage volunteer arriving in France in 1916, freshly untied from his mother's apron strings and facing the sludge of the Somme, or perhaps someone from an earlier generation being handed a pick axe for his first day down the mine, the contrast between the status quo and easy ordinariness I had been used to and the cold plunge into an existential fight for survival in the winter of that year was ruthless.

CHAPTER 2.

The Event

It is so apparent to me now, and I try to be mindful of it daily, that at any one time each of us sits somewhere along the spectrum of physical, mental and spiritual health and throughout most of life the majority of us in Western society hover contentedly in the mid-section of the spectrum, feeling neither great extremes of joy or sadness, pleasure or pain, an average life of fitting in with peers, getting along with neighbours and generally being quite normal; doing regular activities like working, watching TV, reading, supermarket shopping, worrying about paying bills, DIY, gardening, and latterly gaming, social media and online activities. If you are in this position today, please be thankful.

The mid-spectrum of existence is a good position to find yourself in. Most of us will fluctuate in life from the mid-spectrum to either side of it through the years, with some periods spent to the pleasant bright side of the spectrum in times of good health; good spirits; being in love; on happy vacations; celebrating successes; living in prosperity, and so on; while other periods will be spent further to the gloomier side of the mid-line, perhaps during periods of ill health; financial difficulty; bereavement; insecurity; relationship problems; job loss and so on. Thankfully, life for the most part does not linger too long in each extreme and we seesaw continually, finding agreeable equilibrium, for the most part.

If you are an emotionally sensitive person, it's unlikely you are going to be kicking your heels with joy all the time. Indeed, a below average or low mood is more than likely for much of the year if you are sensitive to the world around you and walk around with your eyes open. It's a fallen world we live in riven with war and strife we can count our blessings if we have a roof over our head, are well fed and nurtured by a loving family and social group around us. Ernest Hemingway famously said, "The world breaks everyone, and afterward, some are strong at the broken places". He also said, "Happiness in intelligent people is the rarest thing I know". I can agree with those sentiments.

My story is an English one, but it could easily be a Scottish one, a French one, a German one, an American or Russian one. Western Man differs only very slightly around the cultural edges wherever you travel.

That day in southern England in 1983 started off routinely like previous others. The bus stop on Wycombe Road, Marlow, was a huddled affair where cigarettes were shared and smoked and television programmes and comedy sketches from the night before were dissected and re-enacted.

My brother John and I waited with friends Ronnie and Sarah for the bus to take us to college in High Wycombe town centre. We were all enjoying pubbing, clubbing and partying for the first time, during the latest cultural phenomenon of *New Romanticism*, with its effeminate looking fashions for young men including baggy pleated pants, extreme winkle-picker shoes, button-over shirts, long flick-able fringes and even eyeliner. Girls wore rah-rah skirts, striped leggings and Doctor Marten boots and sported boyish hair trimmed a bit spiky. It was post-Punk harshness synthesised with androgynous gender-bending and without any of us realising it, the rise of homosexual culture. There was loads of other new-fangled stuff going on too: Miniaturisation technologies spawned Sony Walkman cassette players and headphones and Atari and Sega TV game consoles. Home computing had begun with floppy discs and the BBC's Micro; Commodore; and ZX Spectrum computers. Early Apple computers were appearing and mobile communications had started. The richest had bulky car phones installed, while the poorer end of the social spectrum revelled in Citizen's Band (CB) radio with its embarrassing juggernaut-jargon.

At home in Willowmead Gardens, my mum had recently bought duvets known previously as 'continental quilts'. They replaced the ubiquitous candlewick bed linen, nylon sheets and candy stripe pillowcases of the 1970s that were retired into the back of airing cupboards before slipping into a fabric Bermuda Triangle. Downstairs, microwaves pinged and sandwich toasters dripped oily cheese and baked beans on to worktops. Modern kitchen shops with names like 21st Century Kitchens displayed stylish new veneers and dampened drawer mechanisms which ousted fishmongers and ironmongers from the high street. The simple, *Camberwick Green* concept of Britain I had grown up with was disappearing fast. New cars looked more rounded with less metal and lots of matt vinyl and there was a buzz of emergent prosperity in the air.

23

On that fresh November morning, the anachronism of the double decker Marlow-to-High Wycombe bus contrasted with all the modernity as it began its peak-hours morning service via Cressex Industrial Estate. The air brakes hissed and hydraulic doors opened and shut inelegantly behind us as we swung heavily down into our seats as it pulled away. A throwback to the 1950s it was upholstered in rough fabric in shades of russet, ochre and brown with sturdy hide trim. It was a smoky ride where 'stubbers' on the Formica seat backs were still used and a greyish blue fug engulfed smokers and non-smokers alike in *eau de Silk Cut, JPS, Marlboro* and *Superkings*. How people put up with that pollution amazes me now, especially in offices and on aeroplanes. Not so in 1983; smokers ruled.

My friend Sarah flashed an elegant embossed carton containing 20 *Sobranie Black Russian* brand cigarettes. When lit they smelled of sweaty socks. Personally I considered it cool to smoke white-tipped *Kent* or *Peter Stuyvesant*, at least until money from a part time supermarket shelf-stacking job ran out midweek, because by Friday I was smoking *Golden Virginia* roll-ups or sponging filter cigarettes from anyone I hadn't cadged from earlier in the week.

The bus would arrive and disgorge the few remaining students at 8.45 in the sheltered concrete concourse of High Wycombe bus station which was drab and noisy with fluorescent lights, but always dry. After a brief walk to the college entrance, the morning of lectures on Fridays would culminate in a noisy gathering at lunchtime in the college refectory with clattering cutlery and a racket of chattering. Here far more cigarettes were smoked and coffees drank from plastic cups than meals were eaten. Friends would break off in threes and fours to head to one of the many pubs in High Wycombe for a pre-weekend booze-up before returning to the bus station and alighting home on separate buses. I would usually catch the Marlow bus back on Friday a little sloshed, with my brother John and Ronnie. Today it was just Ronnie.

It was also the day of the *Children in Need* BBC telethon appeal co-presented by Terry Wogan and Gloria Hunniford with lots of things happening; fancy dress, people bathing in baked beans and collecting cash in plastic buckets in office carparks and shopping precincts all over the country. This new American-format telethon-event made the day memorable for the right reasons and everyone was in a happy, relaxed mood as businesses and schools had given workers and pupils *carte blanche* to fool around and dress up a bit, reflecting a more upbeat attitude fostered by a growing economy; Britain's recent defeat of Argentina in the Falklands' War, and exciting new music and cultural developments. We felt at the vanguard of something optimistic and had turned the corner from 1970s strikes and those austere British Winters of Discontent, now we had Margaret Thatcher at the helm.

On the journey home at around 3pm as dusk was falling, Ronnie and I discussed getting high, or more specifically 'having a trip' that evening, hopefully to match the fun of a 'magic-mushroom' taking experience we had enjoyed a month earlier. We thought it would be entertaining to go to the pub while 'tripping' too, but magic-mushrooms were highly seasonal, growing on lawns and playing fields from summer to autumn and you had to collect and dry them if you wanted them beyond October. Problem.

A possible solution was provided by the presence of two twenty-something, ginger haired, wispy-bearded goons sitting at the front right of the bus top deck. They visually fitted our cannabis-user profile and seemed like our best hope for either getting hold of some decent grass or something stronger that evening. We moved our seats to sit diagonally behind them when other passengers alighted.

They looked a bit shady, even sullen, and smelled of dirty houses, but they were hippy-ish so surely couldn't be that dangerous. Besides, my friend Ronnie was big for his age, built like a bull and looked like he could seriously handle himself (which he could), and was especially menacing with his geometrically precise flat-top haircut he was sporting. For that reason, I assented to Ronnie's murmured enquiry to the nearest of them:

"Excuse me mate, do you know anywhere around here where we can score some weed?"

They were taken aback; suspicious; a little wild-eyed, and murmured they couldn't help us.

However, around a minute more into the journey, after a brief and inaudible consultation with each other, one of them groped around in a dog-eared wallet and sheepishly pulled out an insignificant and slightly grubby looking piece of blotting paper, 5mm square. He held it guiltily between thumb and forefinger across the aisle from us and said, "I've got a tab of acid but it costs a tenner. That's all I've got."

We readily handed over five pounds each though I was distinctly uneasy about that look of guilt. Was he ripping us off? I didn't trust his awkward eye contact.

Ronnie and I examined the tiny, inconsequential fragment of paper with cynicism. It had a crudely printed Superman in blue, red and yellow on one side and looked like a miniature Roy Lichtenstein painting or the comic strip you got on a *Bazooka Joe* bubble gum insert. The reverse was blank.

Ronnie and I passed it back and forth sceptically and wondered how this trifle of blotting paper could possibly give us the same experience as the full teapot of magic-mushroom infused tea we had enjoyed in October, especially since we would be sharing it between us.

I took safekeeping of the purchase and reaching home, furtively cut the Superman blotting-paper diagonally in half with a pair of nail scissors in my bedroom. After wolfing down a beef stew provided by my mum, I headed the quarter mile to Ronnie's house through the alleyway, optimistically fondling my wallet containing £5, or five beer tokens as we dubbed them, along with the prized tab of acid.

CHAPTER 3.

Mushroom Tea

As I strolled towards Ronnie's house I was looking forward to repeating another magic-mushroom experience similar to one we'd had there one Friday in October when his mum was out at work. The experience had been far beyond expectations and admittedly very good fun, if a little scary at times.

My brother John had already taken 'shrooms' on two or three occasions previously with another friend of his, and had tutored Ronnie and I in the ceremony. John had picked the magic mushrooms from some parkland locally and dried them. When fresh, they were around five centimetres in height, dark-gilled with a 15mm tan cap and darker brown nipple-like protrusion in the centre. We trusted his judgement as he added half a cupful of the dried variety into a large teapot, adding tea leaves and pouring on boiling water. He let the tea brew for 15 minutes.

Straining the liquid into three mugs, we downed the mushroom flavoured tea. It looked grey and tasted horrible. As we swilled the dregs out, the stalks and caps of the re-moistened mushrooms looked like a tangled mess of crushed house-spiders in the bottom of the pot.

Half an hour later, the mushroom-trip started. There was a gradual heightened intensity in the room of…something, followed by a gentle rippling from the curtains and then an intense coming alive of every inanimate object as even the room itself seemed to pump up and down, sway and groove to the beat of the thumping soundtrack of *Mesopotamia* by the *B52s*.

The already-alive things - the budgie, Ronnie, John and myself - were comically energised into a circus of chirping and giggling jollity amidst a backdrop of mounting hallucinations. The artexed ceiling dripped multi-coloured blobs of light and our faces undulated through shades of mauve, lilac and blue as objects danced and span to the rhythm of the music.

It was a lot of fun, though I didn't enjoy it much when it wore off. For a couple of hours after the intense hallucinations stopped, I thought I wasn't going to get back to normal. I did.

I anticipated the LSD would be as much fun, albeit we were going to be in a different environment than Ronnie's living room, but it was Friday night, the best night of the week, so what could be the problem?

Friday and Saturday in the company of friends at the pub with lots of pretty girls was longed for. I loved meeting girls, but had very little confidence speaking to them, especially the attractive ones and I would clam-up unless I had sufficient 'Dutch Courage' before attempting it. So as usual, my aim was to get semi-drunk as cheaply as possible, to loosen inhibitions.

I was fine chatting with the plain-Janes and a little more inhibited though still fairly relaxed with the prettier Bohemian, hippy types; however, the mature, high-heeled, long-legged girls with Farrah-Fawcett hair were unapproachable as I lacked both the financial means and masculine confidence to attract them. I would usually crumble with shyness in their presence.

Although my grammar school, single-sex education helped me be more attentive in class without the distraction of females, it was ruinous to building confidence with the opposite sex. My clumsy dialogue in conversation with women when I was sober was conspicuous. Ronnie had bags more confidence and success with girls. He was manly looking for his age and although I was a good-looking boy at 18, I was still fresh-faced and very immature, with that grammar-school sarcasm and exaggeration-style of humour that carried off Monty Python sketches adroitly, but didn't impress chic girls. Conversely, Ronnie had attended a mixed Secondary Modern school and knew how to chat to girls without nervousness. His athletic build made him attractive to many young women that flocked to the bars in Marlow each weekend. The girls who went to The Crown were predominantly from his old school and most were as sensible as their mothers at 18 and looked like real women much earlier than their peers from the all-girls' grammar schools.

That night, Ronnie and I were both under the impression the LSD trip would be of a lesser magnitude than magic mushrooms and would at best help turbocharge the effects of a few pints of lager. It would be a social enhancement at most, given the miniscule proportions of our 'half tab' each share. I hoped for a more outgoing and amusing routine with the girls than drinking lager alone could muster and we anticipated it would provide a pleasant buzz for the evening.

CHAPTER 4.

Dropping Acid

I can't remember the exact nature of the LSD-taking ceremony. Ronnie and I probably swigged some sherry or *Dubonnet* from his mum's meagre drinks cabinet to wash it down. I just remember us both swallowing our portions simultaneously and checking we had both done so before enthusiastically striding into town.

We stopped briefly in the glare of an orange streetlight to light cigarettes and assess each other's faces to see if we 'looked different' or whether we were feeling something yet. The mushroom trip experience would be our yardstick as to whether the two goons on the bus had ripped us off.

Ronnie said he wasn't sure, but felt as though he was bouncing along more lightly than his usual walk, a bit like he was moonwalking. I agreed with a 'Yeah! Me too,' not really being convinced. We had in certainty wasted a tenner.

It wasn't cold that night, but the damp November air contrasting with the sudden clamour of the warm pub as we entered with its blinking slot machines and video games was abrupt and dizzying. I felt suddenly uneasy and I realised something was not quite right.

The brass of the beer pumps appeared more highly polished than ever with a garishness under the bright bar strip lights too painful to look at. I needed to drink my pint quickly to calm my jumpiness and to stop my palms sweating. Ronnie seemed gregarious and quickly separated from me to chat to various friends. I headed as nonchalantly as I could to keep my rising panic hidden, toward the far corner of the pub by the back door where there was a curved high backed seating booth and a heavy oak table. Here I perceived I would sit more securely, protected from the crowds in the bar. I was feeling increasingly vulnerable, insecure and edgy.

A couple of semi-drunk buddies joined me (I forget their names) and I immediately confessed I had dropped some acid and was feeling a bit anxious and worried. They were amused and indifferent to my rising dread, which made me panic more. I darted outside for cool air and a cigarette. There was no reason to smoke outside in the 1980s, you could generally puff anywhere other than in the supermarket or classroom, but I thought it would help.

It was breezy now and dry leaves skirted around the barrel seats and tables in the yard scratchily. I was noticing peripheral trivia I would normally be oblivious to. I stumbled back inside to sit at the table again but now the atmosphere was chaotic and hostile. I saw people looking at me and apparently discussing me, even people in the distant saloon bar. When I looked at someone, they would deceptively avert their gaze and turned the conversation to something else. Every now and then my eyes would meet someone else's and it was like they were looking straight into my soul. A plot against me was underway and was deviously sophisticated.

I felt like an outsider. Faces of friends began to look odd. Startled, I focused on my hand gripping my beer, but my fingers had become surreal-looking with accentuated musculature, just like *Soft Construction with Boiled Beans* by Salvador Dali. Panic seized me.

Now my mauve-tinged fingers took on a silicone-like texture like airbrush fantasy art. Where had I seen that? Yes. Alan Aldridge's insects in *The Butterfly Ball* or one of those fairground ride murals of impudent Madonna or brazen Olivia Newton John, with *thump-thump-thumping* bass of the music pumping from The Waltzer. I had to get out.

I sprang from my seat and left the garish carnival, fumbling for 5 pence to call a more mature friend, Eric from a phone box in the car park.

Eric answered the phone promptly. Age 32, he was a barman at The George & Dragon pub and I explained my predicament. He'd told me he'd had LSD once before so I figured he'd be a mentor and could help. Bless him, he appeared almost instantly from his home three miles distant.

"Eric, I'm freaking out", I blurted, and I quickly dropped into his car's bucket seats as he drove to the large car park behind the supermarket. Eric began talking in a monotone voice about the time he'd taken LSD and had tried to have sex with some girl and couldn't do it. He seemed amused and relaxed in his reminiscing, not appreciating the terror I was experiencing. He told me to sit tight for five minutes while he phoned work to explain he was running late. A heavy drizzle smeared the windscreen and I noticed dark raindrops running down in hues of pink and green, shimmering against the streetlights. I had seen a similar undulating effect on magic mushrooms, but this time it wasn't fun or fascinating, just frightening. The inside of the car became sinister.

Eric returned with a couple of cans of beer. The alcohol didn't make me any calmer and I found every mouthful difficult, each gulp emphasised. I became conscious of swallowing.

I had another cigarette, fidgeting. Eric didn't smoke but didn't mind anyone else smoking, even in his car. The cigarette crackled loudly as I drew on it. I started to notice Eric's face in the glow. Did he look suddenly surly and creepy?

As I tried to account for the change in Eric's demeanour I unexpectedly felt a startling sensation of motion as though I was being pulled back into a kind of dimensional shift, like being attached to an ethereal bungee cord pulling me into something inhospitable and eternal.

I lunged forward to counter the backwards motion sensation, grabbing Eric by the arms, scrabbling to anchor myself to him, and stammered, "I'm retreating! I keep retreating Eric! Help me!"

Eric's face appeared even darker and his surly expression seemed to say, "I know, we've been expecting this."

In terror I realised the plot to destroy me had been devised for years and Eric was a part of it. Here in his car was the denouement of the previous 18¾ years of my life. A terrifying demise into permanent separation from reality was taking place.

But presently I was back; a moment of clarity returned as adrenaline kicked in.

Did Eric see my panic when I looked at his darkened features? I had to get out of the car before that sense of being on a piece of elastic pulled me away again. I didn't want him realising I knew about the plot. The pulling-away sensation came back. In terror I bolted from the car, abruptly blurting, "I've got to go Eric, I have to walk!"

He shouted, "Are you sure?" and mentioned something about being finished at work by 11pm. I dismissed it and hastily marched away, through the car park, avoiding people by heading up the tree-lined alley skirting my old school-playing fields. Here it was dark and quiet, away from traffic noise and headlights, where I could focus on getting things together and sweat out the drug effects without scrutiny.

Critically conscious of each footstep I seemed to be walking with a ludicrously exaggerated gait, taking profound strides. Passers-by would surely see my long-leggedness and grow suspicious.

In the dim light, my hands were shifting in hues of purple, grey and blue in a feverish goblin strangeness. I lay under a tree in the shadowy school playing field by an old long-jump pit. I developed an additional paranoia that if anyone saw me there they'd believe I was up to no good and phone the police. Then I'd have to confess my drug taking and my mum and teachers would find out and the consequences and shame of being labelled 'a druggy' heightened my agitation.

The light rain stopped and clouds scudded above me so I could just make out faint stars. The breeze rattled the bare branches above into witches' fingers, inquisitive and probing. I tried shaking my head back and forth in short bursts to rattle myself back to clarity. It didn't work and the trip was becoming more intense. I was unable to dispel the false belief the police were on their way to arrest me, so I staggered back the way I'd come to wander aimlessly around random residential streets, walking and walking in the hope I'd snap back to reality by exercising the LSD out of my system and importantly, killing time before returning home to bed. I was fearful that if I got back too early my mum would still be up watching the TV and she would see my anxious state and start asking me too many questions about where I'd been and who with, and I would inevitably collapse into a clumsy, stammered confession of drug abuse.

I'm not sure when the next demented thing started, perhaps in another alleyway, accompanying the rhythmic sound of my footsteps and breathing, but I began repeating a sort of frantic mantra of "Jib, jib, jibber…Jib, jib, jibber…Jib, jib, jibber." I visualised myself now as a different entity with the real me trapped inside a gangly, Dali-esque embodiment of a gibbering idiot. That's where the mantra originated; a kind of frenzied edit of the term *gibbering-idiot* to 'Jibberet' had taken place. I had not only invented a new noun, but had become *Jibberet* personified; a dithering embodiment of wretchedness. I could not let my mum see me in this state.

But I was desperate to return home and hide in the seclusion of my bedroom. The street walking was intolerable and perhaps people were getting suspicious, as I'd paced some streets two or three times now and they may think I was a car thief or burglar. I anxiously returned to the High Street to access the quiet residential route back home via Liston Hall Old People's Home.

Long hours seemed to have passed since I first 'dropped acid'. *Lysergic Acid Diethylamide* was echoing alongside *Jibberet* in my head and time was increasingly difficult to measure or even conceptualise anymore. Minutes seemed like hours, and seconds, minutes. I was horrified to see the second hand on my wristwatch move imperceptibly slowly and even stop entirely for a few seconds. Then I saw it move backwards and then forwards again. Was it 11.30? What did time mean? Could I trust myself to interpret the position of the hands? Could I head home now without being cross-examined?

I realised the trip was becoming more powerful when I cornered the top of the High Street and wandered into one of my brother's drinking buddies, Malcolm. His face seemed a bright sky blue in the glare of the fluorescent lighting of the estate agent's window. He spoke and I blurted some clumsy dialogue back with a fake smile on my face, looking for reassurance: "Man, I'm really tripping out tonight...Ron and I dropped some acid...Do I look alright?" or something along those lines. I wasn't sure how he responded, his words were slurred and in slow motion as he slapped my shoulder good-naturedly and went on his way.

On reaching my street I ducked furtively up the short alley running adjacent to the back garden of my house and squinted over the garden gate to the back door entrance. I could see the dining room and living room beyond were in darkness which meant to my relief my mum was in bed. I quietly approached the house, closing the garden gate silently behind me. Immediately on entering however, my mum shouted from her bedroom, "Is that you, Alan?"

The effort to sound normal was gargantuan. I was in panic-mode, terrified of being found out, but I managed to utter a tiresome-sounding, "Yes."

The LSD trip was peaking now and I had successfully avoided mum detecting my distress. I made it quickly into bed without consequence.

CHAPTER 5.

Bedroom

The bedroom was dimly moonlit through a central gap in the curtains and I could see the street view by moving the right hand border of the curtain by my head. I hoped I could manage the trip better now, uninterrupted by fear of people, however the full effects of the LSD in the dreary light seemed worse than ever. My luminous alarm clock became threatening, as though it would sprout facial features from some half-forgotten nursery rhyme. I turned it around and gazed through the curtains at the high moon for relief, but the moon was shaky, unstable and seemed dreadful.

How long? How long? Had I always been tripping and the rest of my life a fantasy? Was the universe existent only because of my consciousness? Had everything in the world been designed and created to bring me to this point of self-realisation? The terror of infinity gripped me. It was real and it was awful.

I had little concept of duration anymore. For some terrifying seconds, time itself seemed utterly ungraspable and everything I had ever known just one terrible eternal moment as the room rippled around me. "It's always been like this," I pondered, "I just never noticed it before."

Long hours of stress and abject fear had given me palpitations and a painful stitch across my chest. I had probably been hyperventilating too. The thought that the LSD would trigger a heart attack became another background anxiety to add to all the others.

I started to drift into a kind of trance - or vision would be a better description, because I was fully awake; tossing and turning with apprehension. Each time I closed my eyes I could see a strange scene in detail as though my eyes were open and I was really there.

This closed-eye vision revealed a dismal, arid landscape that was rock-strewn with no wind. Standing in front of me in the gloomy half-light were some large, apparently lifeless beings; frog-like humanoids, each standing about eight feet tall and very powerful looking. They were facing me.

I am not sure how many there were. My impression was five, but maybe seven, as it was dark and my peripheral vision was limited. I could certainly make out five silhouetted in a tight cluster with a slice of grim landscape beyond. Each of them stood facing forwards, about three feet apart in a five-on-a-dice grouping. I stood and faced the central figure, just a couple of feet away.

My gaze moved upon this heavy-set monster in a strange, measured scrutiny I had no control over. I was drawn to look upwards from its feet to its face, taking in details and feeling the intensity of its presence. This one had an air of dominance and seemed more powerful than the four (or more) surrounding it.

They were wearing what I can only describe as tight, silvery, padded spacesuits which were warlike, as I could vaguely make out belts and strapping and something like areas of chainmail or mesh on their flanks. They all stood completely motionless as though mummified or dormant, yet they had a strong vibration of evil suggesting their consciousness was stirring within.

I was aware of a kind of gurgling, incoherent speech as though they were communicating. The nearest thing I could liken them to were the *Sontaran* aliens from 'Dr Who' (given the silver spacesuits) combined with the cartoon alien from 'Kaptain Kremmen' from *The Kenny Everett Video Show*, with that same wide slit mouth and greenish grey tinge to the skin. The awful dimness of the light made it difficult to make out any fine details, such as their eyes which just appeared big, dark and shadowy.

I know this sounds more like a description of a daft kids' sci-fi show with the silver suits and the frog-like appearance - comical even, but in actuality the sense of evil exuding from these beings was intense and penetrating, especially in the still silence of that dim, eerie landscape. It smacks of one of those clichéd alien abduction scenarios, except I didn't feel as though I was being forcefully abducted, more like drifting into this strange place as though levitating.

Every time I opened my eyes the narrow, barren scene would disappear, but every time I closed them I would drift back into the proximity of these evil frog-like beings.

This continued exhaustingly throughout the restless night, interspersed with my fretful curtain-shifting to check to see if the moon was beginning to appear normal as it wheeled above the houses. I

36

repetitively checked the alarm clock and watched the interminable minutes drag inexorably towards dawn.

CHAPTER 6.

The New Planet

A cheerless grey light filtered into the room. It was 8am and my mum had started moving about, clearing her throat, flushing toilet, switching on kitchen switches. Normal day for mum, yet fifty tortuous years seemed to have passed since I first took the LSD.

The light of day brought an end to the rippling motion and evil-frog visions, but I was not all there. I had the feeling that I had lost some of my faculties; that I was brain-damaged and was lacking mental lucidity.

Finally, just as I was mustering the confidence to get out of bed, I had another vivid closed-eye vision; an ornate Chinese serpentine dragon soared toward me and as it grew closer I could see the detail of its multi-coloured body and lion-like face as it opened its jaws and regurgitated another dragon; the same size as itself, but a different design. The new snake-like dragon was now in front of the original dragon and both were flying in a serpentine up and down motion, wheeling around in a wide arc. The second dragon then did exactly the same thing, spewing out another flying dragon of a different design and colour from its mouth.

The clarity and the decorative complexity of each of the dragons astonished me and horrified me simultaneously. They looked solid and real. Their eyes stared with dark severity, cruel and indifferent. That was the closing image of the trip*. *I saw a similar dragon-regurgitation vision captured perfectly in a psychedelic illustration by Alan Aldridge in his book, *The Beatles' Illustrated Lyrics*. I am still astonished someone else had also visualised such a bizarre thing as me.

I reticently stepped out of my bedroom to quickly scoot across the landing, passing the top of the stairs to the sanctuary of the bathroom. I needed a reviving shower before I could speak to my mum. I had to be in control of my appearance. I looked drawn and grey, like I was suffering from shock. My hands and feet were icy cold.

The shower did little to refresh me from the empty-headed sensation. My mental capacity felt hijacked, I couldn't think straight. It was an unexpected after effect of the drug and I desperately needed coherence to make conversation with my mum, who was thankfully preoccupied with washing and tidying.

My two brothers laughing and joking together took the focus off me and I was able to blend into the Saturday background routine quite inconspicuously, making a cup of tea, sitting in the living room watching TV and phoning Eric at home to ask him to call around as soon as possible so I could escape the house and tell him about what had happened last night, but mostly to get reassurance from him that my cognitive functions would return.

To my dismay my mum reminded me she was preparing for her brother, my uncle arriving for a rare visit at noon and hoped I would stay for at least half an hour before going out. I grunted I would, even though I thought it was a dreadful idea, but I simply wasn't capable of a counter argument and tried desperately through splashing cold water on my face to snap out of this lingering vacuity. I was dry-mouthed in fear that I had fried my brain permanently. How was I going to talk to my uncle without my nervousness and dread showing; or anyone for that matter who knew me? They would know I had changed. How was I going to do college stuff or get a job, or ever be normal again?

I lay on my bed ostensibly reading, but preparing myself for the biggest act of my life.

I heard my uncle arrive and the chit chat commence. My mum shouted up to me, "Alan, come down and say hello."

I casually ran downstairs two at a time, and cheerfully shook his hand. The conversation was terse with the usual "How are you getting on at school" niceties; "What year?" "What university?" "What course?" "How long?" I stammered back brief answers and he interjected with some talk about his daughter, my cousin, and what she was doing. In the background *Saturday Superstore* was on BBC1 and Eddy Grant was singing *I Don't Wanna Dance*. It looked so disconnected, unreal.

Eric's silver Alfa Romeo pulled up and he tooted his horn. The relief to extricate myself from the embarrassing and awkward conversation was immense. I said my goodbyes and bolted out of the front door, slumping liberated into his car.

Sunshine had replaced the early greyness, but there was no lessening of my anxiety. We wandered around High Wycombe Market, which looked surreal and different. The sunlight appeared synthetic as though replaced by a different category star with a cheerless, hostile beam.

We visited The Falcon pub and the same paranoia as last night that others were eyeing me suspiciously remained, though to a lesser degree. After a pint of lager, Eric drove back to Marlow and I spent the day wandering around the shops to refresh myself. To my relief the mental vacuity diminished.

I caught up with Ronnie in the evening to ask him how his experience had been. I had a *schadenfreude* hope he'd been caught up in a similar nightmare to me, because I was ravaged, distraught and wanted to compare notes. He said he'd been really spaced out and buzzing, but no adverse effects other than tiredness from partying until 3am.

Chapter 7.

A Short Pause

Remembering all the details about the next couple of days is impossible 34 years later, suffice it to say I managed to shake off the worst of the effects, was able to interact quite normally again with my mum and brothers, and just felt very flat, but I usually felt like this at the end of November, exacerbated by the dark afternoons and being short of cash.

The LSD trip was a topic of conversation at college for the next week. I was one of the few people in my generation to have experienced both a magic mushroom trip and now an LSD trip, albeit a bad one. The mushrooms were natural psilocybin, the LSD was man-made. I rationalised that was the reason for the two very different experiences.

In a conceited way I even felt a bit superior, after all, I had experienced something my parent's generation could never have dreamed of and like my heroes, *The Beatles*, knew what it was to 'trip-out'. I had become a member of The Psychedelic Club and could rightly claim a mystical camaraderie with those luminaries from the drug culture of the 1960s such as Huxley and Leary. Pride comes before a fall.

At a deep level my life was disorderly and chaotic through bad choices I had made from fifteen onwards with drinking and partying and a sloppy attitude to the last two years of school. And now, through ignorance and immaturity I had dabbled with something extremely powerful and spiritually dangerous with an attitude of utter recklessness.

But I was back to normal, briefly.

Then something unexpected happened. I can't pinpoint the moment, but the interval of normality which had returned over the last few days upended suddenly. An abrupt, overwhelming sense of despair, dread and fear descended upon me, and it was crushingly bad. I just seemed to wake one morning and everything felt strange and otherworldly. Nothing seemed happy or normal-looking anymore. The dreams I woke up from felt more normal than the new (un)reality I had plunged into.

It seemed my world-view was being beamed to me via an imitation of reality I could call 'Misery-vision'. Not a horror-film-style blood or gore-fest, but an alarming change in perception as though a filter of artificiality had been overlaid on my mental acuity, as you might put a filter on a camera lens to create a new mood. My mental filter however was now delivering a miserable tonal range of depressive hues superimposed onto everything I looked at or even thought about. Even memories were tainted with it including joyful and sunny memories from childhood. These too were suffused with despondency, like a switch had been thrown, gloomifying every thought.

My new world was submerged in a spectrum of grotesqueness and morbidity, undergirded by unremitting fear. I'd heard of 'flashbacks' into an acid trip, but this was different. It didn't feel like I was re-entering the trip - there was a different dynamic - but I knew it was certainly caused by it.

I wanted to die. This was chastisement. Godly chastisement. I wasn't aware of it then, but realise now that the Lord had handed me over to Satan for a while so that my soul might be saved.

CHAPTER 8.

Psychotic Reaction

Sunny days and dull days were no different. Unexpectedly, when a sunny day came it made me more fearful because I anticipated a change in mood, though none came. Every day seemed to bring a startlingly different type of depressive disposition as if my life was flicking through a paint-swatch-from-hell full of dismal ambiances.

I'd had dreary sensations before, but they were fleeting and were soon forgotten about. I remember feeling really depressed when I was about nine or ten years old at home on a grey, Sunday afternoon watching a 1930s *Felix the Cat* cartoon in black and white (or perhaps it was a vintage *Betty Boop*). There was something in the scratchiness of the image, the tinnitus of the sound and the frenzied rhythm of the characters that gave me the shivers.

My new LSD-triggered paradigm however was relentless miserableness with an undercurrent of nursery-rhyme-like unreality. I became jumpy, introspective and fearful. I was suffering slow motion shock.

I started to focus and ponder on the minutiae of life, gazing at objects and textures where previously they'd been unexceptional and insignificant background items. The tiniest bubbles in the glaze of a vase or a previously unseen knot of woodgrain in a doorframe was momentous and Anaglypta wallpaper (prevalent in many homes in the 1980s) was a highly unwelcome magnet for my attention. I would see an eye or often an evil face staring back at me – that 'looking into my soul' sensation accompanied by the notion that the object had a baleful life-force pulsing through it. A discarded tissue on a bedside table could take on the features of a wicked old crone, or a sofa cushion would have to be hurriedly re-plumped to smooth away the crumpled goblin eyes staring into me.

This was schizophrenic behaviour. Madness. Even the word madness terrified me. When I saw the band *Madness* on a record sleeve it was as though the sleeve was affirming my insanity and mocking me. I kept noticing the words *insane* and *crazy* more regularly than I had ever done before on shop window point of sale, in newspaper headlines and on adverts. I heard the words on the radio and TV continually and believed they were subtle accusations directed at me.

I had the vague notion that somehow I could 'pop' my brain in the same way that I could pop my ears to remove the deafness after the swimming pool and find relief, but none came. Sometimes I would shake my head rapidly to see if I could loosen the bubble-like greyness of my mental shroud. It was as though I had a metaphorical goldfish bowl or Perspex bubble inside my head which was blocking normal perception. Was it reversible?

Before I opted for anything drastic, I visited the college library to check the medical and psychology books with reference to LSD and its side effects.

Flicking through a number of medical guides, I eventually found one that listed LSD in the index. Scanning quickly through I reached a page that sent a gradual, growing shockwave through me like that fright you get when a low flying jet flies suddenly overhead as you grit your teeth and stand motionless because your brain can't figure out fast enough what it is, or what to do about it.

Gulping, I gripped the reference book in both hands, fidgeting with the sensation I was going to wet my pants in panic as I re-read the terrifying conclusion:

"*LSD and Mental Illness:* A psychotic reaction from LSD can be a dangerous condition with symptoms related to schizophrenia. Some people never recover from an acid-induced psychosis."

Terror-struck, I was plunged into an even deeper hopelessness than previously. Who was to blame? The Beatles? Yes, The Beatles. They'd indirectly encouraged me and countless others to end up in this despair by promoting LSD as fun and cool. Evil bastards! Did they realise? If they'd had a bad trip like mine they couldn't have. Surely not! Perhaps? Probably not. I didn't know. It wasn't important anymore.

No one properly explained what LSD could do to me. I'd only ever heard the odd story about people jumping from moving cars and windows, not the mental after effects.

My life was ruined; I had no future, just mental anguish 24 hours a day; no relief; no one who understood; no one I could explain things to.

That tiny life-changing snippet of paper, that insignificant fragment, like a tiny mosquito bringing malaria or a tropical worm bringing

44

elephantiasis; this miniscule blot had wrought something worse than physical illness – insanity! I would willingly exchange any bodily infirmity in preference to living with this tortured mind.

CHAPTER 9.

Hallucinogen Phobia

The library revelation embedded a fear of discovering anything further about the dangers of LSD. I did not want the hopelessness of my situation confirmed from elsewhere and was fearful of any discussion even remotely related to depression, mental illness and especially schizophrenia and psychosis. Even the words themselves frightened me.

I had seen for myself the unwashed druggie 'losers' sitting in the college refectory with their obvious mental issues. Here I was statistically joined to them with my own mental affliction. Whereas previously I was an optimistic student - deemed bright enough in English Literature to sit an Oxbridge S-Level paper, with high hopes for the future; liked and respected by many teachers at the grammar school, but now a plodding downbeat in a state of despair. If people only knew how far I had fallen because of that tiny speck of blotting paper.

December 1983 became a blur of dreadful introspections and surrealism. I trudged aimlessly through a kaleidoscope of fear each day, finding some comfort in cigarettes. I had begun to chain smoke to help quell nervousness (I note today how many mental illness sufferers smoke voraciously). Cigarettes were first priority, beer second. Eating was a chore undertaken simply to appease my mum. If it wasn't for putting on an act of ordinariness for her I would have rapidly become skeletal with malnutrition.

You would think that getting drunk would help lift the depression to a degree, but even if I got drunk the torment was there. Alcohol may have dulled my nervousness slightly, but never removed the mental grey-blanket suffocating every healthy emotion. All prior life occasions, celebrations, holidays, joyful events, meetings, memories seemed to me small, distant and otherworldly as this grey behemoth flanked me above and below with every avenue of escape blocked. I knew the normal version of me still existed inside my mind, but was trapped by what felt like an impregnable force-field.

Whatever company I kept, wherever I went, the anguish didn't go away. From college to home, to the pub, to parties, nothing would cheer me and nothing would shift the feeling of unreality or disperse the fogged fantasy world I was shuffling around in. My work suffered, my retaking of A-levels seemed like an impossibility; I could hardly focus on reading a sentence let alone writing an essay in History or English Literature without wanting to curl up and die.

When I wasn't at college during holidays or weekends, much of the time was spent wandering from house to house of friends and acquaintances in and around Marlow, just to find some relief from dark thoughts and ruminations by having a cup of tea and a cigarette. These distractions helped a little, but increasingly I perceived some acquaintances were starting to view my repetitive presence as unwelcome and I was conscious of being a burden.

Parents whispered while I was shuffled upstairs to chat in a bedroom or smoke in a kitchen with an embarrassed looking friend, but such was my desperation for company to divert me from the myriad of anguished thoughts I shrugged off any awkwardness. I walked miles and miles to seek new company and it's why during the week at college I felt more rested than spending a Saturday or Sunday marching from street to street, house to house, bar to bar.

Mercifully, I had two friends who seemed to understand some of my predicament. One, Andy a classmate from the grammar school was retaking the same A-Levels as me, and the other, Mike a very entertaining friend who came from High Wycombe had an amazing sense of humour. Even with my depression I was able to laugh at his jokes.

When I explained to Andy about the LSD experience he was fascinated because he assured me he understood the type of depression I was referring to and explained he had it too, but not triggered by LSD. I couldn't quite believe he had the same level of despair as me, but nevertheless Andy was a relief to talk to because I didn't bore him when discussing my misery and my bizarre thoughts and weird dreams. He seemed to 'get it'. He certainly shared my concerns about mental health and said he was experiencing terrible depression, undiagnosed because like me he feared going to the doctor's. He talked tongue-in-cheek about the relief of death.

Mike however had been diagnosed with depression and regularly consulted a psychiatrist. During our time at college, Mike's doctor had prescribed him a big purple pill on two occasions to help him 'get back to normal'. The pills were so big he explained they were hard to swallow and he had to take them while the doctor watched. Whatever the pills were they seemed to send Mike into a thoroughly depressed state for up to a week before he came around again.

Sitting in the college refectory at lunchtimes, smoking and chatting, was preferable to being at home. My mum didn't allow smoking in the house and the whole home scene felt claustrophobic and restrictive. It was cosy, but I felt trapped and though I loved my mum deeply I was desperate to be with my peers, especially Andy and Mike, as we shared the bond of tortured minds. My mum didn't have a clue about my tormented state, let alone theirs.

Mike would often discuss his ZX Spectrum computer and how he could programme it to play video games. Everyone in 1984 was amazed by the rapid explosion of technology and the ZX Spectrum made video gaming accessible to people at home for around £100 for the computer and £10 for each game. Many games you had to input yourself with code. In February 1984 he invited me to his home so he could show me a couple of video games he had bought and games he had programmed himself. He was always talking about BASIC and ASCII code and 'getting the syntax right'. I was clueless. For a prank Mike even went into Boots the Chemist in the Octagon Shopping Precinct one lunchtime and programmed the networked computer screens in the window with an obscene message instead of the 10% OFF Home Computing. We all thought this was hilarious and that Mike was a genius, typing out strange looking coded language so effortlessly and getting a result.

One Saturday in early March I took the bus to Mike's house and spent an afternoon there. Mike had a couple of very big-pixel platform games by today's standards with gaudy red, green, blue, yellow, pink and white graphics on a black background. I was fascinated watching his games load from chunky cassettes and hearing the upload noises which sounded like robotic voices, Morse code, gongs and squeals combined.

The first cassette Mike loaded was called *Valhalla*, a Viking Saga role playing game where text instructions were input and your character could talk to other characters. I was temporarily distracted from my wretchedness by this interesting technology. Another game was a science fiction-themed platform-style 'shoot 'em up'. Mike showed me which keyboard buttons to press, but I preferred to watch him play.

Soon I felt unsettled. The game had a mood to it which heightened the sense of unreality I wanted release from. There was a maddening repetitiveness in the graphics, especially from the rotating red radar dishes on the hillside and a feeling of malevolent intent from the arcing and buzzing transformers which the player had to avoid.

Those transformers were hideous. I sensed the arcing electricity was reaching out, connecting directly to my brain's circuitry, searching deep into my soul to destroy me. My palms started sweating and a panic attack ensued. I had to leave straight away.

The video-gaming experience took me to a new level of despondency. I felt there was nothing I could do to penetrate the blockade that stopped me having a happy thought. My mind was in prison. Mental illness was something I truly grasped now; it was all about types of unhealthy mood: A miserable mood; a terrified mood; a trembling, anxious mood; a paranoid mood; a despairing mood. It wouldn't be described as illness if it was a good mood; a positive mood; or a joyful mood, would it?

There was no 'snapping out of it' either. I had been wrong about what depression was, I had misunderstood the enormity and intensity of it and the control it exerted. It was an evil, dark grey power that overwhelms a person.

I went home on the bus, mentally ill.

CHAPTER 10.

Bleak House

My life was a maelstrom of weird thoughts and gloomy moods so isolating in their hellishness that I felt I would eventually reach a tipping point and descend into terminal insanity. Each day had a never-before-experienced dismal cast to it. There was nothing that linked each day's distinctive despondency to any past sensation.

All memories of joy appeared polluted, as though the feeling of happiness was being blocked from coming through. A psychological paint-swatch of depressing tones daubed each morning, afternoon and evening in a despairing new hue or frequency. Whereas a standard emulsion chart has appealing sunny labels like *Crystal Cove, Highland Heather, Peach Melba* and *Raspberry Dawn*, my mental swatch ranged through a murky spectrum of monochromes: *Sepia Smog; Belsen Dusk; Shipyard-Smokestack; Corroded Noon.*

When exhaustion finally compelled me to sleep, my dreamscapes were closer to my remembered version of reality than my new world perception. Asleep, my thoughts were more authentic than my waking consciousness which had become a dystopian science fiction saga. Bad dreams however were significantly more frightening than ever. One night in the early spring of 1984, I had a dismal, fragmented nightmare about being lost in a far distant zone of space; the Earth and all its history unremembered; just me as a single conscious soul in the loneliness; misplaced in cold eternity with three gloomy geometric shapes – a white and a pink octahedron and a red pyramid floating there pointlessly. The dim remoteness of the location and the monotony of the slowly rotating shapes was terrible. I took it to be a glimpse of death; eternal separation from all life, joy, soul-to-soul contact and comfort.

If you could share the experience of this lucid dream and its eternal quality, I assure you you'd also wake up terrified; praying to God for mercy in frantic desperation like me. I scrambled back to consciousness and instantly started pleading to God to free me from all the misery by letting me die, without me having to resort to suicide (as it would hurt my mum and family too much). A quick heart attack or stroke would do it. I pleaded.

Death did not come. I therefore started planning what I might do to end the misery quickly and I was drawn to the idea of jumping off a local road bridge onto the hard shoulder below. This would be very quick and I began to imagine the sensation of falling and what I would be thinking as I fell. If I could just walk up to the bridge and hop over the top without overthinking it would be the best route. If I started looking down, I would lose my nerve by rationalising the pain of impact and that horrible concussion sensation, however fleeting it may be.

A sudden supernatural event brought the route of suicide to the frontline of options. A detailed vision flashed into my consciousness like a heavy boot stamping violently on my mind's-eye. The image I saw lasted just a fraction of a second, but was so vivid it embossed my memory for years.

I was presented with a picture of an old man, in a tragic-looking blue dressing gown and slippers, lonely, insane and pathetic; moping along a clinical mental institution corridor. In spite of the hollow eye sockets and drawn grey cheeks, terrifyingly I could see it was me in the future, shuffling along as the final ravages of insanity ebbed my physical strength away.

Choking in panic, the shock sent me reeling onto my bed in the dimly lit room. It was clearly a future image of me at around 70 years old, or as I believe now, it was a future *possibility* of me.

This bleak revelation I understand now was a demonically created fake vision designed to affirm my hopelessness and send me decisively onward to kill myself. Something evil was manipulating my mind so I would run out of excuses to stay alive and 'do it' sooner, there was simply no other explanation for this unexpected and crystal clear image other than it had been planted in my consciousness by an evil force wanting me dead.

It almost worked. I visualised walking to the bridge in the glare of the orange carriageway lights and looking at the tarmac below. But what if I did jump and that distant outer space vision was at the end of it? I would never get back. That idea and the thought of my mum grieving and wondering why I'd jumped stopped me. It would be crushing for her and she seemed so happy and content in her homely little world. She dearly loved me too, as did my siblings.

I would just have to continue to wait for a heart attack. As things were I had a continual range of anxiety pains across my chest, shooting pains in my arms and head with all the worry and angst. The expectation of some form of circulatory collapse wasn't too difficult to imagine. My mental problems were blossoming with physical side effects.

CHAPTER 11.

Bed Tremors

The weeks of torment continued with the desperation for death present daily. Easter came and went and days of sunshine and spring passed me by without any feeling of renewed hope or vigour. A stark coldness highlighted everything, even the early spring daffodils in the garden appeared wretched.

There was a brief change of scene in mid-April 1984. I visited my sister in Newcastle to attend a cousin's wedding. It was a Friday when my mother and brothers and I took the train from London, Kings Cross. We usually got the rambling National Express coach from Victoria Station as it was much cheaper, but my mum had been saving coupons from the back of Ariel packets for discounted express rail tickets promoted by that creep, Jimmy Savile on the train ads. We arrived late morning at my sister's house. I needed a short nap as the previous night I had been to the pub and was still a bit hungover. I lay in the sunny upstairs guest bedroom and closed my eyes.

I got that closed-eye vision thing again. Although I was tired, I was awake and could see the room was sunny and bright with my eyelids shut. Funny thing, I'd never experienced this closed-eye vision until after taking LSD – it was like an illicit spiritual eye had been opened. I could see the pillows, the patterned duvet; the curtains; pictures on the wall; mantelpiece ornaments and books on the bookshelf. I could see the house roofs opposite in the sunshine, all with my eyes closed. Suddenly I sensed the arrival of an evil presence in the room. I still had my eyes shut and felt immobile. The bed started shaking violently. I was terrified. The evil presence was hovering beside me. I couldn't see anything, just felt its presence and opened my eyes to see the bed still shaking. I tried to shout for help and couldn't. I wanted to call out to my sister but my mouth was paralysed. I started trying to recite The Lord's Prayer and just managed to slur out "Owwurrr Farrrthrr". Promptly the bed stopped shaking and the room was released from the evil presence and returned to normal. I bolted downstairs hiding my distress and didn't tell anyone what had happened.

My cousin was married the next day. I can't remember much about it, but I know I was extremely depressed - the new normal. I do remember going to bed that night. I was in a sleeping bag on the floor in the downstairs guest room adjoining a wide hallway and one of my brothers had the bed alongside me. At around 2pm I started to get the closed-eye vision back and an unsettling expectation of an evil presence approaching. This time my vision floated out of the bedroom to meet it, drifting toward the hallway, viewing the scene as though I was standing there and anticipating something happening on the staircase. The stairs had three steps and small stairwell turning right onto the main flight, before reaching a second stairwell and top landing. Half way up, revealing itself through the banister rods, I saw a strange electrical arcing materialise as though electrical power was conducting through the walls and ceiling like a Faraday cage; a little at first, and then increasing to a noisy crackling and buzzing. This buzz and crackle grew intense and plasma fingers reached toward me from the stairs connecting with my head as my body lay paralysed on the floor in the downstairs bedroom.

The sensation of vulnerability was overwhelming. An uncomfortable electrical flux sensation stabbed inside my skull so painfully I began groaning in pain. The stinging, arcing tentacles from the stairs preceded the appearance of a most horrible entity. I say *entity*, because it wasn't a man; it initially looked like a brown, heavy looking gas, like bromine, which swirled and coalesced into a smooth, defined shape about twelve inches in height, the shape of a bowling skittle or large tan coloured baby-bottle teat. This thing was moving downstairs, discharging electricity at me like an evil Van der Graf generator or Tesla coil.

The piercing electrical buzzing reached deep inside my cranium accompanied by the tingling of plasma and agonising electric crackles. The sense of evil was overpowering. Unmistakably I was in the presence of something very dangerous, much more powerful than me, and its intent I concluded, was either to get inside me or to kill me. My head seemed to be on the verge of exploding in acute pain when I mustered the intense effort to remember the words of The Lord's Prayer. Without speaking, just thinking the words, "Our Father Who art in heaven..." the event ended abruptly, leaving me relieved and disorientated in my sleeping bag. It was the only prayer I had on tap from memory, and it had apparently stopped the attack.

My psychosis had turned a fearful corner. The bed-shaking and now this. Both experiences had involved a palpable physical dimension with buzzing in the head and a 'fitting' sensation, a bit like epilepsy I speculated. I was terrified of it happening again and gravely concluded my situation was worsening.

Returning to Marlow, there was mercifully no re-visitation from the skittle entity. Regardless of what mental-health label my condition would have been classified under I knew I wasn't delusional. The electrical flux-firing fiend had a physics-based scientific reality to it in spite of the fact no one else saw it. The scientific world would ridicule this conclusion, but like 'invisible' radio-waves which we accept as fact because text books explain how radios work, this paranormal experience had electrical and plasma-physics written all over it.

The unknown and mysterious things of the world that science can't explain are either ridiculed or ignored. There was more to these two frightening events than my imagination playing tricks on me. In both cases I felt the presence of something external approaching me that was extremely menacing and which intended harm. In hindsight my mental problems were being influenced by something supernatural. I didn't make a big deal about the correlation at the time, but in speaking The Lord's Prayer (even though the words of the prayer were more eloquently 'thought' than spoken) both events had been subjugated instantly.

In 2009 Marian Keyes, the renowned author also experienced a psychosis with similar symptoms to mine, except hers wasn't triggered by LSD, it just happened one day at a social gathering when a strange buzzing sensation in her body preceded a complete mental breakdown. In an article in the Daily Mail she quoted:

"Whatever was wrong with my brain wasn't physiological; it was emotional or spiritual — or something that doesn't have an acceptable name."[3]

I wrote to Marian Keyes suggesting that she should reach out to the Lord. She didn't respond. However, if my mental illness had a supernatural cause, I concluded that going to church might help me.

I had been nominally Christian all my life and had been schooled in ostensibly Christian environments, though had never really grasped the theology behind it. As a family we acknowledged the celebrations of Christmas and presents, and Easter and Easter eggs, but my only church experiences had been at Boy Scout's Parade in the local Church of England (CofE) church, or tagging along when my sister and brother-in-law attended, so I could spend time at their house for an hour or so afterwards, providing a refreshing change of scene from boring Sundays at home.

The church experience had been so mind-numbing, I remember fainting on a couple of occasions and repressing yawns throughout the whole tedious ceremony, especially during the dreaded sermon.

Like most children, we were lectured at school about how lucky we were to be living in a Christian country as we read about David and Goliath or Daniel and the Lion's Den as infants, with more complicated stories during our early teens. I remember for school homework I illustrated the Transfiguration of Jesus with him wearing an Apollo 11 style glowing space suit, in deference to Erich von Daniken's *Chariots of the Gods.*

Although I understood that Jesus was called the Son of God, I didn't know what this meant, hadn't a clue about who the Holy Ghost was, and even less understanding about God existing as a Trinity and taking on human form in the person of Jesus while retaining One God status.

Nevertheless, I decided to revisit church to see if I could find enlightenment and above all, hope. I had nothing to lose. I didn't even care if any of my friends saw me entering All Saints Church in High Wycombe with its grand stained glass windows that weekday in early spring. However appalling the idea of being spotted going to church was among my peers, my desperation for relief prevailed and I left the college refectory at lunchtime to investigate.

I sat in the middle pews and read the ornate scrolling on the stained glass windows. There was the familiar Jesus image I had grown up with in storybooks and school; a long-haired 'hippy Jesus' wearing ivory toga and sandals. He was lifting up a child in his arms and the text read: *'But Jesus said, Suffer little children, and forbid them not, to come unto me: for of such is the kingdom of heaven.'* When I saw the word *suffer*, it affected me, although the meaning of the word in its context means 'allow', that day it spoke to me with double meaning. I was strangely comforted by that window. I felt like a little child wanting Jesus to heal him from desperate anguish.

CHAPTER 12.

Low Summer

The frightening spring of 1984 stretched into a fearful and dismal summer. I had hoped that longer days and a more upbeat rhythm to life would somehow pop me out of my insanity-bubble.

I tried to meditate on happy summer-time memories from childhood while sitting in the garden and focusing on the beauty of flowers, but every effort failed. However hard I strained, I couldn't break through the blockade inside my head. Like seeing through a sepia-tinted glass, every happy memory was blighted by a depressing post-industrial vibe, and even the sunny flowers in the garden looked severe in the sunshine, appearing artificial and other-worldly; the opposite of wearing rose-coloured spectacles.

As one depressing week at college merged into another weekend of dissolute behaviour, the week for exams came and went. The A-Level retakes which I hadn't revised for became a futile brick wall I had to hurl myself over so that I didn't look like a total failure although I felt like one. I had been too busy keeping a grip on the last vestiges of sanity and managing my play-acting of being normal in front of my mum to focus on academia. I had no concern for History, Geography and the grindingly miserable English Literature studies which focused on the 20th century poetry of Ted Hughes, W H Auden and Sylvia Plath. Was modern literature designed to make people feel suicidal? It was all so nihilistic and forlorn. It mirrored my mood exactly.

The relentless pursuit of seeking out other people's company as a distraction against disturbing thoughts was exhausting. Like a condemned man in his cell playing cards and making small talk with the jailer to divert his attention from the approaching march to the gallows, I was simply biding my time until death came. It didn't matter to me now how much I smoked or drank or indulged my flesh as these were my only comforts.

When you are miserable, bereft and hopeless it is tempting to indulge in reckless living. Today I recognise how easy it is for the despairing (whether the root is financial, emotional or spiritual) to engage in reckless behaviour - drug taking; sexual promiscuity; criminality; indolence; adrenaline-inducing extreme sports (no less a sign of needing to fill a spiritual and emotional void as the others). All these perilous and messy attempts to give definition and meaning to life are grounded on a lack of peace.

At one point in late May, I spent a long weekend boozing in Wolverhampton, taking the National Express coach to visit a school friend at Wolverhampton Polytechnic halls of residence. He had spent the last 11 months in Business Studies there.

Wolverhampton seemed weird and unnatural; a treeless place of plate-glass and concrete with graffitied bus shelters and soulless industrial estates. It looked harsh and unwelcoming in the early summer sun. My friend was playing a Cat Stevens Greatest Hits cassette in his room for most of the weekend during which we smoked pot, drank and partied in the halls and local pubs. He sneered at me, almost loathingly when I explained my depression and how I thought that Rolls-Royce motorcars looked evil. I had become the loser on a road to failure.

In spite of this, after the weekend he invited me to spend a couple of days with him in at his family home, probably as a distraction against the boredom of being stuck with his mum and dad 24/7. They were picking him up for the holidays and it would save me getting the coach all the way home as he only lived 15 miles from Marlow. It was a welcome suggestion for me, although his parents who had previously thought I was a bright, well-mannered boy and a good example for their son when I had last seen them, both looked at me aghast in my unshaven, trench-coated state and said we both looked like 'Hickory Holler's Tramp' whoever that anachronism from their 1950s world was.

Of course, they were clearly singling me out with the slur, but were trying to be less harsh by bracketing us both under the same insult. I could tell they were disgruntled with the idea of putting me up as a lodger for the next two days, and tried to persuade me to be dropped at home in Marlow, but my friend, more worried about the banality of being stuck in a quiet Buckinghamshire village by himself countered their reasonable arguments and insisted I was to stay with him until Wednesday.

I became despondent during the two hour journey to their home. There was a dreadful atmosphere, and I don't just mean from the parents; I could handle that, but in the sunshine the turquoise-tinted glass in the plush Mercedes car had initiated a desperate new phase in my depression. One would think that the intense aqua light so reminiscent of bright swimming pools in spring sunshine would impart a positive and upbeat backdrop to the luxury interior of the ivory leather upholstery, but instead it furnished an oppressive, ascetic glare reminiscent of 1940s clinical trials and Nazi experimentation, tempering the faces of the car occupants in a menacing aqua hue. I gulped claustrophobically, breathless and drowning. How many more miserable, despairing moods could my brain muster? Even in bright sunshine things looked disquieting at best, terrifying at worst. I had considered that living in California basking in sunshine would be better for mental health than shivering in the drab industrial streets of a European city with its winter chill and urban poverty, but now I realised that when you're gripped by a severe mental health issue, your external environment is largely inconsequential. With intense negativity controlling your perception of reality even the most pleasant climates and scenic views are shrouded in horribleness.

CHAPTER 13.

A Dreary Outlook

According to psychiatric reference books, my affliction would probably have been classified as a form of posttraumatic dissociative *depressive psychosis*.

While regular people can understand common sensations of anxiety and fear, the terrors of a depressive psychotic are so extremely outlandish and varied that if you are a sufferer, it is nearly impossible to explain your myriad of experiences and emotions to a sane person. Even if you have the vocabulary to do so, getting them to appreciate the fluctuating sensations of madness is frustrating and usually received with a polite and sympathetic head nodding as they make their excuses to leave.

Unlike 'The Blues' or feeling a bit under the weather which we can all relate to and receive sympathy for, depressive psychosis delivers so many capricious mood swings and atmospheres affecting your frame of mind they are too crazy to articulate. I couldn't just say to someone, "Hi, I'm feeling intensely suicidal today because I saw a factory chimney and its charred matt texture was so overpoweringly gloomy and nasty, it has created in me a sense of despair so great that I really have no option but ending it all." Or, "I have just seen a logo on the side of a van representing a symbolic person, but the wiry-looking legs and arms and the faceless ball of the head-shape is making me terribly morbid and anxious."

"Nuts!" they would think and have me put away. Indeed, a few months ago I would not have understood either, but now I did. I really got it; I understood what mental illness meant in all its mottled, speckled, rough, smooth, polymorphous and fearful varieties.

In like manner, one rainy Sunday afternoon I had stayed at home watching TV with my mum when an advert came on for an insurance company showing a stick-man character in a dark Tim Burton-esque style of animation as seen in *Corpse Bride* and *The Nightmare before Christmas*. The animated character walked from shop to shop, ostensibly looking for a better insurance deal.

My mum surprised me when she exclaimed that the stick man (it actually looked more like a pipe-cleaner with two big eyeballs) gave her a 'horrible feeling inside'. I knew precisely what she meant. I also had an abhorrence toward that lanky pipe-cleaner thing because recently at night, as one more nightmarish outgrowth of my psychosis budded, I'd experienced closed-eye visions of a crude worm-like thing with curled bristles sprouting from its reedy body in a random, untidy manner. It was almost the same design as the TV stick man. I had found this deeply unsettling and wondered if, far from being a figment of my imagination whether the thing I'd glimpsed in my mind's eye was some kind of demonic entity my spiritual goggles had revealed, facilitated through the illicit opening of my 'third eye' through LSD. Was this worm-like vision the entity's true form? It seems quite possible that it was the case and would beg the question, is there an inherited tendency for entity attachment (given my mother recognised the hideousness of the thing on a subconscious level at the very least)? The idea that individuals could share a common aversion to such weirdness and are able to articulate a suspicious dislike of such oddness supports the concept of Carl Jung's *Collective Unconscious*; that part of the mind containing memories and impulses of which the individual is not aware, yet is common to mankind as a whole and originates in the inherited structure of the brain.

Incredibly, many years later I had this *Collective Unconscious* idea confirmed while watching a news article about a recently discovered fossil of an extinct marine creature the scientists had named *Hallucigenia*. Although it didn't share all the characteristics of the pipe-cleaner thing on the advert, the artist's impressions nevertheless had that disturbing strangeness about it clarifying that whoever had named the creature had also recognised it was something which had broken away from normal reality with a demented hallucinogenic weirdness about it. Other images of a similar genre, and which, during my psychosis could easily have triggered a profound sense of despair were on the B52's album cover, *Bouncing off the Satellites*; and Orbital's *In Sides*, all sharing the common theme of nightmarish unreality with images that certainly look like entities.

The contemporary art designs of some album covers seem deliberately intentioned to create mental dissonance. That goes for animation in general with many styles of cartoons and computer graphic imagery very disturbing to a mentally ill person with the capacity to tip the balance of an already miserable day into a hellish experience.

If a sane person wants to understand something of the mood of depression experienced by a sufferer, there are one or two films readily available on YouTube and other digital platforms that have the uncommon ability to tap into the recesses of even a healthy mind and trigger a reaction. I don't recommend anyone with mental illness views them, but Frank Zappa's music video, *City of Tiny Lights,* encapsulates the morbidity and outlandishness of certain moods of psychotic depression, as does the film *Eraserhead* by David Lynch. I can't bear to watch either. A carer perhaps may want to look at these to grasp the sense of unreality and atmosphere of depression that can overwhelm a sufferer. Salvador Dali was also able to capture demonic madness in many of his paintings too. *Sketch for Destino* is a particularly disturbing artwork.

What, I wonder did Middle Ages' psychosis sufferers experience? What hallucinatory visions did they see corresponding to their time? Possibly something comparable to the Dutch artist, Hieronymus Bosch's paintings of grotesque people, devils, human-hybrid monsters and dismal scenes of Hell with its torture, suffering and decay.

Technology aside and with a few cultural differences, the mood of a seventeen year old boy or girl from 1500AD probably wouldn't differ that much from the mood and hopes of generations of teenagers in the present day, sharing as we do those common threads of experience and human nature alongside the changing lilt of the seasons affecting the thoughts and disposition of a person. Even so, I am certain that mental illness may be more terrible today thanks to the influence and sheer volume of contemporary media, particularly television that gushes a fountain of disturbing and surreal imagery to dramatically undermine the disposition of a person.

Canadian author, Henry Makow Ph.D. exposes this eloquently in his "Illuminati" trilogy of books, showing how culture has been hijacked to deliver a satanic, X-rated rendering of Visual Arts, Performing Arts and Conceptual Arts, as we grow daily more accustomed to watching perversion and violence without blinking an eye. There's always some group or person pushing the boundaries of acceptability even more towards total depravity. It appears that media are designed to both promote consumption of goods and services (as well as teaching us what to think) while simultaneously disturbing, assaulting and depressing us at a psychological level.

TV was always more a curse than a blessing during my psychosis with some programmes dangerously mood-tipping. However, I admit some programmes helped distract me from my depressed state.

Before my psychosis I was not a great lover of sport, yet tennis, football and anything upbeat and real-worldly like athletics and motor racing I discovered could divert me from the worst of my ruminations. Conversely, any TV show relating to fantasy, space and science-fiction had to be avoided. The latter genre was both claustrophobic and agoraphobic simultaneously; any kind of artificiality was oppressive.

Back in 1984 there were only four channels available on English TV, and with no VCR player in my home there was a very narrow entertainment window. I was easily outvoted on sport if a film was on another channel. Comedy was okay as long as it wasn't alternative or madcap. Spike Milligan and Monty Python were no-no's, but Dick Emery, Benny Hill and Morecambe and Wise were okay.

The yearning I had for the tiniest glimpse of remembered normality was priceless. I felt that if I could get back to ordinary feelings just for a few seconds it would be a permanent route of escape, something I could clutch onto which would catalyse further recall of 'normal thinking' in a snowball effect. If I could only break a little hole in the mental Perspex sphere that was blocking my perception and exploit it until it cracked clean open, as a chick pierces its eggshell, I was sure I would eventually crack through my prison walls and find glorious, healthy ordinariness on the outside.

Daily, the possibility of finding that escape route evaded me as a lack of peace and restless quest for peer companionship was winning me a reputation, even defining me through binge-drinking, marijuana smoking and being a party animal. I was the King of Joking Around when I was boozing and could put on a remarkable act of being the life and soul of the party, though inside I was dying. The world looked upon me as an agreeable fool, but I knew I was simply lost.

I received my retaken A-Level results in August, which were surprisingly the same mediocre grades as previously. I anticipated worse grades considering I'd barely skimmed through the required reading in English literature and had been unable to mobilise any effort with Geography studies at all. My mother was accepting, if a little disappointed, but I couldn't have cared less. I had slumped into an apathy about everything where nothing mattered except getting better. I had already rationalised that if I could swap my mental affliction for anything physical I would do it, but of course that wasn't a deal I had any influence over. I concluded too that I was feeling worse every day, with more new and bizarre psychological issues to contend with. The variety of unhappy moods, frightening concepts and miserable philosophies which high summer evoked was astonishing. What was usually the most upbeat time of the year with sunny days and light nights felt oppressive and hopeless.

Nevertheless, the autumn would be different; whatever tortuous mind-trip my brain might have me on in September it would at least be from a new vantage point since I'd secured a position at a London University to study English Literature or at Liverpool for Social Studies. I opted for Liverpool given that I had always wanted to experience the city of The Beatles and figured the change of scene may do me some good. The choice of Social Studies was by no means a career move, but simply a course undemanding enough to enable me to focus on getting better without the distraction of having to put much effort into course work.

Liverpool was a disaster. After meeting some wild new acquaintances who were party animals like me and who recognised a fellow clown, I ended up moving out of halls of residence within two months and living in a grim upstairs flat above a Building Society office in a noisy street called County Road in Walton. This district of Liverpool, like many others in the early 1980s was impoverished and burglaries were rife. The Toxteth Riots had taken place just three years previously a couple of miles away, and I had a steel-reinforced back door to stop break-ins. The whole situation was not conducive to any improvement in my condition and it was here I gave up on all pretensions of being a social worker, spending more and more time smoking dope and drinking. The money ran out, I didn't attend lectures or hand in course work, eventually leaving at the end of the winter term in March 1985 with a sizeable bank debt added to my mental burden.

When I returned to Marlow I was nearly emaciated and my mother was shocked that my body hardly made an impression under the duvet cover - I looked like a gaunt head resting on a pillow. Although food was not my priority, it was admittedly a relief to eat properly again. I had experienced days of hunger in Liverpool and although I immediately had to sign on the dole to pay my mum rent money until I could get a job and sort my life out, the return back to Marlow was better for me physically, but mentally I felt like an abject failure.

The impoverishment of my situation and the letters from the bank had the effect of propelling me out of bed into a search for work. Within a week or so, I was unloading lorries in the warehouse for the catalogue store, *Argos* in High Wycombe alongside Ronnie, my brother John and a few others from school and college. They were all surprised to see me back in Marlow so quickly.

I rapidly paid my debt off and began working at Argos reliably and efficiently, even doing overtime. It was a good distraction as I had to concentrate on finding items from a sheet within a timescale and making sure the cage was loaded onto the right lorry at the right time. It was hard, sociable work where I was able to chat to other people of my age and older ladies and gentlemen who were good-natured and friendly. The only downside to the work was on rainy days when it was very dark and gloomy in the warehouse and this could affect my mood.

As I was earning reasonable money this afforded me the opportunity to go out more and see friends in the evening. My best friend from college, Andy was still a big support to me in the early spring of 1985. He really seemed to share some of the common symptoms I was experiencing with my psychosis, offering me some relief in understanding my plight was far from unique.

We both however continued to live a dissolute and reckless lifestyle. One night of binge drinking partly funded by Andy in High Wycombe left me in an even more miserable state than previously. Smoking marijuana and going to a party in a block of flats ended up with me separating from Andy and having a meaningless hook-up with a girl in a rubbish-strewn ditch in the early hours before trudging the seven or so miles back to Marlow on the grey, gravelled edge of the soft-shoulder on the motorway. I pondered if I could get any lower.

A hangover with psychosis is a rock bottom experience. Physically you feel shot, but mentally you really want someone to put you out of your misery.

CHAPTER 14.

Climate Change

I headed into Marlow town centre just after lunchtime on an overcast Sunday, and I slumped at the bar of The Crown Inn, putting on a cheerful disposition for the bar staff there. I was chatting to Iain, a young man of around 21 who had been, at times, on the wrong side of the law. I am not sure what his offences were, but they were of a petty, non-violent nature. He was intelligent and a polite person.

The church bells of Marlow All Saints Church were ringing optimistically. I had mentioned to Iain that I'd walked home from High Wycombe in the early morning after a night of boozing at Oceans nightclub and in a jocular, confessional tone admitted my life had reached a point of degradation I hadn't expected, especially having once been considered a bright grammar school boy.

I told him about how LSD had affected me and said something like, "Yeah, I sometimes think I should heed the call of those bells, maybe it might be a good thing to go to church."

At once, his demeanour changed, he looked at me with a keen sparkle and said he had started going to church, the Baptist one, and hurriedly handed me a couple of leaflets - small Christian tracts. He promptly ushered me around to the quiet back bar and briefly highlighted the tracts' contents insisting I should read them. He then did something which made me cringe and I had to check around that no one was in earshot. He asked me if it was okay to pray for me. I blushed, nodding.

He spoke a prayer relating to me directly, something along the lines of "Heavenly Father, please bless Alan and guide him with the reading of these booklets that you would give him help." I said Amen with him, uncomfortably.

He told me that after I had read the booklets it was important I had access to a Bible. I told him I had a small Gideon's New Testament from school and he said I should start reading it daily.

I thanked him and shuffled off, flushed and embarrassed at the public prayer-recital, but telling him I would give it a go.

He didn't realise just how hungry I was for some intervention and how desperately I devoured those two Christian tracts he had given me. One was all about how Jesus creates a bridge between sinful man and Holy God, illustrated by a small diagram of a cross acting as a bridge connecting a crowd of sinful people at the bottom of the page to the word 'God' at the top. It had various short Bible verses and explained how sin separates us from God and dooms us to perish for eternity. I understood the reality of Hell (at least from the viewpoint of representational suffering) very clearly now and I eagerly sought out what I could do to be saved from it.

Depression had shown me that rather than being symbolic, there was a state of mind and mental turmoil that existed at a spiritual level that was so awful even in this life, that if the soul did continue after death, through some kind of sub-atomic law of plasma physics, not yet understood, the idea of enduring that for even a short period of time was intolerable. Far from seeing Hell as a medieval concept for superstitious peasants, it seemed to me that the possibility of existing in some form of conscious electro-magnetic tormented energy upon death was entirely plausible, after all, I had glimpsed infinity and timelessness during my trip, and even if it was delusional, it was a delusion that felt real and produced genuine terror, so what was the difference?

It was hard-hitting stuff, but I'd already been hit hard and the words in the leaflets gave me a new hope. I was desperate to believe in their validity and when I reached the final spread when it asked if I wanted to go to Jesus in repentance and in faith for the forgiveness of my sins and go to Heaven instead, there was no contest. Even as I walked home I sensed there was no time to waste. I speedily recited the Sinner's Prayer in the back which read:

What to Pray: *Dear God, I am a sinner and need forgiveness. I believe that Jesus Christ shed his precious blood and died for my sin. I am willing to turn from sin. I now invite Christ to come into my heart as my personal saviour."*

I was reassured by the next paragraph which went something like: *If you have prayed this prayer and meant it, you are now a child of God and have eternal life. You have just begun a wonderful new life with Him. Welcome to the Christian community.*

It is staggering to me now that throughout all my nominally Christian schooling and visits to Church of England churches from an early age, there was never a mention of how salvation is attained for an individual. If it was, I clearly had missed it because I grew up with the belief, like the majority of people, that you had to be a good person and that at the end of your life somehow the good deeds would be weighed up in the balances against your bad deeds and you would enter through 'The Pearly Gates' if good deeds outnumbered the bad ones. Not once had anyone taught me the simple truth of how salvation is really accomplished (see Chapter 43, How to Be Saved). It took the intervention of that young man at the pub to point me in the right direction.

CHAPTER 15.

Sunny Spells

Within a few seconds of praying, a ridiculously coincidental climatic event occurred. Like a visual cliché, the sunburst unexpectedly through thick layers of anticyclonic gloom and for a few joyous seconds bathed me and 20 metres or so of ground about me in warm sunshine before returning to heavy cloud again. It sounds unbelievable yet I felt the Light of the World had responded to my prayer by shining those lovely rays down on me, brightening the rain-soaked pavements for a few brief moments. Looking up, I gave a gasp of gratitude, because for my part it was affirmation my prayer had been heard and that forgiveness and salvation was imparted. I felt a powerful spark of hope ignite within.

I was upbeat – the first time I had been anything other than despairing since the LSD. I started to pace home briskly to re-read the leaflets in the quiet of my bedroom and was keen to thumb through the pages of my Gideon's New Testament as recommended by Iain. I had been given one of those pocket-sized burgundy Bibles at school a few years previously.

I kept thinking about that sunburst. It surely was more than an amazing coincidence, wasn't it? The sky had been so overcast and dark and continued to be so. Such a deep bank of stratus stretching from horizon to horizon would scarcely have released such a clear beam of sunshine in such a limited area - shining right upon me - without some supernatural hand guiding it.

But the more I thought about it, the less incredible it seemed. It probably was just a coincidence and not really a sign at all. Perhaps I was giving mental assent to something I wouldn't typically have noticed. But then again, I was weather-obsessed and would truly have been surprised to see sunshine on such a grey day even without having spoken that prayer.

However, other doubts immediately started to creep in. Had I actually even demonstrated belief when I said the prayer? Was I really 'saved' at all?

The leaflet said that if I had faith in Jesus I would be saved. I flicked through the Helps section in the Gideon's Bible to see if it offered any advice. It declared in the Gospel of Matthew that Jesus said:

"If ye have faith as a grain of mustard seed, ye shall say unto this mountain, remove hence to yonder place; and it shall remove; and nothing shall be impossible unto you." (Matthew 17:20)

And again, for those lacking faith the Gideon's Helps section pointed to another verse under the section 'When Doubts Come':

John 7:17
"If any man will do his will, he shall know of the doctrine, whether it be of God, or whether I speak of myself."

The verses sounded old fashioned as it was a King James Version Gideon's Bible, but we had read this version in school for years in Religious Studies and school chapel. I was also used to reading poetry and prose for A-Levels and these archaic words spoke to me at a deep level. Even though I didn't fully understand them they were soothing, powerful and rang true.

Then a thought just arbitrarily popped into my head suggesting to me that since I'd had enough faith to even say the sinner's prayer in the first place it was recognised as sufficient *mustard seed faith* for God to grow it. It was an unusual thought, because it dropped into my mind, apparently from outside of me, not something I would think.

It clarified that if I really had no faith at all the prayer would *never* have been said, whereas my desperate plight had brought me to a point of grasping for some hopeful straw to cling to and I had responded to God's call for my salvation, however weakly; reaching out to Jesus using the tiny faith I could muster. It was more than enough.

On the Sunday evening, I attended All Saints Church in Marlow. It was the biggest church in the town, next to the bridge over the Thames. My old Religious Studies teacher, Doctor Day was the Canon there. As is the tradition, he was meeting, greeting and shaking hands with people on the way out of the church. I tried to avoid him and sidle past, but he saw me and exclaimed, "Poskitt! What are you doing here, boy?" He was surprised to see me there alone, especially given my fluctuating interest in the subject of religion in the classroom over the years. However, I could barely speak and just looked at him forlornly as tears started to well up in my eyes. He spoke kindly and reassuringly saying, "Go home, Poskitt. You need to go home."

I went home, choking back tears. This was the first time I had been able to cry since before taking the LSD.

I went to bed that evening feeling that something transformative had happened and that a sunburst within me had also taken place. The thick dark clouds enveloping my soul had been breached. I slept peacefully.

CHAPTER 16.

Early, Perilous Spiritual Steps

A week or so later, a friend of mine from school invited me to a Spiritualist Church in High Wycombe. My expectation was that it would be a regular church service with hymns and prayers, but instead of pews, altar and stained glass windows, it was more like a village hall, with blue plastic seats arranged theatre-style on a parquet floor and a stage area where people got up, muttered to spirits and imparted messages to the audience. I was initially intrigued, but rapidly grew bored and unimpressed that not one of the mediums had tapped into my situation, or even had a message to me from my dad which I felt would have been a certainty had they been genuinely able to contact the spirits. Rather, they were coming out with lots of trivial generalities, the likes of which caused some in the audience to nod and murmur knowingly. The atmosphere in the place was dark and oppressive too. Jesus wasn't mentioned at all. He wasn't there.

Afterward, we attended a group meeting at some 40-something female's house, but I got the impression it was an excuse for divorced, middle aged women and some very plain-Janes to approach young men. The house was full of chatter and one woman was gossiping about one of the girls' sex lives, which I found titillating, though inappropriate as even I knew churchgoers shouldn't do things like that. Later, I discovered the Spiritualist Church had nothing to do with Jesus and like many other organisations, the word Church at the end doesn't automatically confer Godly credentials. I was very much a 'baby Christian' and had no idea about which church or denomination to attend over another. This was a danger area for me, as I was truly seeking God now, and could easily have been pulled into one of the cults like the Jehovah's Witnesses, Seventh Day Adventists, Christian Scientists or the Mormon Church since all of these were available locally and were actively seeking new converts. I also attended a couple of services in the Roman Catholic Church in Marlow, but was so bored with the pomp and ceremony of the thing and formalism of the service, I didn't go back. None of the churches I attended so far were giving me any answers.

However, in spite of questioning the benefits of attending church, for the next two weeks I almost ate up my Gideon's Bible, desperate to hear more uplifting words to feed my hungry soul, ravenous for the hope it contained. This small Bible that had been collecting dust on the bookshelf was my lifeline and provided me such spiritual comfort that I carried it with me at all times like a security blanket. I started to read it at work in the toilet cubicles at Argos while having a cigarette break and at any other opportunity. The dreariness of my Argos warehouse job was transformed. The work felt light and the lack of intellectual demands in my role as a 'picker' allowed me to focus and meditate on the hopeful words from my Bible. I would also pray regularly and there was comfort in prayer now that I understood that Jesus had enabled direct access to God the Father, making me spiritually alive.

I had a reasonable guess as to what spiritual death must feel like. Mental illness had provided me with more than enough material as to guess at the existential horror of it.

Before asking Jesus into my life and trusting in Him, I had been spiritually dead in spite of the fact I'd thought I was 'a spiritual person'.

I'd read Buddhist literature; and done some Hare Krishna chanting and other things with an Eastern philosophical bent including Ba'hai, all of which certainly contained some spiritual truths, but now I had experienced Jesus, I realised all this other stuff wasn't *the* truth. I'd been hoodwinked by false religion.

Nothing had improved in my life through reading Buddhist or Hindu books and pamphlets, and things couldn't have been much worse after LSD. The various religious teachings I had previously experimented with may not have landed me in the mess as I was in, but they hadn't helped. Hinduism now seemed ridiculous with its elephant-headed and blue-skinned multi-limbed gods and goddesses, and the George Harrison- Hare Krishna gibberish of repeating endless mantras was hard, meaningless graft.

I came to understand the difference between worldly spirituality and true spirituality; the latter energised and enabled through Jesus Christ. All these other religions had taught me was that I had to *give this* or *do that* to earn spiritual points. Like a platform video game, I had to skill up and earn my way to the next level through learning mantras, saying repetitive prayers, breathing exercises, or getting spiritual rewards for doing good works, so that eventually I would attain *Nirvana, Paradise* or some other concept of Heaven. Yet my small red testament told me that Jesus had done all of the necessary hard work and had paid the price for me to be completely forgiven by God and enter Heaven just through believing that he had made me acceptable to God by his own blood.

It sounded too simple, but the more I read from my school Bible the more I became convinced this was the real deal. The words were alive with truth and it especially clarified why evil exists with an explanation in the front section that made total sense – that the devil is a real spiritual being and the enemy of God and Man and that all the misery and problems in the world stem from his influencing the affairs of man in opposition to God.

Satan is devoid of love. That is the problem with him. He can only love himself. Jesus however, is love made perfect, both toward God in total obedience to his laws, and toward Man, loving us in spite of our lack of love towards him.

I look back today and realise that the chance meeting with Iain in the pub was the defining moment and turning point in my life and it also marked the rapid decline of my psychosis. It was nearly two weeks now since I had prayed on the way home and though I wasn't noting down my feelings in a diary or journal I remember that I stopped envisioning suicidal thoughts and there was an immediate decline in anxiety.

It is vital here to state that it wasn't my prayers alone that were helping my situation. Iain and his church were praying for me regularly during this period. They showed me so much love in praying for me, and Iain even cycled miles to my place of work to give me uplifting Christian music tapes.

I still had episodes of fearfulness and disquiet but they had become tempered now by the positive words I had read in the scriptures about me being a child of God and that no one could ever grasp me from God's hand. The bizarre thoughts were lessening too. Rolls Royce motorcars no longer looked malevolent, just expensive.

Chapter 17.

Taming the Party Animal

One thing that hadn't changed was my habit of going out on Friday and Saturday to get drunk with friends and smoke marijuana. The 'get hammered at the weekend' habit was part of English teenager cultural identity and was particularly rife in small-town Buckinghamshire. Most of the late teens and twenty-somethings were doing the same as me, especially young men. The 1980s had a few girls getting drunk, though not as prolifically as the 'ladette culture' that would be promoted a decade later by *The Spice Girls* and their handlers in the late 1990s.

I hadn't considered getting drunk and stoned as 'sinful' behaviour, though I certainly understood their negative side effects like hangovers and feeling maudlin the next day. However, even with my marijuana smoking a change was beginning to occur. I began to contemplate God while I was 'stoned'.

One very strange event occurred when Ronnie, myself and a couple of other friends, Paul and Pete were driving by the river in Maidenhead at around 1am in the morning, smoking marijuana in Paul's mum's car. It was midweek, and we all had a common vision or hallucination which happened on the road adjacent to Boulters Lock. Driving past the lock on the left, the pavement opposite attracted our attention. Hundreds of chiffon scarves appeared to float down from the sky in a myriad of colours. As we drove closer under the confetti of chiffon we saw a very tall man, clearly illuminated, almost the height of the lamppost he stood under, wearing a shepherd's costume with a herd of around twenty sheep next to him. Dumbfounded, we drove past this vision, mouths open in astonishment, simultaneously exclaiming "What the …?"

I brought this up a few times in conversation over the next couple of weeks and no one wanted to talk about it. I thought their reticence to discuss the matter extraordinary. Whatever this vision was I still do not understand the relevance of it. Was it a vision of protection? Were four reckless boys driving around under the influence of drugs in a sports car being protected by the Great Shepherd, Jesus or one of his angels? That could have been it. Perhaps though it was a spiritual deception given that we were smoking marijuana, though if it was, I can't see what the aim of the deception was.

However, the most notable of all the strange events in the immediate aftermath of my early Christian walk was two weeks later on a Saturday morning. I'd been invited by a couple of friends from the grammar school to a London Squatter's party. I didn't dare mention it to my mum as the word 'squatters' would have horrified her, but since the address was in Bermondsey I had to catch a coach from High Wycombe into London.

I waited in the shelter of the big bus station and sat down on one of those uncomfortable plastic wall seats that flip down from vertical to a horizontal position, just a little bigger than a child's swing seat. There were three seats in the section and all were now taken. A young woman with a pushchair and baby turned up. She looked fraught and tired and I thought she would appreciate my seat. I offered it to her and she took it gratefully. It was then it happened.

From somewhere beyond myself I felt a warm, compassionate presence approach me and then enfold me from both without and within in overarching love and security. I am hesitant to use the word benevolence as it has become a cliché for those sensations when people describe the presence of God, but that is truly what the sensation was - benevolence 360 degrees - above, below, around and inside.

There was no expectation of anything happening that day. It was God's grace moving upon me. I felt like that *Ready Brek* porridge advert where the boy walks to school with a rosy glow all around him after eating a warming bowlful. Even the severity of the concrete bus station had mellowed; all seemed softer, calmer and the people looked benign though a little sad and lost. For precious minutes I perceived the bus station and everyone in it bathed in peace and blessedness. Even the noise of airbrakes and departure announcements appeared muffled or detached and I felt a deep empathy and love for every person I looked at.

Whereas I would normally be unconsciously critiquing them for their size and shape, their facial expressions, their clothes, their class, their manners and demeanour; what I was doing now was totally out of character. I was looking at them lovingly, captivated by each person's uniqueness; realising they were altogether wonderful and beautifully made; young and old, skinny or overweight, black and white, some with shopping bags, others with cases; some reading a book or paper, others scrutinising timetables. I loved them all the same, from the

76

unkempt and unwashed to those who were in the full bloom of youth and attractiveness. I loved them all without favouritism. The presence that was with me was tangible; warm, holy and perfectly loving, and this love which embraced me from all directions was energising. I was given the most sincere desire to love and reach out toward every person I encountered.

The warm benevolence continued to enfold me as I got on the bus for London. The atmosphere was exquisite and compassionate. I sat in the centre of the bus in the left hand window seat. It was empty apart from the driver and someone else in the row of seats at the far back. Just before we set off, two very well dressed older gentlemen in smart suits got on and sat directly behind me. I thought this was strange since there were so many seats on the bus available. I felt the same compassionate warmth towards them as the bus pulled away smoothly into the town centre and onto the motorway heading for London. The two men talked behind me in pleasant, mellifluous tones. They were discussing something about Heaven and angels. I don't know what exactly, but their tone was kindly, reassuring and spoken with a soothing, ethereal gentleness.

I felt enraptured on that journey as though spiritual knowledge and insight had been poured into my head. Most of all I cared about people. I really hadn't cared much about anyone but myself before and that was the crux of the matter. For the first time in my life I really loved other people more than myself and I felt I could sacrifice everything for them. I was seeing people as Jesus saw them, as essential and priceless. Wherever I went that day I felt immense tenderness and wanted to bless everyone in any way possible. I was loving, invigorated and full of joy. No more mental illness. All the turmoil in my mind had been swept clean away and I'd been released from prison. I could barely remember what the feelings of psychosis felt like. I was upbeat with a new purpose in life and spring in my step. Hope had returned.

I took a lift to a high floor in the tower block where the party was to take place. It was just 3pm and too early yet, but I knocked on the door hoping one of my old school buddies was inside. With no response, I headed back to the lifts to find a café and come back later. A young girl, around 21 joined me in the lift down. She was unkempt, though pretty, with matted hair and a large brown rat on her head. I had never seen anything like that before, and normally I would have been shocked and disgusted. Instead, I felt she needed kind words. I judged her, but not in a negative and hypocritical sense like, "She is doubtless a dirty heroin addict and is such a loser having a rat on her head; stay clear in case you catch head lice." Instead I was drawn to ask her, without fear or repugnance if it was her pet rat. She said yes and I enquired of its name and told her I thought it looked very healthy and well looked after and asked what she fed it. Her whole demeanour lit up when I spoke with her and she left the lift, walking into the street with a big smile on her face and a lightness in her step. I had touched her with the presence of God by speaking to her lovingly, with true sincerity.

That night the Squatters' Party was filled with very Bohemian types who were being evicted the following week. I was surprised to find various Christian books lying around on coffee tables. There were other New Age spirituality books too and various Underground Comics, but the people, although young and struggling were not the big drug-taking losers that we are taught to expect from squatters. They were intelligent and interesting with some junior doctors in training living in the flat as it was free digs in an otherwise very expensive city. My friend from London who had invited me, now works in international development setting up water infrastructure.

In spite of having such an intense and powerful spiritual experience with great spiritual insight, I still smoked marijuana and drank until the early hours of the morning, falling asleep on a sofa. Throughout the party I felt the presence that had arrived with me in the bus station slowly distance itself from me without altogether leaving me.

The question I ask myself now over three decades later, is why was God so gracious to me when I was still immersed in dissolute behaviour? Like all Christians there is that lingering worldliness that stills clings on tenaciously like some rotten chewing gum on the heel of your shoe even when you get 'saved'. It took me a while to understand that Christians are not sinless, but if they are truly saved they do 'sin less' than before their salvation.

The Holy Spirit's work is ongoing in a believer and it takes some longer than others to shed old habits. I believe to the day we die there will be a struggle with sin in a Christian's life. Thankfully I was learning that all my sins were paid for in full by the sacrifice of Jesus at Calvary.

Colossians 1:13-14
For he has rescued us from the dominion of darkness and brought us into the kingdom of the Son he loves, in whom we have redemption, the forgiveness of sins.

Forgiveness of sins was such an easy free gift for me to accept, though had I not had the bout of mental illness, perhaps I would never have come to see my need. It's why Jesus said of those who were rich in this world and cushioned from worldly troubles that they would rarely ever come to the place of salvation, the foot of the cross.

Matthew 19:24
"...It is easier for a camel to go through the eye of a needle, than for a rich man to enter into the kingdom of God."

My mental illness ended abruptly, as a child waking from a fever rapidly returns to full health, and those vicious, horrible demons had been swept away by something much more powerful.

I had been delivered from psychosis by loving, spiritual intervention, and the shadowy evil entity or entities that had gained internal access to my brain chemistry and electromagnetic thought processes like parasites, were expelled.

The Holy Spirit had taken up residence in my soul, sealing me with the assurance I was now one of God's children.

Jesus said he would send the Spirit to us to be our Helper, Comforter, and Guide and he doesn't renege on his promise.

John 14:16
"And I will ask the Father, and he will give you another Counsellor to be with you forever".

For 35 years now I have pondered my experience almost daily, and wondered how many countless others have been saved from mental illness by Jesus Christ.

There will be objections from well-meaning non-Christian religious people who will claim that their belief system is just as valid and that if I had been a Muslim, faith in Allah would be equally curative; or that a Hindu prayer to Krishna would have been as effective; or a New Age advocate may claim it was simply my 'positive thinking', belief in myself or faith in *'insert any alternative god here'* which pulled me out of the pit I was in.

Secular psychologists on the other hand may assert my experience was delusional especially given the rapid pendulum-like swing to happiness, classically symptomatic of bipolar mania. They may also attribute my sudden cure as just a coincidence or explain in a convoluted way that the positivity rendered by a feeling of hope within me had caused a flood of serotonin which overwhelmed my mental negativity, like a placebo effect; or that the drugs had eventually been flushed out of my system causing a return to sanity etc.

I realise that some religious experiences are often misdiagnosed as symptoms of mental illness and vice versa, with psychiatric symptoms explained as spiritual experiences. I get it, I really do and understand all the objections. Scepticism can be a healthy safeguard against deceit, however, as Shakespeare's Hamlet so eloquently put it, *"There are more things in heaven and earth Horatio, than are dreamt of in your philosophy."*

When I experienced that benevolent force coming upon me in that bus station it had a physical warmth as well as spiritual dimension to it. Similarly, when an evil cloaked figure attacked me in bed as a child (see Chapter 20, Spiritual Attacks), it had a powerful crushing force which caused my bed to creak and arms to ache in the effort of trying to push it off before it dissolved into an invisible extra-dimensional spirit form.

Carl Jung the brilliant Swiss psychiatrist and psychoanalyst would understand this cloaked figure as his allegorical 'shadow' concept and not as an evil entity existing apart from a person. I don't deny we all have our own 'allegorical shadows' existing within, but I am compelled to believe there are real shadow entities too.

What caused me to be susceptible to such paranormal phenomena? I hope to answer this in the following chapters as I believe there are many factors which make a person more vulnerable to demonic or spirit possession and psychosis; with both phenomena in my view being inextricably connected.

Getting possessed does not have to be deliberate. You don't need to invite demonic spirits in by saying, "Please enter my house!" Any action that opens that door such as tea-leaf or tarot reading, or smoking a joint may do it. Even bringing home an item with an occult attachment to it, like an African mask or dragon ornament may open a gateway. Evil spirits can exploit the smallest chink in your spiritual armour to assault you.

In my maturity, I recognise that in 1983 at 18¾ years old my spiritual defences were not just in poor repair, they were almost completely shattered and I was a prime target for oppression or possession by demonic entities. In addition to the trigger event of taking the LSD, other events and actions in my childhood had also softened me up to the likelihood of spiritual attack and a major psychotic episode occurring.

CHAPTER 18.

The Door Openers

During childhood, I had two unforgettable encounters with the supernatural; at age seven and ten years old; one of which could be described as a *spiritual attack*. I detail these two distressing events in Chapter 20, but first I must mention that prior to the age of seven, and in total contrast to these later frightening incidents, all of my earliest spiritual or mystical experiences were very positive and provided my first evidences of God. Though I did not frame God in any biblical sense, I yet instinctively believed in a spiritual or heavenly realm as early as two years old.

I have amazing recall of very early childhood, which surprises many people, but occasionally I enjoyed rare moments of soul-refreshing perception where my vision of the world was suffused in a gentle, Paradisal light. One of the most notable of these early 'heavenly realm' encounters happened one sunny morning in the garden when I was just over two years old (c. July 1967). I was squashing some succulent plant leaves between my fingers and kneeling on the garden path in the bright morning sunshine while gazing at the pink, lilac and white Virginian Stocks growing in the border alongside. The smell of the vegetation, the warmth of the ground, the hum of bees, and the lush moistness of the plant leaves I was investigating connected me to the beauty of Creation for the first time. As I gazed deeply into the petals of one of these small lilac flowers trembling ever so slightly in the light breeze, I became overwhelmed at its delicate beauty, and in a rush of emotion, I shivered as a thrill of elation ran through me and I gasped with joy. Simultaneously a presence of great love and kindness enveloped me, reaching into my soul as though saying, "This is love." I would often return to gaze at Virginian Stocks in later years to have the same feeling affirmed, with a gradual decline in the sensation as the years passed, until puberty when I stopped getting it anymore. It is now just a far off memory of a memory. C S Lewis affirmed a very similar sensation and termed it as being *"Surprised by Joy"* in his book of the same name.

Just a little later, when I was three years old, my dad would take my brothers and I on our tricycles to ride around a very compact, tree-shrouded park a couple of hundred yards from our home, called Melville Park, while my mum would do housework or make dinner. On the way, my brothers and I would ride over an arched railway bridge opposite the small West Monkseaton train station and I remember one late afternoon looking at a spring scene through the diamond patterned metal screening of the bridge. I recall garden plots and allotments with hawthorn hedges, and a solitary cherry tree bordering scrubland full of weeds and rusted things which adjoined the clinker-strewn railway line itself. The scene was unkempt, a little desolate and quite unremarkable and I only remembered it because of the strange dreams that happened later. In these dreams this commonplace scene would be enriched into a vision of beauty and strange sadness.

The dream would begin with me floating soothingly in a kind of out-of-body detachment above the back garden at night. Not a breeze stirred and the garden was faintly lit by glowing flowers; from anemones to carnations and Sweet William, columbine and lupins; all aglow with a shifting bioluminescence igniting the darkness of the warm night.

It was a lovely sensation floating around; feeling protected and nurtured while slowly traversing the garden plot enraptured by each shimmering bloom which gleamed softly in the warm stillness.

Gradually I would ascend higher and higher until I surmounted the rooftops opposite and drifted toward the railway bridge by Melville Park where my gaze would be drawn toward the lonely cherry tree with its wonderful blossoms dropping like pink snow in the gorgeous pre-dawn glow, making a delicate, tinselly sound. The whole scene encapsulated a strange aching forlornness, which was yet exquisitely happy.

Waking up was a disappointment. I say waking up, since I was always in a semi-conscious state when I had the experience and could even control the directions I travelled in.

The Romantic poet, William Wordsworth believed children are born with a natural connection to God and Heaven, a link that dwindles in adulthood. He clearly cherished similar spiritual experiences and wrote, *"Trailing clouds of glory do we come"* and *"Some thoughts lie too deep for tears"*.

I felt privileged to have also had these joyful and lovely moments. These sensations dwindled as I moved from toddler to mature child and I never did enjoy this dream again beyond seven years old though I do remember when reading John Keats's *Ode to a Nightingale* at seventeen,

82

feeling the memory of the dream sensation almost whisper to me when I reached the verse which said:

"The song I hear this passing night was heard in ancient days
By emperor and clown, Perhaps the self-same song
That found a path through the sad heart of Ruth
When sick for home, she stood in tears amid the alien corn..."

On reading those words, the emotion of that dream hastened back and was sweetly recalled in a momentary rush of exquisite happiness. Like Ruth in the poem, I felt a growing realisation that my true home lay elsewhere and was inexorably calling me towards it.

CHAPTER 19.

Nursery Rhymes, Tonsillitis and Fabric Conditioner

Having covered two very positive mystical experiences, it is also essential to outline some of the more negative childhood developmental episodes which contained components of the mental illness I was to grapple with later.

These episodes clustered around periods of illness, especially bouts of tonsillitis, and manifested as very uncomfortable mental sensations and jumbled perception which caused great distress and which I describe in more detail shortly.

Borrowing again from William Wordsworth, who wrote in his poem, 'The Rainbow', *"The child is father of the man"*, I believe that foundational experiences during childhood are crucial factors in how we both perceive and conduct ourselves in the adult world. That is basic psychology.

As a boy with a vivid imagination there were abundant domestic sources for my fears to latch onto. Ordinary household objects became a source of mild worry at one end of the fear spectrum to outright terror at the other. To adults around me such fears seemed silly and my parents and older sister would gently humour me and joke about them. However, I am convinced today that some of my fears were likely incited by the demonic realm or that my fear in and of itself attracted spiritual oppression to some degree. Remembering the terror that some dreams imparted, I was much more concerned when my daughter had nightmares than most parents are, being sure that some sleep experiences cannot simply be ascribed to 'having a bad dream'.

In winter 1967, I almost died from sickness and diarrhoea, and was physically weakened for many months afterward. This period of illness followed a visit to a local vaccination clinic. Against my mother's better judgement she had decided to get my brothers and I vaccinated against polio (after watching a scare-mongering public information film about children being paralysed and living the rest of their life in an iron-lung). I remember trudging uncomfortably to the clinic with my mother and brothers in the pouring rain wearing a stiff plastic white mackintosh and recall with horror the tattered anatomical chart on the doctor's wall of a 'skelington' with pink and red musculature cutaway and staring, googly eyes. This unpleasant visual imprint coupled with other tactile reminders of the clinic such as the whiff of surgical spirit and disinfectant comingling with the pain of blood tests, icy stethoscopes and screaming toddlers, culminated in very unpleasant memories and a healthy distrust of vaccinations.

The doctor gave us some foul-tasting brown paste on top of a sugar cube and a lollipop as a pay-off. This mercifully was our only childhood vaccination. We never got any more after that, especially since a young boy in my street was brain damaged because of a jab given to him as a baby. He had to have bars up at his bedroom window to stop him jumping out. The 'polio cube' left me prone to terrible ear infections and general malaise for months and I was compelled to wear a rough wool balaclava to protect my ears from the cold. In this run-down state, I believe I was sensitive to stuff that my brothers were not aware of and became a deep thinker, philosophising about various subjects far in advance of my tender years, as I lay in bed.

My first memory of terror came about after an introduction to nursery rhymes via Hilda Boswell's *Treasury of Nursery Rhymes* from the early 1960s. Hilda was a famous children's illustrator and painted beautiful children's watercolours, however, the combination of the grotesqueness of some of the nursery rhymes and her correspondingly uncanny illustrations were disturbing. There was a pale green crescent-shaped man-in-the-moon made from cheese and an even scarier painting of the North Wind personified, blowing a gale with his plump, puffed-out cheeks, pitching a galleon upon a dark, stormy sea. However, the worst image for me was on the *Old King Cole* page. The dreaded illustration presented Old King Cole's 'fiddlers three' as impish beings with rubbery-skin textures, probably due to the imprecise print origination process used in that era which gave their skin an ambiguous quality. My brothers would delight in chasing me around the house thrusting the Old King Cole page at me and taunting, "Merry Old Soul! Merry Old Soul!"

Some of the Enid Blyton *Noddy* books too, with their primary colour pictures of wobbly-men, houses with faces and prancing pixies sent similar shudders through me, but dreams of being pounced on by the Merry Old Soul Fiddlers were particularly distressing and more like night terrors than simply nightmares.

I had a range of other childhood fears to contend with too, such as the loud, tornadic sucking of water down the bath plughole; thunderstorms; and cobwebs, notably a lingering, dark cobweb draping the rusted iron shoe-last in the corner of the garage. The garage was empty save a top-loader washing machine and mangle; two shelves housing half-used paint pots and old biscuit tins containing all manner of nails, nuts, bolts, curtain hooks and grimy, oil-smeared things. I would skirt past that shoe-last and dash back into the adjoining kitchen whenever the requirement to go in or out of the garage arose. In a similar fashion I would also avoid looking too long at the sinister shadows cast by the 1930s Art Deco glass lampshades in the upstairs toilet and hallway respectively, causing me to duck and shrug every time I walked under them.

There was an issue too with the new refrigerator, a luxury item in England in 1969. This would frequently whirr and vibrate without warning, usually when I was alone with it in the kitchen. My mother reassured me it was simply the 'Thermostat Man' inside switching it on and off. Far from easing my mind, this heightened my anxiety as Thermostat Man mentally morphed into an eerie, faceless version of TV's *Homepride Flour Man* with his bowler hat.

Amid all the terror of cobwebs, shadows and the fridge man, further cause for concern arose with my mum's oft-repeated ditties and rhymes. The first was the fairly innocuous, *"I saw a ghost eating toast halfway up a lamppost"*, which she occasionally voiced at breakfast or lunch if toast was involved. I pictured a ghost hanging halfway up the lamppost opposite my bedroom window trying to peer in at me. I didn't like the idea of that.

The second and by far the most sinister ditty went:

Yesterday, upon the stair
I met a man who wasn't there.
He wasn't there again today
I wish, I wish he'd go away...

To a young and impressionable boy, the idea of meeting an invisible or ghostly presence on the stair was just one more reason to either stay upstairs (if no one was downstairs) or stay downstairs if no one was upstairs. This presented problems if I needed the toilet, because there was only the upstairs loo in the house. If I did have to run the gauntlet of the staircase I would rush what I needed to do, flush the toilet and then hurtle back downstairs dangerously, three stairs at a time, always with that hairs standing up on the back of the neck sensation as though something pursued me. (N.B. The ditty about the ghost on the stairs had no connection to the plasma flux entity from Chapter 11. The location of the incident is coincidental despite the obvious Freudian connection.)

Another horror could be found in my sister's single bedroom. She had a small selection of 45 rpm records from The Beatles to The Kinks as well as a collection of LPs, usually borrowed, and which did the rounds among her friends. One LP in particular caused me nearly as much anxiety as Old King Cole, and that was a record by Chicken Shack: *Forty Blue Fingers Freshly Packed and Ready to Serve*. The LP sleeve showed a tin can with a photograph of blue fingers inside. The image seemed so illogical that my childish instinct was to reel back in terror. How wise children are. They notice things that adults are inured to and react in fright when their simple wisdom perceives something as irregular or unnatural.

Similarly, just a few years ago, as though duplicating my early sensitivities, when my daughter was just two, there was a toddler's television programme where a storyteller's house was personified with a large talking-face on its gable end. To an adult it was quite innocent looking, but to her tender mind it was just plain wrong. Just the mention of the BBC's *Step Inside* was enough to send my daughter sprinting in fear from the living room into the arms of the nearest adult.

Sensitivity is one attribute my daughter certainly acquired from my DNA, and there is nothing mentally ill about being more sensitive to moods than others. It perhaps affirms a more developed imagination or at least an aspect of the personality that is more esoteric than exoteric. It is probably fair to assume that certain personality types are therefore more prone to mental illness than others, for example I would assert that a child with a passion for real-world practical stuff like *Meccano* is less likely to be disposed toward psychological problems than one who reads fairy stories, fantasy books and science fiction with its various monsters, fiends, goblins and aliens.

In the same way my daughter shares my sensitive nature, it is curious to note that many of my closest friends over the years could also corroborate the commonality of dreams and other sensations which I had deemed to be entirely unique experiences. These friends could also describe in detail dreams very similar to those that had often disturbed my sleep in childhood, and which later were to re-emerge in a more severe form during psychosis.

One of these dreams I would term the '25-Watt Dream' after a friend coined this most apt description for this dismal dream genre. The backdrop for it was always indoors in a sullen collection of rooms with the whole atmosphere saturated in sadness or threat, illuminated by a dim 25 watt bulb, the light of which cast dark and menacing shadows on people's faces. During my post-LSD psychosis, this particular dismal mood sensation would often frame my waking hours. Visually the dreamscape is similar to the cinematography of David Lynch's 1977 film *Eraserhead* which portrays mental illness and psychosis extremely graphically. The 25 Watt Dream also reminded me of an excerpt from Byron's poem *Darkness*:

"...The brows of men by the despairing light
Wore an unearthly aspect, as by fits
The flashes fell upon them; some lay down
And hid their eyes and wept; and some did rest
Their chins upon their clenched hands, and smil'd;
And others hurried to and fro, and fed
Their funeral piles with fuel, and look'd up
With mad disquietude on the dull sky..."

It was indeed a dark kaleidoscope of dismal sensations which prevailed throughout my 18 months of psychosis. A girlfriend termed her similarly occasional dark moods 'grey-blankets' which leads me into the next significant and frequently experienced sensation of infancy:

I can only describe it as my 'Smooth and Ragged Dream'. Dream is not the ideal term either because it happened when I was drifting in and out of sleep in a mind's eye vision where I could see a motionless grey curtain-like backdrop. The backdrop was highly reminiscent of an image used in a much aired TV advert image from the early 1970s for Comfort Fabric Conditioner where matted fibres under the microscope before and after the application of Comfort showed a rough and smooth effect respectively.

The motionless grey curtain had accompanying tinnitus-like sound effect of static, similar to an analogue television between channels and caused an unsettling sensation within me wavering from mild discomfort during its monotonous smooth appearance, to a feeling of outright confusion and chaos when the microscopic fibres of the curtain suddenly turned ragged.

This was, I thought a unique aberration experienced only by me until my friend Tim described the exact sensation one night when we were discussing dreams in the pub, and then amazingly I heard someone else describe it years later on TV in even greater clarity. The latter description was tragically given by Lena Zavaroni, the childhood singing prodigy from Scotland, in a documentary about her life and her struggle with anorexia and mental illness. On a website dedicated to Lena[1] she described in greater detail what seemed to be the same sensation I experienced:

*"The time at the clinic seemed to bring a little happiness to her life, and Lena quickly managed to put on weight reaching just under 6 stone, but she explained to Peggy that she was fearful that there was a neurological problem that the anorexia clinic could not cure. **She referred to it as 'static' describing it as a veil of greyness and noise, where she couldn't feel a hug, or hear a kind word...** "I feel as though I have given away my soul. I don't have it any more. I feel dead inside..."*

When Lena returned home, she fell into her old ways. Living alone, claiming disability allowance and receiving help from the show business charity 'the Water Rats', she became obsessed with her 'static', and became convinced that the only hope she had, would involve neurosurgery. Eventually a surgeon at the 'University Hospital of Cardiff' agreed to give her a Leucotomy, a controversial operation that was only carried out in extreme cases of depression. She had said that she could not live with the increasing torment and suffering that came with the illness..."[1]

I was stunned when I read that. This was some kind of neurological thing that other people were also experiencing. What was it? Where does it come from?

Whether or not this sensation had anything to do with my susceptibility to mental illness later is unclear. What is clear, and taking a spiritual view of the matter, anorexic Lena could certainly have been influenced or possessed by a depressive and destructive spirit, partially controlling her physical, intellectual and spiritual function; eventually destroying her through promoting loss of appetite; nausea on sight of food and utter despair.

For me, this unpleasant grey static sensation was experienced more throughout early childhood, and more frequently during periods of illness and fever, especially bouts of tonsillitis which I was prone to. Delirium was the term my mum used for it when I tried to explain what was going on in my head during the semi-consciousness of these dreams. They broadly ranged from general sensory confusion to panic.

One of the other memorable delirium images which would form during a high temperature was a mental comparison between a very large, heavy iron ball (like the one Indiana Jones ran from in *Raiders of the Lost Ark*) juxtaposed alongside a tiny, sharply pointed needle. The huge imbalance between the mass and texture of the two objects could provoke the most intense feeling of panic.

This *big-small* sensation would occasionally morph into the conviction that one of my hands had grown massive, contrasting horribly with the rest of my physical proportions, causing further extreme alarm.

In addition to the disproportionate body parts and comparison of massive *vs* tiny or blunt *vs* sharp, the fever dreams would often be accompanied by a nauseous feeling of motion and a sense of travelling across a large black and white chequerboard floor. I would be moving in one of the chequered channels in a monotonous and steady conveyor-belt fashion, when suddenly all chaos would break loose and the channel I was in would flex upwards and downwards in tumultuous and chaotic loops, as the orderliness distorted into reeling pandemonium.

Noteworthy is the fact that these fever dreams were similar to sensations I also experienced during post-LSD psychosis. What is interesting too is how so many people, friends and family included, are collectively acquainted with the same sensations. Reading online forums and discussions about fever dreams and mental illness have also made me aware of how commonplace some of these strange thought processes and mental ideations can be. This is perhaps somewhat reassuring for mental illness sufferers who can appreciate that they are not alone in their experiences and that many other people share their bizarre thoughts and feelings. I would suspect that people who are susceptible to delirium-dreaming during fever could also be more predisposed to mental illness than those who are not.

There are some occult schools of thought, which believe that illness can cause a weakening or rupturing of the protective aura around an individual, allowing access to entities. Aura or not these feverish episodes are fiendishly unpleasant and are imbued with a hellish consistency, lending some credibility to the argument.

CHAPTER 20.

Spiritual Attack

Whether or not these horrible sensations from childhood were caused by spiritual entities attempting to weaken or exploit early possibilities of depression in me is very debatable, however, what I am convinced of is there are a variety of access points, portals or doorways which enable demonic forces and evil spirits to enter into the home of a person and frequently, the person themselves.

Let me say something crazy-sounding now.

"Daily there may be a legion of spiritual entities trying to gain access into your home and control the body and mind of you or a family member."

There, I've said it.

This is a controversial statement and to the majority of people who are spiritually blind and do not understand the danger, it sounds ridiculous, however the claim I make is not unreasonable, especially since evidence for the supernatural is no longer just the domain of religious people, but the secular establishment is now admitting to belief in such abstract concepts as *extra-dimensional portals* and *intra-dimensional entities*, notably from experiments with particle collisions at CERN in Switzerland where the search for the so-called 'God Particle' and the production of anti-matter continues apace. The paranormal is crossing over the boundaries from superstition into scientific fact.

There are secular extremists who reject all spiritual things with disdain. I find this attitude to be scientifically as well as spiritually unenlightened especially given that the brain is a miraculous organic electrical circuit with truly amazing capabilities.

Nikola Tesla, the genius physicist of the late nineteenth and twentieth century said: *"If you want to find the secrets of the universe, think in terms of energy, frequency, vibration."*

Spirit is not outside the bounds of scientific explanation. How can science rationalise such things as magnetism, radio transmissions, microwaves, radiation, and plasma energy; all invisible to the naked eye; all exerting a force, yet in the same breath declare invisible spiritual things as folly?

Scientific research proves that people can have their moods changed with the appliance of microwave radiation as well as hear voices from inside their heads through the application of Long Range Audio Effects or 'Voice of God technologies' developed by the military[2], so why are spiritual things dismissed with a roll of the eyes?

The scientific establishment who deal in abstracts themselves (look at CERN and its use of religious symbolism and terminology to explain its experiments) are arrogant, hypocritical and dismissive of millions of scholars and thousands of scientific geniuses blocked from the mainstream debate who see and understand a Creator's hand in nature's astonishing complexity. With the same vehemence that Roman Catholicism derided Galileo, mainstream science also mocks those who believe in the supernatural.

I lost any scepticism about the spirit world and paranormal activity very early on. My first compelling evidence of the supernatural came one night as I lay in bed when I was seven. It was the first of two very frightening childhood encounters with what I believe was a powerful force of evil.

As triplets, my brothers and I shared a room with our three single beds arranged in a row, dormitory-style with me in the middle with my bed head just under the central bedroom window and the foot of the bed facing the wardrobe opposite. The year was late 1972 or early 1973 and it must have been autumn or winter because the presence of a coarse wool blanket and woollen bedspread on top of the cotton sheet for warmth implied it was cold. The sheet was tucked in under the mattress to the left and right and I felt secure.

It must have been between 1am and 4am in the morning when it happened, because there were no street sounds and it was very dark. The house was completely silent too, so mum and dad were asleep, but something had woken me.

I was drowsy, though conscious of another presence in the room in addition to my sleeping brothers. I squinted groggily at a cloaked figure – the outline of a man – standing at the foot of my bed.

He was tall and dark; a deep black silhouette against the lesser darkness of the rest of the room. Bizarrely, he was wearing a Napoleonic style cocked hat (for years I mistakenly described this as a fedora). I could tell he was staring at me.

Aside from the cocked hat, the figure was startlingly similar to the silhouette logo on the Sandeman Port bottle - Zorro-like, though Zorro's cloak was hip-length whereas the heavy cloak this figure was wearing went all the way to the floor, just like the character on the Port bottle.

Within seconds the figure had moved quickly and purposefully from the bottom of the bed to directly on top of me and was forcing my blankets over my nose and mouth trying to suffocate me. I glimpsed the head and the hat above my face, but I couldn't see any facial features at all, just darkness. It was terrifying, but my adrenaline kicked in and I tried to scream under the muffling of the wool blanket, simultaneously writhing and pushing upwards from under the sheet with both arms to get the horrible heavy weight off me. I was trying to shout out for my dad, and just as I thought I was going to pass out in fear and breathlessness the figure dissolved into an orb of black above my head.

I shouted for my dad again but there was no response, and again; no response. I was too scared to get out of bed to go into my parents' room, and too frightened to go back to sleep. Eventually I must have nodded off. I told my mum and dad about the experience in the morning which was brushed aside as a bad dream.

When I told friends at school about the cloaked man they said I had seen Dracula. I knew it wasn't Dracula. Dracula was kids' stuff. This was a vile entity that tried to murder a seven year old boy. I have recently understood this entity is a commonly encountered 'shadow being' called 'The Hat Man' and have also heard that it is termed a *Djinn* in Middle Eastern culture, however I think it was a fallen angel.

Science would call this encounter *sleep paralysis*, but I say, if it's sleep paralysis why do so many people experience this same cloaked and hat wearing entity? Also, what if the paralysis comes from the entity's power itself? It seems to be entirely possible that sleep paralysis does not necessarily derive from within a person or their particular sleep pattern, but from an external power source.

Sceptics may ask what reason would an entity have in attempting to kill a child, or in tormenting a child with fear. I speculate two reasons. Perhaps demonic entities can guess at the progression of a child from a spiritual viewpoint, predicting that he or she is on a path to Christian spiritual enlightenment and salvation. Because they are satanic, i.e. on the opposing side, this is a threat to them and they attempt to stop that person maturing in their faith. They can do this by possessing a person

before that person comes to a complete knowledge of the truth in Jesus. I would guess that the fear-instilling element energises the greater possibility of a successful possession or increases the effectiveness of a spiritual attack. I don't understand the precise dynamics of this, but believe that entities are empowered by fear and can gain control over the mind of a person more readily by using the negative energy of fear in hauntings or frightening poltergeist activity.

Whatever the scientific basis for haunting is (and I believe that subatomic physics has some answers) there was a good three year interval until the next frightening event happened. I was just under 11 years old and staying at my Auntie and Uncle's house in Maidenhead, Berkshire.

Their home was a modern, three storey townhouse just two hundred metres from Boulters Lock and the River Thames. We spent many happy summer and spring holidays there up until my dad died in early November 1975. A month after my dad died my mum told us that my sister and my brother in law would drive us down for Christmas because the idea of spending it at home without my dad would be too much to contemplate. My brothers and I were delighted at the change of scene and it would be the first time our idyllic summer holiday destination would be experienced at Christmas. We were very excited.

It was between Christmas and New Year's Eve, possibly the 29th December, when I woke at around 1am in the upstairs double bedroom. I saw the outline of a woman in the room who I assumed was my mum as she was leaning over my brother's bed, seemingly tucking him in. I drowsily enquired, "Mum, is that you?" No response. Then, "Auntie is that...?"

The woman didn't respond but calmly wheeled around and walked out. I screamed for my mum insisting I'd seen a ghost. My Auntie was the next out of bed and then my brothers and older cousin were awake, wondering what the commotion was.

I was told I'd had a bad dream and spent the rest of the night with my mum in her single bed in the room next door. It was a most uncomfortable night as it was hot, and I was very afraid. My mum fell asleep again quickly, and once more, I was alone, listening intently between her breathing; staring at the slightly open door into the darkness of the landing beyond until sleep eventually came.

94

The next morning I recall lots of hushed chatter by the women in the household talking about who the woman could have been. I'd heard them agree that it was 'Nana' (my mum's mum, the grandma who died of lung cancer before I was born). I wasn't meant to hear all of this, but I happened to be in earshot of my cousin who was in her early 20s and interested in anything to do with spirits and Ouija boards and I overhead her speaking about it in the kitchen through a serving hatch.

The next night was also spent in my mum's room. It was so uncomfortable, but I couldn't bear the idea of going back into the bedroom and seeing that ghost again. By night four, a day or so into the New Year of 1976 I'd had enough of sleeping in a sweltering single bed with my mum. Besides, the fear had worn off somewhat, so I returned to sleep with my two brothers.

I slept solid until around 1am, when something woke me. I anticipated seeing the 'ghost' standing in the room, but there was nothing there. It was just me and my brothers, however the air seemed charged with a threatening energy.

In the bristling silence I sensed a presence approaching. I quickly pulled myself upright in bed and turned myself to face the door, gripping the candlewick blanket in terror and listening intently. Did I really hear a noise on the landing? I dared not breathe as I eavesdropped the silence.

I could hear my heart thumping, faster. Then it came again, a small and furtive creak followed by silence, then two seconds later another short creak, purposefully, inexorably moving toward the bedroom door.

I dared not even blink, but just stared hard at the dim door outline which was slightly ajar. Another creak. It was nearly at the door. The room prickled with anticipation. Two seconds later, another creak. Now it was just outside the door, and then, *creee-eeak*. It was right outside the bedroom door.

My heart was pounding rapidly as the fear was overwhelming. At the instant I reached what was a pinnacle of terror, the most wonderful thing happened. I heard a calm and reassuring voice. My dad! He had been dead for six weeks, but I heard him, or at least a very good impression of his voice, in assertive clarity speaking from *inside* my head. The tone was gentle, though firm: "Don't worry pet, it'll be alright."

Momentarily I felt a loving and uplifting presence blow like a warm wind right through me. It was the most delightful sensation I have ever had and nothing has matched it since. Like a heavenly breeze, this tender, warm gust blew through me like a soothing zephyr and my whole body felt as though it had become pure spirit for a brief two seconds, with every cell, molecule and atom bathed in loving peacefulness and total release from fear.

The evil presence approaching from the landing was forgotten, whatever it was, and I slumped against my pillows in a delightful, refreshing sleep for the rest of the night.

This was 'peace' as I had never felt it before. That rush of warm wind certainly felt like a breeze from Paradise and it made me realise in later years that when people talk about peace on TV, they don't fully understand its true nature. This peace that I encountered certainly felt like the real deal; living, vibrant yet utterly restful and it seemed completely energised by love.

When I told my mum the next day, she was astonished at my experience and told me that the words I had heard were the final words dad had mumbled to her as he was carried out of the house on a stretcher by the ambulance men before he lapsed into a coma and died from a cerebral haemorrhage two days later. The words I heard from inside my head however weren't mumbled, they were clearly spoken.

I didn't know it then, but my father had become a dedicated Christian in his late 40s after being a New Age aficionado and dabbler in Hinduism, Buddhism, Ba'Hai, Kundalini Yoga, Transcendental Meditation and practically every other occult spirituality for most of his life until his early 50s. My mum had told me that once, during his *yogic* breathing exercises he had come hurtling downstairs, terrified. He had "seen something" which made him as white as a sheet and he didn't want to discuss it. Whatever terror he saw no doubt catalysed serious doubts within himself as to what spiritual direction he was actually headed in and in his final five years his road to enlightenment was entirely Christ-focused.

This is the end of the first section. The following section covers my views on the subject of mental illness from a spiritual viewpoint, what demons are; how and where they operate and whom they afflict.

Part Two – *Spiritual Truths*

CHAPTER 21.

More Questions than Answers

The previous chapter describes a personal encounter with the supernatural – a haunting. Was it my dad or a deceiving spirit? I didn't have a clue about deceiving spirits at the time, only years later after my conversion, so I firmly believed it was my dad. (I have to swing back and forth a bit in time here and refer to scripture to give a better answer).

Biblical texts clearly explain that Satan's favourite disguise is that of an angel of light (see Chapter 33, *Channelling*, and Chapter 36, *Angel Worship*). I also believe that fallen angels and demons have the capability to mimic dead people (including relatives) if they choose to and they are sufficiently acquainted with human physiology to generate deceptively pleasant feelings within a person, particularly someone whose spiritual defences are down.

Jesus Christ himself will be impersonated in the Last Days. The Bible says false Christs and false prophets will deceive the multitudes and people will believe *lying signs and wonders*. Jesus said that when this *Great Deception* event comes even the very elect of God will nearly be deceived, such is Satan's power to mislead.

Matthew 24:24
*"For there shall arise false christs and false prophets and shall show great signs and wonders, insomuch that, **if it were possible, they shall deceive the very elect.**"*

The deception will be so powerful, people may even hear clear voices speaking to them from within their heads. (See 'Voice of God technology' below).

Of course, with the understanding I have today about salvation, I realise that since my dad was a Christian when he physically died, he didn't spiritually 'die' because he was spiritually alive in Jesus just as the Bible promises to those of us who are 'in faith'.

In Luke 16:22 Jesus talks of the dead going to either Paradise or Hades immediately upon death in his parable about Lazarus and the Rich

Man, and this is indeed what the Jews believed (that souls of good men went to Abraham's bosom, or Jewish Paradise before the physical resurrection). We also have evidence for this in Revelation where dead martyrs are conscious, not sleeping, under the altar in Heaven and are given white robes and told to rest for a little while:

Revelation 6:10-11
"And they cried with a loud voice, saying, How long, O Lord, holy and true, dost thou not judge and avenge our blood on them that dwell on the earth?

"And white robes were given unto every one of them; and it was said unto them, that they should rest yet for a little season, until their fellow-servants also and their brethren, that should be killed as they were, should be fulfilled."

Would the spiritual danger threatening me that night have been enough to allow Jesus to permit my dad's spirit (that was resting in Him) to reassure me very briefly with his presence under His (Jesus's) patronage? Only God knows.

What I can say is that the feeling of a warm Paradisal wind blowing through me was absolutely authentic and my dad's voice unmistakable, talking to me from *inside* my head. The voice was clear and strong.

The brain is a highly complicated organic electrical circuit, and it does indeed respond to certain frequencies. Nowadays, I believe there are certain frequencies that the brain can pick up especially when certain doorways have been opened and access has been enabled. If you need some scientific clarification about the brain being able to do this I suggest you look up 'Voice of God' technologies online where *ELF* or Extremely Low Frequency microwaves have been used in military applications, able to communicate directly to the brain in words or music, bypassing the standard route of ear canal to eardrum. Whatever spiritual method of communication was used when my dad spoke to me from inside my head possibly operates on a similar basis.

However, as stated previously, Satan and fallen angels can also pull off very clever deceptions.

Although at the time the experience utterly convinced me of the reality of Heaven, I was guilty of retelling the tale hundreds of times without any reference to Jesus Christ or my dad's Christian faith and may have inadvertently given unsaved people the idea that when you die you can get to Heaven without Jesus. That would make such a deception highly worthwhile for Satan.

I had in fact been praying in my bed for many nights to *"Jesus and God and Daddy"* in the weeks that followed my dad's death. I can't remember the specifics of what I was praying for or about, (I know I was very worried about dying of the same thing as my dad at any moment).

Those dark weeks in the immediate aftermath of his funeral were the first time I had prayed sincerely to Jesus under my own volition and not forced into prayer at school assembly. Without realising, I had taken my first steps in faithful prayer, in sincere entreaty, but I admit, and I didn't understand it then, I shouldn't have been praying to my dad. I was channelling his spirit inadvertently.

Nowadays I believe that deliberately or even accidentally channelling a spirit (as I did) or any attempt to contact dead people and animals is a magnet for demonic *familiar spirits* and they are very clever, even giving you authentic sounds, smells and sensations to deceive you.

So, although my dad was, as a spirit-filled Christian 'spiritually alive' in Jesus Christ, there is only rare biblical evidence of dead *saints* contacting the living (when the Witch of Endor conjured the spirit of Samuel in 1 Samuel 28:3-25 and on the Mount of Transfiguration where Jesus was speaking with Moses). I'm not saying it couldn't or doesn't happen, but aside from God's Holy Spirit, angels sent from God are usually the only ministering spirits that communicate physically with people in the scriptures. That means incidents of dead people contacting us will be deceptive and demonic communications designed to lead us astray.

Was I really that privileged to have had my dead dad speak to me? I have analysed the facts and think that although the experience seemed utterly authentic, I believe the likelihood it was a demonic impersonation of my dad to be compelling. I think the evil spirit could have used the spiritual energy of my terror to empower it and it did this to attempt to trick me and others through my retelling of the event, into believing in Spiritism or the 'universalist' New Age doctrine about going to Heaven without any reference to the necessity of Jesus in getting there.

Demons are intelligent and resourceful, but most of all they have no mercy and are utterly ruthless. They will pretend to be your dead son or daughter, brother or sister, mum or dad and get you to feel sympathy that you open your heart to them. They can also give you authentic lovely feelings when they want to as well as false visions. The real deal is they want to take you to Hell and the Lake of Fire, the so-called 'second death' where you are separated from God for ever, because misery loves company and they have nothing to lose.

Such are the risks of channelling spirits knowingly or unintentionally.

Another time I accidentally channelled a spirit was when my much loved cat, 'Biggy' died. He was run over by a car.

As I was burying him in the back garden I remember talking to his spirit, kind of whispering, "Goodbye Biggy, you were a lovely cat and we'll miss you," or something similar. That evening a classic poltergeist entered my home. A pungent smell of cat urine suddenly materialised, entirely confined to a localised area near the bedroom door for around 20 seconds - the smell came and went as though an odour-switch was turned on and then off. Simultaneously with the arrival of the odour came a hideous groaning sound travelling around the inner doorframe, moving through the neighbouring wall and into pipes where there was a clanking reverberation toward the direction of the airing cupboard, reaching the water boiler, which amplified the awful clanking. A final loud groan culminated in a sudden loud bang. The water boiler electrics had violently short-circuited. A new boiler had to be installed later that week.

That was a sobering lesson in the dangers of speaking to the dead, whatever the species. An evil spirit had been attracted to the atmosphere of mourning in my home, and was energised by my terrible sadness and my attempting communication with a dead animal, albeit inadvertently. This evil entity was able to move through walls and into electrical circuitry. I shall never forget that unearthly, horrible groaning sound.

CHAPTER 22.

Spirit is Not Unscientific

So what is an *evil spirit* and a *good spirit*? Where does each come from? Anyone who has had a supernatural experience will tell you that it was no figment of their imagination. Often the supernatural event will manifest in something physical such as electrical current fluctuations, or movement of objects, even physical attack and levitations of people.

As a boy, I had been culturally programmed into believing ghosts were dead people coming back to haunt us or tie-up unfinished business here on earth. We see countless films and media depicting ghosts as such. After my LSD trip however, I adapted my viewpoint.

I believe that ghosts are exclusively spirits or entities that are either holy-angelic or demonic in origin and that the souls of dead people never linger around. Angels are spiritual beings that at times take on physical form, and the good angels in the Bible when giving messages to people, *always* took the form of men.

I believe that when people die they go to either Heaven or Hell immediately after death and not so-called limbo or Roman Catholic 'Purgatory', (designed by counterfeit-Christianity to extort money from grieving people). There is debate about whether people have 'soul sleep' before being awoken for judgement, but that would still exclude people coming back to communicate with the living.

That is not to reject the possibility that a horrifying event like a murder may not leave a kind of sub-atomic imprint on the atmosphere of a place, leaving a spiritual marker of sorts. When Cain killed Abel, the ground itself seems to have become a spiritual pointer to the murderous act.

Genesis 4: 10
"And he said, What hast thou done? The voice of thy brother's blood crieth unto me from the ground."

It is perhaps why people see apparitions when the atmosphere is right, perhaps a kind of spiritual 'weather phenomena', but such events are rare and I believe are much more likely to be a demonic impersonation, and certainly not the person who was murdered communicating from beyond the grave.

Jesus said that when the righteous are resurrected from death they will become like the angels.

Mark 12:25
"For when they shall rise from the dead, they neither marry, nor are given in marriage; but are as the angels which are in heaven."

As mentioned in the preceding chapter, the biblical examples of dead people communicating from the beyond the grave are incredibly rare and all share one thing in common. They are *redeemed* souls.

The Witch of Endor was able to contact the spirit of (redeemed) Samuel at Saul's request, invoking him from beyond the grave:

I Samuel 28:15
"And Samuel saith to Saul, Why hast thou troubled me, to bring me up?"

Also, during the Transfiguration, Moses (and Elijah, who didn't die, but was taken to Heaven alive) appeared, speaking to Jesus:

Matthew 17:1-3
"And after six days Jesus taketh Peter, James, and John his brother, and bringeth them up into an high mountain apart, And was transfigured before them: and his face did shine as the sun, and his raiment was white as the light. And, behold, there appeared unto them Moses and Elias (Elijah) talking with him."

All the examples of 'ghosts' in the Bible therefore are of God's *redeemed* people who can on very rare occasions appear to men and even speak with them. However, there is no biblical precedent of *unredeemed* people being able to visit the living in a physical or spirit form. Therefore ghosts of people who haven't been redeemed must be viewed as deceiving spirits or demons.

Demonic entities can fasten themselves to a location and will be very familiar with the activities of a person or persons in a household and even attach themselves or possess susceptible *living* people within the household, hence the term 'familiar spirit'.

When a person dies the familiar demonic spirit is able to freely mimic the individual it attached itself to when they were alive. It is why ghosts often appear as family relatives. Some fortune-tellers will channel the familiar spirits attached to their customers, receiving from these *familiars* real details about the person they 'haunt' or the person's close family members, with astonishing accuracy. These evil entities have been around for thousands of years and understand how to gather Intel on people.

I warn the reader, if you attempt to contact dead relatives or pets, you will only reach these familiar demonic spirits who will try to deceive you into believing you are speaking with a loved one or give you messages to trick you into taking a particular action, especially to give you false life-direction.

I also made the mistake of channelling spirits deliberately through a Ouija board when I was 15 years old with unhappy repercussions. I will relate this episode later.

CHAPTER 23.

Old-Fashioned Truths Meet Modern Psychiatry

A quick quiz for you.

Whose name is spoken more than any other, and in more places?

Not sure? Here's an easy way to find out.

Go to the office and have a conversation, or turn on the TV. Watch a movie; read a paperback.

Have you got it now?

You'll hear the most important name in history used hundreds of thousands of times in your lifetime, spoken now as a curse term rather than as a blessing.

"Jesus Christ!"

"Jesus H. Christ!"

"Jeezus!"

"Oh my God!"

"OMG!"

You may hear many other derivations with perhaps some spittle, venomous intonation or profanity added to it.

Have you ever wondered why? Why is it that you or perhaps your husband, your wife, your son or daughter, your friends and colleagues are using the Saviour of the World's name as a curse word or inconsiderately blurting it out like some cheap insult, hundreds of times a week, thousands of times a year?

Why would a name from 2000 years ago still be so much on the daily lips of the general public (albeit abusively)?

Or, let's turn it around. Why don't people hiss out "Allah!" or "Oh my Buddha!" or "Lucifer!" in those expletive moments instead?

I'll tell you why.

Because Jesus is *so* important.

Important both to those who love Him and to those who hate Him.

Satan hates Jesus and wants to trample his name under foot. Satan wants you to hate Jesus too. He wants you to get so used to using the name of your only hope for salvation as a curse word that you will subconsciously curse the idea of coming to Jesus for deliverance. Call it 'subliminal aversion therapy' or programming.

Our minds are a battleground between spiritual truth and deceit; spiritual health and sickness.

I cautioned in the introduction that this book is written from a Christian perspective. I have affirmed my belief that mental health is as much a spiritual matter as a physiological one and I have, through suffering myself, been in the privileged position to get to grips with many abstract ideas and philosophies that never would have arisen had the mental illness passed me by. My LSD-induced psychosis was a life-changer, horrifying at the time, but ultimately leading indirectly to spiritual enlightenment and salvation.

As more than three decades have passed from the end of my psychotic episode, immediately coinciding with my acceptance of Jesus Christ (I understand atheists may mockingly attribute this to a heightening of my delusional condition, but that is to be expected), I have sought to understand the basics of psychosis and explain it from a spiritual perspective, especially relating the cause of some mental illnesses to either an entity or entities exploiting a physiological weakness to enter into a person; or possessing a person through a spiritual open-door.

Once within a person, I surmise that a residing entity/demon may alter brain chemistry either through deliberate action (creating electrical stimulations of the right amygdala and causing negative emotions such as fear, stress and melancholy), or simply through some other chemical or electromagnetic reaction triggered by its presence, affecting both the chemistry and circuitry of the brain, dramatically altering mood and processes of logic.

This is back-to-front reasoning for a psychiatrist who would state that a chronic stressful episode (like a bad trip on LSD, menopause, PTSD or say the trauma of an abusive childhood) increases the stress hormone cortisol and affects many brain functions, putting a person at risk of mood disorders and other mental issues. Of course, this is a logical assumption and in many cases will certainly be true; but in actuality, I believe the root cause of some types of mental illness is not fully understood.

I would agree that chronic stress increases cortisol levels while reducing levels of vital neurotransmitters, like serotonin and dopamine (the happy chemicals) and that low levels of these leave a person depressed and prone to addiction. However, I consider the strong possibility that entities enabled by a spiritual door-opening event such as occult channelling or taking mind-altering drugs like psychedelics or certain prescription drugs, could also be the cause of 'brain chemistry alteration'.

The action of a drug within the body, or the adrenaline released by severe psychological trauma can also open a metaphysical door to spirits, which have the power to consolidate their presence within the mind and manipulate brain function on purpose, or even involuntarily due to being a filthy spiritual squatter within the brain circuitry.

Without science being willing to accept the presence of a spiritual world however, it is not currently possible to prove that an entity could do this scientifically. To an unbeliever in demonic forces my hypothesis would be as ridiculous as suggesting that unicorns cause mental illness.

However, the hypocrisy of Science and its numerous outlandish claims should not be ignored. On the one hand, scholars who cling to a material explanation of the universe including many within modern psychology, assume there are two separate branches of existence: a concrete physical one, which they think is true reality because they can touch it; and a spiritual one. The latter they mockingly deride as a delusion for weak-minded people who cannot cope with the idea of nothingness after death.

However, remembering W. Clement Stone's famous words, "Truth will always be the Truth regardless of lack of understanding, disbelief or ignorance", I assert Christian theology is never at odds with true science, and the two should be complementary.

I recall a science fiction story by author, James H. Schmitz, called *Grandpa*, about a planetary ecosystem where one of the attributes of the planet's ecology was bodily takeover of benign, larger lifeforms by smaller, sinister ones, causing formerly nonthreatening creatures to become hostile, against the normal placid characteristics of the host organism. The planet had various parasitic creatures that could attach themselves to their preferred choice of host creature and assert control by connecting to the animal's nervous system using an organic-synaptic link. The story had clear metaphors for demonic possession and spiritual parasitism.

Similarly, I am now certain that given the right conditions, demonic creatures and evil entities that usually exist at a frequency invisible to the human eye can infiltrate and connect with a person to affect and alter the emotions and actions of the infiltrated 'host', to the entity's benefit and the individual's detriment.

Benefits to the entities – essentially wandering evil spirits - include having a host body to reside in where they can indulge in those things their master Satan would encourage, primarily *stealing, killing and destroying*. They can do this much more effectively in a body whereas as wandering spirits they are more impotent, potentially able to oppress a person, rather than 'possess & oppress' simultaneously.

As wandering spirits alone they may be effective at creating fear through apparition-like, poltergeist-like behaviour, but their main desire is to control a host mind and body from within. By doing this they can also carry out an assault on society, corrupting both the host and society at large to cause as much destruction as possible against their enemies, God, and Man, made in God's image.

This would occur through controlling the spirit of a person to indulge in destructive behaviour which may include unhealthy and excessive sexual pursuits, especially perversion (often leading to abortion or unwanted and abused children); covetousness and greed (leading to selfish accrual of resources while others starve); cruelty (sadism to others as well as to the host body through self-mutilation, eating disorders etc.); destructive thinking, especially to curry thoughts of suicide within the host by sowing mental confusion and anxiety; other forms of violence and murder; encouraging reckless behaviour; drugs, addictions (leading to despair, homelessness) and so on.

This list is just the tip of a large iceberg. I surmise that different demons and evil spirits have wide ranging partialities and preferences that individual humans can accommodate more readily than others, hence the variety of demonically-inspired forms of behaviour, with each entity creating specific symptoms and havoc within the mind and body of every host.

In order for the host individual to regain control over their mind and body, the entity(ies) either have to voluntarily leave the person and never come back or be forcibly removed or usurped by something stronger. It is likely that entities tasked with driving a person to suicide (in spite of the fact they like to reside in a host body) do so because it is easy for them to move into new human real estate given the many gaping spiritual doorways of modern humanity.

People need to wake up to this alternative reality: Spiritual forces exist. Our ancestors in the Middle Ages who believed in demons, faeries and night terrors were not as gullible as people think, in spite of their Christian religion being controlled at that time by an ignorant and narrow Roman Catholic system so theologically sick it was almost spiritually lifeless. Rome had seriously departed from the teaching of the Bible and was engrossed in real heresy and traditions of men with legends and myths so intertwined with its dogma that it was almost impossible for the common man to access truth from error - and there lies the rub - our world has been so immersed in 'fake Christian news' with fables about *stigmata*, disgusting bony relics oozing saintly grease; or idolatrous weeping statues dripping blood, that true Christian faith; the reality of the Holy Spirit; and the life transforming power and love of Jesus Christ, is the baby that has been thrown out with the bathwater.

I sympathise with the atheist. Atheists rightly reject the false teachings and superstitions of paganism and religious cults. If some warped version of Christianity was all that was offered to them without a Bible providing a reference and anchor point, it is no surprise they have chosen a rationalist path with a visible, material foundation that makes some sense to them; however, as renowned physicist Stephen Barr wisely points out, "How ironic that, having renounced belief in God because God is not material or observable by sense or instrument, the atheist may be driven to postulate not one but an infinitude of unobservables in the material world itself."

Atheism today is as mired in uncertainty and fantasy as pagans were in the Dark Ages. Instead of bowing down to statues and idols, atheism bows down to the talking heads of television and lecture halls who worship the concepts of infinite parallel universes, quantum mechanics and multiverses – all undergirded by the nihilistic sacred cows of reductive materialism i.e. Big Bang and Evolution theory; the *pseudo-sciences* we have been taught are true by 'experts' and 'scholars' from our earliest schooling.

Atheists are essentially spiritual prisoners, blinded by Satan and deceived by secular education; completely unaware a spiritual war exists. Instead of being abrasive toward atheists or any believers in false religion, it is a Christian's job to warn them by speaking the truth in love.

My argument is this: invisible things are no less real because they are invisible. Spirit is as real as the wind - an invisible pattern of energy - just as electromagnetism and microwaves are real; or radio waves; radioactivity; plasma energy; and the very topical 'dark matter'.

I predict that the dogmas of Atheism and Materialism are on their last legs and mankind will soon succumb to a form of politically-correct Luciferian 'techno-spirituality' or 'Occulture'. My guess is that it will be a revived version of the Alchemical tradition, embracing Transhumanist Artificial Intelligence alongside spiritual abstracts - a form of sexualised spirituality where sin goes unrecognised and its adherents will violently persecute Christianity as outmoded and intolerant.

CHAPTER 24.

The Truth is Out of This World, or Perhaps Not...

Spiderman vs *The Green Goblin*; *Obi Wan Kenobi* vs *Darth Vader*; *Big Daddy* vs *Giant Haystacks*; *Yin* vs *Yan*; *Light* vs *Dark*; *Good Cop* vs *Bad* Cop. The rivalry between good and evil is the world's favourite entertainment genre. The world is fighting many battles, but the ultimate war is invisible and is a spiritual one for your soul.

The main monotheistic religions: Judaism, Islam, Christianity, Zoroastrianism; and the polytheistic religion of Hinduism, all affirm the existence of a devil and evil spiritual forces, demons or *djinn*, however I unapologetically believe that Christian theology alone can explain wholly and without contradiction the real characteristics of the supernatural realm as well as the reason for the existence of these powers and how they operate in our world, bringing suffering and despair.

All other religions are satanic counterfeits which contain some truth, for sure, but contain enough false teaching to keep their adherents firmly away from *the Truth*.

The word for demons in the Greek language is *daimon* and appears over 75 times in the Greek New Testament and is translated in the King James Version of the Bible as *devil*.

The Bible provides many passages about the existence of fallen angels and demons. Indeed the whole of the Bible from beginning to end and our spiritual battle is predicated on their existence.

Christian theology understands possession happens when one or a number of such devils/spiritual entities/evil spirits enter and control the mind and intellect of a person by merging with that person's consciousness. An evil spirit merging with someone's consciousness is not a healthy situation. This book is grounded on my belief that demonic or spirit possession as well as spiritual attack are key reasons for many psychiatric afflictions resulting in a whole range of diverse global problems.

In Jesus Christ's ministry, he often confronts demons and demonstrates his power over them as well as giving his disciples power to cast them out:

Matthew 10:1
And when he had called unto him his twelve disciples, he gave them power against unclean spirits, to cast them out, and to heal all manner of sickness and all manner of disease.

We also know from Scripture that Satan who was one of the highest angelic beings (Cherubim) fell from Heaven with a third of the angels who also became evil with him (Ezekiel 28:18; Matthew 25:41; Revelation 12:4). Generally speaking there hasn't been much demarcation made between fallen angels, demons, devils and unclean spirits by Christians who tend to lump them all under a singular category of either evil spirits, devils or demons.

However referencing 'The Book of Enoch' which is not in the canon of Scripture, but nevertheless was considered Scripture by many early Christians with verses from the book alluded to by both Jesus and his disciples, there is a clear hierarchy delineating demons as a category of spirits deriving from the fallen angels and their procreation with man.

It is stated in the Bible (in Genesis 6:4) and The Book of Enoch* that *Nephilim* were the giant offspring of the original fallen angels breeding with humankind. These Nephilim were later destroyed in Noah's flood. The spirits of the drowned Nephilim continued as earthbound disembodied entities always looking for a body to inhabit through which they might once again cause evil. According to The Book of Enoch, it is these spirits of the *Nephilim* which are the demons and evil spirits we know today, although they are not in the same category as fallen angels who were created beings and were originally good angels before their rebellion against God.

God's holy angels, unlike demons can appear in a bodily form, always appearing as men (when on earth) in spite of the artistic tradition to give them wings or feminise them. Fallen angels also appear to be able to take on different forms - from men to monsters - whereas demons do not have their own bodies and that is why they seek a host to possess. Demons can possess a person or occasionally an animal they are working through.

It also seems that fallen angels and demons can manifest as ghostly apparitions or *deceiving spirits*, i.e. spirits that mimic our loved ones who have died; also known as *familiar spirits* as they are very 'familiar' with the person they are mimicking either because they once possessed the living individual or were attached somehow to the home of the dead person. (See Chapter 22).

The New Testament infers that the giants or *Nephilim* came into the world again after the flood, inter-breeding with Mankind.

Genesis 6:4
*"There were giants in the earth in those days; **and also after that**, when the sons of God came in unto the daughters of men, and they bare children to them, the same became mighty men which were of old, men of renown."*

These *men of renown* would account for the various Greek and Roman legends of superhumans like Hercules and Nimrod as well as the Titans and other legendary heroes from Roman and Greek mythology. These were 'god-men' of supernatural ability and strength. In addition to causing violence and sin (rebellion against God and His commandments), the Nephilim were also corrupting the human bloodline.

Possess or Oppress?

Demons or unclean / evil spirits are not human spirits, and will attack us in a number of ways. Examples provided in the Bible include:

- Physical illness

- Mental impairment

- The spread of false doctrine

- Spiritual warfare

- Possession

As well as possession, there are many examples of demonic *oppression* and spiritual attack in the Bible. Evil spirits can and do afflict a person while remaining external to them, specifically in relation to Christians who, though their souls are safe due to the Holy Spirit residing in them, can experience demonic *influence*, either through temptation or through the actions of other people and the satanically-grounded culture around them.

These are *the fiery darts of the wicked* mentioned in Ephesians 6:17; indicative of a weapon that stings us and penetrates us to some extent, but can be quickly yanked out. Demons will continually attempt to disrupt and cause problems in a Christian's life using these methods.

If you want to see this in action, type in 'Street Preaching' on YouTube and watch demons spring into action from within people to disrupt the preaching of the word of God.

CHAPTER 25.

Why Do Demons Possess People?

The ultimate purpose of fallen angels and demons is to keep us from salvation available through Jesus Christ. They want revenge on God and so they want to destroy Man, the pinnacle of God's creation made in His own image.

Destroying us physically and spiritually is their goal. They want to devastate our physical and mental health and remove all joy from us, always distracting us from the true source of hope and love, Jesus Christ.

Demons will attempt to demolish our relationship with God, with family and with other people; relishing the idea of increasing our depression, our pain, anxiety and terror. They want to make us insane by twisting our thinking and perceptions. They can do this through deceptive thoughts such as putting the idea into a person's head that he or she is a total failure and has no worth or future, or by influencing other people to cause pain to undermine us and to keep us focused on hating our fellow human beings. This activity leads to social problems at a local level and eventually culminates in unrest and war at an international level.

When Adam and Eve succumbed to Satan's lies in the Garden of Eden God declared a judgement on Satan:

Genesis 3:14-15:
"And the LORD God said unto the serpent, Because thou hast done this, thou art cursed above all cattle, and above every beast of the field; upon thy belly shalt thou go, and dust shalt thou eat all the days of thy life: And I will put enmity between thee and the woman, and between thy seed and her seed; it shall bruise thy head, and thou shalt bruise his heel."

God announced that Satan would ultimately be destroyed through the seed of the woman. A human woman would give birth to a male child who would one day defeat Satan. This was the first prophecy of the coming Messiah, Jesus Christ. Satan was warned of his end in advance and was trying to destroy the human bloodline that would bring in the

Messiah. For this reason he set out to corrupt or destroy any Godly child that could potentially fulfil the prophecy.

The first Godly child born, Abel was killed by his wicked brother, Cain. Cain was banished and Adam and Eve gave birth to another son, Seth. When Seth was born Eve stated: *"For God, said she, hath appointed me another seed instead of Abel, whom Cain slew."* (Genesis 4:25).

Although not explicit in Scripture, it seems a key plan of Satan was to corrupt the actual DNA of Mankind. By corrupting the 'seed of the woman', Satan could prevent the birth of the sinless Messiah, who of course, was prophesied to come from a woman. God said that Satan too would have a 'seed'. The Nephilim were Satan's attempt to ruin God's plan of salvation for humanity.

The evil Nephilim giants and their fallen angel parents were much more powerful than the feeble humans which they dominated. To accelerate the depopulation agenda, the satanic angels and their offspring encouraged and promoted every corrupting influence possible especially sexually 'uncreative' practices of Sodomy or homosexuality. Abortion was also taught by the fallen angels as well as warfare and making weaponry; taking drugs (sorceries), and encouraging idolatry (paganism). The fallen angels' agenda also included teaching humans to wear make-up and jewellery no doubt to incite lust and fornication which would lead to greater promiscuity, adultery, social turmoil and abortion.

As a result of Satan's efforts, God proclaimed that all flesh on the Earth had become corrupted.

Genesis 6:5
God saw that the wickedness of man was great in the earth, and that every imagination of the thoughts of his heart was only evil continually.

Humanity was on the verge of being wiped out through DNA corruption, as no hope of being saved from sin exists if you are part Nephilim or part fallen angel. Thus God judged the Earth with the flood, saving just Noah and his family and *the seed* that would lead to the Messiah.

Genesis 6:9
*"These are the generations of Noah: Noah was a just man and **perfect in his generations**, and Noah walked with God."*

Genesis 6:12

*"And God looked upon the earth, and, behold, it was corrupt; **for all flesh had corrupted his way** upon the earth."*

Genesis 7:13

"In the self-same day entered Noah, and Shem, and Ham, and Japheth, the sons of Noah, and Noah's wife, and the three wives of his sons with them, into the ark."

This is such an amazing proof of God's power that He was able to use just eight people to carry the uncorrupted bloodline (they were generationally uncorrupted by Nephilim interbreeding) which would lead to the Messiah, in spite of all of Satan's pre-flood efforts. Of course, when Jesus Christ ended up sacrificing himself for mankind at Calvary as an atonement for the sins of all those who would believe in him, Satan knew the game was up, and his judgement had started. The only game-plan Satan has now is to carry as many people with him to eternal punishment as possible, so he attempts to make people blind to the grace of God by keeping them in ignorance about the salvation offered through coming to Jesus in faith and repentance.

Demonic possession and spiritual attack is a powerful way the devil exerts his influence today and it's very much on the increase, particularly through the influence of drugs as well as occult practices and countless satanically-inspired religions so that no one is immune from its ravages either directly through possession and oppression, or indirectly through living with or in proximity to demonically-possessed people.

CHAPTER 26.

What are the Symptoms of Demonic Possession?

Possession and spiritual oppression as an invasive or attacking spiritual force have symptoms. Some are physical, but most are psychological.

It is clear from the Bible that demons contribute to or cause mental and physical disorders, but it is also vital to understand that not everyone who has mental illness is possessed, though a spiritual cause cannot be ruled out as a person may be under spiritual attack rather than outright possession. Misdiagnosis is common.

Incorrectly thinking a family member is demon-possessed when they are going through a bout of stress, anxiety or nervous exhaustion will deliver a wrong response to their treatment.

Mental illnesses that manifest with supernatural phenomena such as poltergeist activity, shadowy figures in the bedroom at night, or the ability for clairvoyance will certainly have a demonic root and it is my belief that 'hearing voices' will also be indicative of a demonic presence at work especially when those voices are barking commands to kill oneself or others.

Classic auditory 'hallucinations' usually diagnosed as a component of schizophrenia may range from sounds of little children crying; whispering voices; heavy breathing; mocking laughter; lying voices saying that family members or loved ones are in a plot to destroy the person; marching and drumming noises and many more. The reason I mark such auditory 'hallucinations' out as demonic is that they are designed to torment, to instil fear and to distract an individual from normal living.

In the Bible there are various classifications of spirits, and demonic possession has a range of symptoms from discernible mental disorders and physical illness to (more rarely) unnatural strength and violent conduct, as well as the ability to spread sophisticated false religious doctrines; divination and fortune-telling. It is apparent that demons and evil spirits have distinct personalities, individual attributes and capabilities.

Scripture shows that in most cases the person possessed had done something which caused him or her to be possessed (see Chapter 31, 'Possession in the Bible'), though possession can also be due to generational, environmental and other factors.

Depictions of possession in modern culture are misleading and based upon films from Hollywood, notably *The Exorcist* and *The Haunting of Emily Rose*. Films always portray demonic infestation in extreme fictional forms for cinematic impact and scare-factor.

While rare cases of possession do manifest in a very conspicuous manner, *The Exorcist* movie and others like it mask the subtlety of symptoms inherent in most cases of possession by portraying victims with spinning heads, projectile vomiting and having ridiculous ceiling-crawling abilities, to the extent that possession as a subject worthy of serious discussion becomes far-fetched and derided. This is deliberate.

Demonic possession is usually well hidden within the multilayers of someone's personality because evil spirits are secretive and can embed themselves deeply into a person's character over a period of time so that the person and the demon(s) exist almost as a duality (depending on how many spirits are residing). Multiple personality disorders may be symptomatic of multiple spirit possessions.

Interestingly, possessed people rarely understand they are possessed, neither do they display significant symptoms and it often takes spiritual discernment to recognise spirits residing within an individual.

Occasionally however, evil spirits do betray their presence by manifesting blatant side effects such as psychological problems that may include various forms of psychosis and schizophrenia, as well as physical symptoms from epilepsy / 'fitting' type reactions; bizarre body contortions and abnormal vocal changes such as speaking in the voice of a small child (if an adult), or vice versa; growling and snarling like a dog; unnatural changes to features such as facial tics, scowling, lustful grimacing and extreme rage. If you have ever been unnerved by an individual just by looking at them you will know what I mean.

Newspapers commonly use the headline, 'Face of Evil' for murderers and rapists, and we have phrases like, "I didn't like the look of him" or "so-and-so gives me the creeps". Sometimes we encounter someone so possessed we reel in shock when our eyes inadvertently meet their scrutiny, giving credibility to the phrase, 'the eyes are the windows to the soul'. The eyes are after all a physical extension of the brain.

A possessed individual may sometimes use vile and profane language or display perverted or fetishistic sexual appetite. Other strong demonic pointers include self-harming from cutting, piercing or burning, to suicide attempts, as well as extreme dietary disorders such as gluttony and/or purging, though other factors may also be at play in all of these behaviours, so discernment is key.

More commonly, possessed or spiritually oppressed individuals display severe depression and are at risk only to themselves because the demons plaguing them are bent on their destruction through tormenting them with despair, fears and putting suicide ideation into their thought processes. Often voices are heard supporting the lie that the person is a failure, encouraging suicide.

I have heard it said that an indicator of a possessed person whether or not they display psychotic symptoms, can be an extreme aversion to Jesus Christ. I am not convinced that possession will confer a hatred of Jesus in all cases, it will depend on the level of infestation and will be entity-dependent, with the culture and belief system of an individual also playing a role. It must be said though, that the indignation when Jesus Christ is mentioned even in polite conversation these days is profound and is culturally reflected in the twisted portrayal of Christians in entertainment genres as either neurotic control freaks or evil cultish abusers; sentiments continually pushed by a controlled, anti-Christian and atheistic media bias. Many celebrities and cultural influencers who are possessed themselves attack Christian values in an agenda focused particularly on changing the attitudes of the young. (See Chapter 38).

Many celebrities are controlled by spiritual entities that cause them to exhibit extreme Narcissism. Narcissistic Personality Disorder is not classed as a mental condition, but a character trait, however those who have NPD are the classic sociopaths and psychopaths who seek to control and dominate others for personal gain; financial, sexual or otherwise. Because such individuals account for around 7% of the population, their selfish behaviour patterns are so commonplace that the spiritual component of their sociopathic actions goes unrecognised.

The stark polarisation in society between those who love God and those who hate him is well advanced, whether that is through unbelief or active persecution. The figurative separation between God's sheep and Satan's goats is reaching its denouement.

CHAPTER 27.

Who is Susceptible?

Why do some people get spiritually attacked or possessed and others don't? Was I possessed or simply under extreme spiritual attack? (I don't know for sure, but I certainly never had a hatred of Jesus Christ which may mean that I was under spiritual attack or oppression rather than possession. Why were my brother John or my friend Ronnie unaffected who were also taking drugs?

Well, perhaps they were without realising it; perhaps by a lesser demonic entity or entities than me, affecting them differently and changing them subtly and secretively. Was I under assault from a much more powerful entity or group of entities? I can't be certain. I may just have been in the wrong place at the wrong time, with my particular circumstances and history making me a more convenient target. Only God knows.

It would of course be wrong to attribute every depressed mood or angry outburst or lustful desire to the presence of an evil spirit, however when destructive emotions, unnatural desires or fears start to occupy a person's consciousness unrelentingly, to the extent they can no longer control their anger; conquer a dangerous lust; disperse a lingering depression or even quell the temptation to kill others or themselves, then the notion that they may be spiritually oppressed or possessed has to be taken seriously.

In the West we are not programmed to attribute spiritual causes to life's problems and crises. You don't wake up one morning feeling depressed or suicidal and blame it on demons. It is not a cultural norm. Demonic oppression or possession is the last thing people attribute their moodiness and antisocial behaviour to. Why? Because we're conditioned to look to science for the answers.

Even within the Church the concept of Jesus casting out real demons and devils is scorned among many professing Christians who find the whole idea old-fashioned. This is no surprise. The Church by and large has become worldly and spiritually blind. Spiritual blindness will ascribe physical causes to a spiritual condition and will use material means to address the symptoms.

As a result, in the Post-Modern era, possession is not an acceptable diagnosis and mental illnesses that may arise as a result of possession are categorised as neurological conditions symptomatic of psychosis with physiological origins and will be treated using the latest drugs, counselling and group therapy.

Holy Spirit-filled Christians however are acutely aware of a spiritual dimension around them and can't fail to detect the evidence of spiritual warfare operating throughout the world as a rising tide of evil sweeps through every continent.

No one is immune from spiritual attack. Even Jesus had to contend with Satan a number of times in the wilderness where he was given clear visions by the devil to try and corrupt him and destroy his mission of salvation:

Matthew 4:8
Again, the devil taketh him up into an exceeding high mountain, and sheweth him all the kingdoms of the world, and the glory of them.

And in the Old Testament madness is even viewed as a divine punishment or testing:

Deuteronomy 28: 27-29
The Lord will afflict you with madness, blindness and confusion of mind

In the Book of Job, Satan's spiritual attack against Job was permitted by God in order to test Job's loyalty and to develop his patience and character.

Job 7:13-15
*When I say, My bed shall comfort me, my couch shall ease my complaint; Then you **scare me with dreams and terrify me with visions** so that I would choose strangling and death rather than my bones.*

Job was an obedient servant of God, so his afflictions are an example of how even good men can be tried by mental and physical disruptions to their life; however, more typically, disobedience toward God and his commandments will undermine our defences against spiritual entities and open us up to a higher likelihood of demonic attack.

Like flies to faeces certain activities will attract the attention of demonic entities. To shield us from satanic attacks we are directed in Scripture to obedience and to use the Word of God as a 'sword' against attack as well as to carry the 'shield' of faith in addition to wearing a figurative 'helmet' of salvation and a 'breastplate' of faith and love.

Ephesians 6:10-17
Put on the whole armour of God, that ye may be able to stand against the wiles of the devil. For we wrestle not against flesh and blood, but against principalities, against powers, against the rulers of the darkness of this world, against spiritual wickedness in high places.

Wherefore take unto you the whole armour of God, that ye may be able to withstand in the evil day, and having done all, to stand.

Stand therefore, having your loins girt about with truth, and having on the breastplate of righteousness; and your feet shod with the preparation of the gospel of peace; above all, taking the shield of faith, wherewith ye shall be able to quench all the fiery darts of the wicked. And take the helmet of salvation, and the sword of the Spirit, which is the word of God.

Another weapon we use against Satan is prayer to God, through Jesus.

Ephesians 6:18
Praying always with all prayer and supplication in the Spirit, and watching thereunto with all perseverance and supplication for all saints.

There is nothing in the Bible that suggests Christians, who are indwelt by the Holy Spirit can be simultaneously possessed by demons.

1 John 4:4
*Ye are of God, little children, **and have overcome them**: because greater is he that is in you, than he that is in the world.*

1 Thessalonians 5:23
*And the very God of peace sanctify you wholly; and I pray God your whole **spirit** and **soul** and **body** be preserved blameless unto the coming of our Lord Jesus Christ.*

Most would say that a believer can experience oppression (or very strong influence) by demons especially if the demonic forces are given legal ground to do so, such as through deliberate sin and backsliding behaviour. The flesh is like a puppet to whatever we feed our spirit.

The Bible tells us that different spirits can build strongholds in a person's life. Accordingly, it is highly probable that most unsaved people will be possessed by demons/evil spirits and they can only escape possession through the power of Jesus. As said, most possession goes unrecognised because it doesn't blossom into severe mental illness and an unsaved person's character may actually be partly demonic and reveal itself in antipathy toward God, through unbelief; through conflicts; greed; envy; lust; hatefulness; thefts; murders; sexual promiscuity; unforgiveness and a host of other destructive personality traits. That is a controversial statement to make, but I think it explains many of the problems and conflicts in the home and society at large.

I have a hypothesis. I can't be dogmatic about it, but I perceive that when we are new-born babies we have a naturally strong defence-mechanism against spirit possession, probably more so than at any other time in our life which lasts usually until puberty when we start making moral choices. It's why toddlers and younger children rarely display signs of mental illness, whereas, unfortunately, many adults do. That is not to say some toddlers and babies are not prone to spiritual attack or possession. I think they can be under certain extreme circumstances, especially if they or their parents were sexually abused or if there are generational occult practices within a family.

I saw a distressing television documentary a few years ago about a four year old sweetheart of a little girl who was plagued from the age of two with ideations that a 'horrible, dusty old lady' was getting into her mind and saying horrible frightening things to her on a daily basis. This poor young girl was scared out of her wits and terribly depressed and restless. Her parents seemed to think it was something physiological, but I believe it was spiritual. How she became so afflicted is a mystery, but perhaps some drug given to her mother in pregnancy; perhaps a vaccination administered as a baby, or an inherited predilection or other reason (see Chapter 34 'Drugs and Sorcery'). Demons will exploit any opportunity to attack and don't care if it's a child or adult they afflict. They have no mercy.

I don't know what happened to that poor little tot, but I prayed for her release from that awful mental bondage and I am sure other like-minded Christians also recognised what I saw and prayed for her.

CHAPTER 28.

Environmental Factors

Anyone blessed with even a little spiritual discernment cannot overlook the mounting psychological problems and social issues on a local, national and international level.

There is no doubt that poor social environments can influence development of mental illness, not least because evil spirits are attracted to dark and challenging socio-economic conditions.

On the nightly news we see deprivation, economic woes, toxic environmental pollution, general unhappiness, anxiety and clinical depression as emblematic of modern life with a grim topping of war crimes; mass murder; abortion; serial killings; cannibalism; and other acts of perversion and cruelty so morally evil they defy categorisation.

Of course, these things are not new to our generation, but I have a hunch that the severity and magnitude of such social problems and atrocities are being influenced by an escalation of demonic power which is reaching a critical level.

Areas of high population and overcrowded city environments in particular provide a feeding frenzy for spiritual predators. The wailing sirens and strobing red and blue lights of social distress are symptomatic of an ailing system with selfish corruption continually gnawing away at the broken behemoth we call civilisation.

Eventually, the vice-ridden monster lashes out with a need for war to gorge itself. Look at Iraq, Libya, Syria, Somalia, Yemen and Sudan: Destruction, death and misery are all definite indicators of strong demonic influence at home and abroad as elite controllers vie to snatch assets and exert their power over a region and its people.

War is like a health spa for demons, creating a domino effect of social problems as infrastructure is destroyed, populations migrate, cultures clash and social support structures crumble causing more chaos and hardship.

Aside from warzones, on a smaller scale there are many demonic hotspots; both magnets for and energised by spiritual entities at a local level. These include the brothels and crack houses of red light districts; the drug peddling night clubs and bars; the casinos and gaming dens; as well as the abortion and euthanasia clinics. The demonic dynamic operating in these places is palpable.

Key symptoms to look out for when demons are infesting a particular area or neighbourhood include:

•   Violence and social disorder, districts where drug abuse and prostitution is rife

•   Areas of despair and marginalisation of people; homelessness

•   Places where businesses go bust, repeatedly in the same location

•   Homes where marital problems and relationship breakdowns repeatedly occur

•   Locations that feel eerie and disturbing. Places you don't feel comfortable in that trigger negative moods; perhaps a certain street, house or even a room in a house or hotel. If you notice you were happy and then you walked into a place which makes you feel miserable or ill-at-ease it can indicate the presence of unclean spirits

•   Poltergeist type phenomena: Thumping noises, ornaments breaking or flying across the room, drawers opening, power surges and lights flickering on and off, strange sounds and unexplained voices.

Living in a high-rise block of flats in a depressing urban setting, with a pervasive anticyclonic gloom, coupled with low prospects, loneliness and perhaps a crippling physical infirmity, is more likely to create the conditions for demonic activity and a depressive mental illness than living in a pretty detached house in a rural setting; with loving family and friends; a great social network; healthy diet; low stress; financial prosperity and lots of fresh air and sunshine.

Physical disposition is as important to our mental state, as much as our mental state is towards our physical health. We are body, mind and spirit. That does not mean all people living in deprivation will be depressed, and neither does it mean the affluent escape the trials of mental illness/demonic problems; far from it, but generally having a pile of money in the bank and a supportive family and social network around you can help cushion some of the worst physical aspects of psychosis.

The Bible says that there are certain places on the earth where the land is cursed. One of the ways this occurs is the sins of the inhabitants. If things such as séances, magic, sexual perversion, incest, adultery, or murder have been practiced in a home or region, then demonic spirits have a legalistic right to inhabit there.

Leviticus 18:24-25, 27
*"Defile not ye yourselves in any of these things: for in all these the nations are defiled which I cast out before you: And the land is defiled: therefore I do visit the iniquity thereof upon it, and the land itself vomiteth out her inhabitants... (For all these abominations have the men of the land done, which [were] before you, **and the land is defiled**)"*

Demonic forces may often inhabit old prisons and places where murders and ritualistic magic have taken place; mental hospitals too are known to have many problems with unsettling and creepy ambiance and hauntings are commonplace. After the inmates die, some familiar evil spirits appear to linger in the area. Of course they can easily get into our homes too if we openly invite them in through occult practices and divination; drug use; sexual promiscuity; blasphemous language and so on.

There is no location on earth which is immune from demonic forces. Don't believe TV and films which suggest being inside a church or hanging a crucifix in the home is able to protect against them. That is a myth. Churches are buildings and crosses are just objects and can become idols if we trust an object to help us and not rely on faith in God.

Of course, we must proclaim the work that Christ did for us on the cross, but I have always thought it strange that we should look at the object of our Saviour's execution with reverence, instead of on the person of Jesus Christ himself. Would we wear mini electric chair symbols around our neck or hang up pictures of a lethal injection gurney if Jesus had laid down his life on one of those? Just my opinion, but when you see blasphemous popstars like Madonna or Lady Gaga wearing crosses you have to think about whether the cross-as-ornament has any efficacy.

However, the importance of the cross as the means by which the Saviour bore our sins must not be lessened. The cross symbolises ultimate sacrifice and atonement for sin. This legal transaction in which God the Father transferred to God the Son the penalty we deserve is absolutely key to salvation (see Chapter 43, How to Be Saved). That's what Peter means when he says, "He Himself bore our sins in His body on the cross." Jesus Christ bore your sin on the cross too, but you must take Him up on the offer of forgiveness. If you turn to Him, you will be delivered from the penalty of sin which God justly must impose.

So, if we do feel the need to wear a symbol that states we believe in Jesus then we should make sure he is put on in our hearts before we wear him on the outside for the world to see, because if we are truly living a Christian life, people will know we are Christian; and conversely if we are acting sinfully do we *really* want to give the world an excuse to call us hypocrites, bringing reproach on the name of Christ?

CHAPTER 29.

Measuring the Immeasurable

If demonic power is escalating on a global scale, it would mean cases of possession are on the rise in society and if my theory is right, mental illness must also be increasing. And it is, statistically.

While there's no accurate measure to count just how many people are living with demonic infestation or demonic oppression there are statistics about mental illness.

American research shows that people disabled by mental disorders and qualifying for Supplemental Security Income (SSI) or Social Security Disability Insurance (SSDI) rose nearly 150% between 1987 and 2007 — from one in 184 Americans to one in 76. For children, the rise is even greater - a thirty-five-fold increase in the same period. Mental illness is now the leading cause of disability in children.[4]

Demonic energies work through people and take advantage of their personality defects to create conflict and instability at the level of the individual, family, society and nation. Without protection from God, evil spirits create havoc in people's lives at a physical, emotional, intellectual and spiritual level.

I wonder how many people in your neighbourhood might be suffering because of demons, yet assume that because their symptoms are so commonplace and typical of modern living they never really understand the cause of their unhappiness; mood swings; anger; sexual perversions; difficulty holding down relationships/friendships; minor or major addictions and so on.

The degree of demonic influence over an individual is also dependent upon what type of spirit it is, whether it's a single powerful demon or a multitude of lesser demons or a mixture of the two. The symptoms displayed to the outward world depend upon the type of spirit. Some symptoms manifest noticeably, others are understated, or invisible, for example in the case of a clinically depressed person with suicide ideation who puts on a brave face and acts 'normal' - my story. Conversely, an extremely violent spirit or group of spirits perhaps empowered by street drugs for example, may show their hand in violent psychopathic rage, extreme sexual promiscuity and murder.

Psychiatry uses standard, industry-recognised statistical assessment tools/interview techniques to establish a diagnosis of mental illness. These tools are based on environmental, genetic, biological, and psychological categories and risk factors to establish possible cause and type of mental illness. The spiritually open-minded in psychiatric medicine need to consider the possibility of possession or demonic oppression as causal or contributory factors in mental illness too, because unless they do, mental illness will remain a chronic disease, never eradicated, just 'managed' through various drug and counselling protocols. And who really benefits from this? The pharmaceutical companies certainly. It is in their financial interests to push mental illness management through a lifetime of drug treatment. Like the Cancer Industry which operates a similar protocol, finding an outright cure for a disease jettisons the need for intervention and wipes out profiteering.

Western society today largely ridicules the notion that evil has a supernatural source, deferring to a humanistic interpretation of morality. Even the classification of 'what is' and 'what is not' evil is up for debate with the doctrine of *Moral Relativism* insisting that because opinions differ about what is good and bad from person to person, evil can therefore be both good and bad simultaneously depending on your viewpoint. Twisted logic indeed.

People are increasingly afraid to voice any strong opinion, feeling compelled to leave all controversial viewpoints at the altar of 'tolerance'. Voicing loving criticism no longer has a place because political correctness calls any criticism 'hate', which is further latched on to by lobby groups supporting a particular perversion, or extremist position, and consequently morality in society is in an irreversible tailspin.

The public is confused and fearful. Sensitive individuals can no longer pretend that things they are seeing on TV and reading in the newspaper are unexceptional. Evil seems to be unveiling itself in increasingly creepy and menacing ways. From killer-clown attacks to horrible pornography online; murders; rapes and war crimes. Of course murder, rape and war crimes are not limited to this generation, yet even staunch atheists admit things are getting worse and are holding their heads in their hands in perplexity, as the disintegration of society unfolds daily with increasingly bizarre and horrifying events.

Demonic influence, if indeed it is behind this dramatic upsurge of evil, appears to be snowballing at an alarming rate with global conditions making society more susceptible to spiritual deception and demonic depredations through a variety of factors, not least the cultural endorsement of immorality under the banner of tolerance.

Possession has also moved from being subtle and furtive, rarely manifesting its severest symptoms, to increasingly overt and highly observable, especially with the arrival of fearful new synthetic drugs opening spiritual doorways (see Chapter 34 'Drugs and Sorcery') and causing chaos on the streets and within the prison system. Visible demonic possession is also seen in people who intentionally enter trance-like states as part of a tribal ritual, or when channelling spirits.

Within certain cultures, particularly those practicing witchcraft as part of the national religion such as in Haiti, the Dominican Republic, parts of India, Africa and Indonesia; it is not unreasonable to estimate that a high proportion of the population is possessed and the rest of the country affected.

Examples are given by Cross-Cultural Therapist, Richard Castillo in his book, *Culture and Mental Illness*. Such trance-like states include *Amok*, culturally endemic in Malaysia and Indonesia from which the phrase 'running-Amok' derives with the condition causing an individual to lose their sense of self so that they grab a weapon and run through the village attacking people. Later, the perpetrator has no memory of the actions and usually they are excused from any liability for their behaviour even if someone died.

Similarly, a condition called *Grisi siknis* among teenage girls and women of the Miskito Indians in Nicaragua involves assaulting people with machetes or self-mutilation. Other possession trances include *Indisposition* in Haiti; *Falling Out* in the Bahamas; and *Latah* (in Malaysia) where individuals look possessed, making violent jerking motions and freakish postures; trance dancing; mimicking other people; throwing things and so on.

Also, in Western cities, users of the 'bath salt' drug *Flakka* display profoundly violent and reckless behaviour toward themselves and others with horrifying self-injury and deliberate mutilation characteristic of the drug effects.

CHAPTER 30.

An Evil Elephant in the Room

Spirit infestation is wide-ranging and complex with mild to extreme variations, affecting individuals differently and contributing to many diagnoses of mental disorder including schizophrenia spectrum; bipolar; depression; anxiety; trauma disorders; dissociation; eating disorders; sexual and gender dysfunction; borderline personality and Narcissism disorders; OCD; Tourette's Syndrome and so on. It can also manifest in physical symptoms such as long term weakness and malaise, characteristic of that baffling medical conundrum called Chronic Fatigue Syndrome (CFS/ME). Of course this is a highly misdiagnosed disease, but when it cannot be tied to allergies, vaccination reaction, endocrine or autoimmune and thyroid disorders there is always the possibility that it may have a spiritual cause with very real and distressing physical symptoms for which only Christian spiritual deliverance will provide a cure.

You can throw prescription drugs at these problems and you can attempt to treat the fringes of these afflictions at a certain level through various therapies, but if you don't understand that there is a spiritual cause behind some forms of mental disorders, physical illness and even commonly accepted sexual aberrations, you will never address them.

I would be bold enough to state that occasionally even psychiatric conditions with a neurodevelopmental basis like autism or ADHD; or a neurocognitive one like dementia or brain injury could open a person up to spiritual problems and attract demonic spirits like vultures to a carcass. Unless you are protected by God's Holy Spirit anyone can be at risk.

Secular psychiatrists when dealing with some diagnoses are unfortunately like blind men groping in the dark, touching various appendages of a big demonic elephant in the room and never seeing the full spiritual picture. At best they may tranquillise the demonic elephant with a cocktail of drugs, but as soon as the drugs wear off it wakes up and starts stomping around the room again. It's why mental illness is often a chronic condition and one requiring a lifelong administration of psychotropic medication to ever-increasing concentrations as the body builds up tolerance to the drugs.

It is noteworthy to mention that in the early 1990s I lived in a flat in Newcastle, next door to a group of schizophrenics who were 'Living in the Community' as it was termed back then, when government cuts forced many psychiatric hospitals to close.

It was obvious to me these young men had spiritual problems and revealingly, they knew it too.

I had an opportunity to speak informally with the father of one of them in the local pub and he heard my story with interest. I was asked if I could speak to his son who, it turned out was a highly intelligent Oxford University student who had also taken LSD which had caused him to terminate his academic career in entirety after developing schizophrenia.

This young man and three other fellow sufferers came around to my flat at the request of the father to hear me repeat my story. Not one of them doubted the spiritual dimension of their disease and they seemed very relieved that I had recognised it as such. They were comforted to be talking about spiritual things and I gathered they were very sceptical of their psychiatrists who just didn't get it, seeing their illness as physiological and not understanding their demons were real.

When I gave them Christian literature including a Gideon's Bible, some Christian tracts and various Christian music tapes they received them with delight and immediately wanted to go off to discover if their affliction could also be cured in the same way mine had been, by the direct intervention of God.

I don't know what happened to them after that; I didn't see them again as I moved from that district of Newcastle, but I hope they found the blessing of forgiveness and healing through Jesus Christ as I had done. It is shameful that I didn't actively seek out these individuals further to provide them with ongoing support, prayer and pastoral care; however, in spite of my inaction, I hope all of them found some blessed peace arrive in their lives and a release from their afflictions.

If you are a mental illness sufferer and have reached this point in my book, thank you for reading my story. Do not be alarmed if your initial prayers do not appear to lead to an immediate or noticeable decline in your problems. Although my cure came about almost instantaneously I am aware that everyone's situation is different including which demons may be affecting you along with other influences that affect your disposition such as drug use (prescription or otherwise); and cultural and social issues surrounding you.

The key thing to remember is your salvation and deliverance does not depend on how *you* feel, it depends on God's unfailing promise that all who come to him through Jesus he will never turn away. (See How to Be Saved, Chapter 43).

John 6:37
"All that the Father giveth me **shall come to me***; and him that cometh to me I will in no wise cast out."*

CHAPTER 31.

Possession in the Bible

At this point in my book it is highly appropriate to discuss what The Bible says about spirit possession. Examples of it pepper the pages of Scripture with much of Christ's ministry dealing with casting out demons.

The most extreme example of possession in the Bible (certainly from outward appearances) can be found in the Gospel of Mark, Chapter 5 where the man living among the tombs had a whole legion of unclean spirits within him causing him to self-harm and violently attack other people.

Mark 5:1-9
And they came over unto the other side of the sea, into the country of the Gadarenes and when he was come out of the ship, immediately there met him out of the tombs a man with an unclean spirit, who had his dwelling among the tombs; and no man could bind him, no, not with chains, because that he had been often bound with fetters and chains, and the chains had been plucked asunder by him, and the fetters broken in pieces: neither could any man tame him.

And always, night and day, he was in the mountains, and in the tombs, crying, and cutting himself with stones. But when he saw Jesus afar off, he ran and worshipped him, and cried with a loud voice, and said, "What have I to do with thee, Jesus, thou Son of the most high God? I adjure thee by God, that thou torment me not."

For he (Jesus) said unto him, Come out of the man, thou unclean spirit. And he asked him, "What is thy name?"

And he answered, saying, "My name is Legion: for we are many."

Another example of severe possession is found in the person of Mary Magdalene who was cleansed of seven devils by Jesus.

Cases of possession resulting in physical illness are also apparent, and can be found in Matthew 12 where an unclean spirit affects a man, making him deaf and dumb and also in Matthew 17 where a young boy's possession produces side effects of fitting similar to epilepsy:

Matthew 12:22
Then was brought unto him one possessed with a devil, blind, and dumb: and he healed him, insomuch that the blind and dumb both spake and saw...

Matthew 17:18
And Jesus rebuked the devil; and he departed out of him: and the child was cured from that very hour...

There are examples too of subtle, intellectual possession in the variety of false prophets and prophetesses who we infer remain physically unaffected by the possession, yet mentally they are used and manipulated by spirits into spreading false prophecies or divination (fortune-telling), witchcraft and sorcery as the examples below show:

Acts 13:8
But Elymas the sorcerer (for so is his name by interpretation) withstood them, seeking to turn away the deputy from the faith.

Then Saul, (who also is called Paul,) filled with the Holy Ghost, set his eyes on him, and said, 'O full of all subtlety and all mischief, thou child of the devil, thou enemy of all righteousness, wilt thou not cease to pervert the right ways of the Lord?'

Acts 16:16-18
And it came to pass, as we went to prayer, a certain damsel possessed with a spirit of divination met us, which brought her masters much gain by soothsaying.

Other references relating to the reality of demons include:

Luke 4:33-36
And in the synagogue there was a man, which had a spirit of an unclean devil, and cried out with a loud voice...

1 John 4:1-3
"Beloved, believe not every spirit, but try the spirits whether they are of God: because many false prophets are gone out into the world."

1 John 4:4
"Ye are of God, little children, and have overcome them: because greater is he that is in you, than he that is in the world."

Luke 10:17
And the seventy returned again with joy, saying, Lord, even the devils are subject unto us through thy name.

Matthew 4:24
And his fame went throughout all Syria: and they brought unto him all sick people that were taken with divers diseases and torments, and those which were possessed with devils, and those which were lunatic, and those that had the palsy; and he healed them...

Ephesians 6:12
"For we wrestle not against flesh and blood, but against principalities, against powers, against the rulers of the darkness of this world, against spiritual wickedness in high [places]..."

Acts 5:16
There came also a multitude out of the cities round about unto Jerusalem, bringing sick folks, and them which were vexed with unclean spirits: and they were healed every one.

The Bible also makes it clear that Jesus cured people from physical diseases who were not possessed, so not all healings were directly related to possession as in healing of the lepers in Luke 17.

CHAPTER 32.

Common Causes of Possession Today

There are many routes for demons to take entry. For the most part we become more prone to demonic possession over time, particularly in those years immediately following childhood when we lose our innocence, become embroiled in worldliness at a spiritual level, and start to approach life with selfish ambition alongside a desire for physical self-indulgence which often accompanies a lack of self-control; partying; drunkenness and drug taking; sexual promiscuity; and reckless behaviour.

There is a kind of softening-up of our will which takes place, a weakening and opening up so that over time we become more vulnerable to the possibility of possession or oppression. I know, it happened to me.

One thing in and of itself may not get us possessed, but in conjunction with something else it may just be the big door-opener which lets demons in.

Imagine having multiple locks on a front door: a Yale, a mortice and a couple of bolt fastenings. Nothing is going to get into that door easily without first weakening the bolt fastenings, then the mortice, then the Yale. Then bingo! The door opens.

Entry by a front door is just one route into a house. It is the most common access, but there are many others. Other entrances may be an open window or weak side door or even through the cellar or roof. Some burglars push a small child through an open hopper or awning window so that once inside, locks on the main door or window can be opened to let the adult in. Demons, like people are spectacularly varied. Smaller and weaker demonic spirits may act as a vanguard for much more powerful spirits who gain entry later.

Apart from dabbling in the occult religions or witchcraft (white or black), and deliberately inviting a demon into you, the other key routes for demonic oppression or possession include, drug use, sexual immorality and perversion.

Imagine for example doing the Ouija board in conjunction with drugs, either simultaneously, or even separated by months or years of time. It doesn't matter to an evil spirit that's been in proximity from childhood waiting to find entry. Perhaps it noticed you did Tarot when you were 15 and although it couldn't make it inside of you then, it stuck around waiting for the main door bolt to be unlocked by the Ouija board when you were 17, gaining entry; and then when you smoked marijuana or got dangerously drunk at 19 was able to bring some of its friends to lodge inside of you too. Then at twenty you suddenly reach a life-crisis of depression, perhaps with addiction problems, an eating disorder or penchant for self-harming, along with reckless sexual promiscuity or lewd behaviour, and everyone including yourself wonders how you got into this tragic position.

The strength of an individual's spiritual protection is diverse, varying from person to person depending on culture, social circumstances, actions of the person and even ancestry. Certain religious philosophies, cultural backgrounds and belief systems can soften-up an individual to entities that seek their destruction very early in life. Indeed, for some people, their spiritual doors are already subjugated or highly vulnerable from birth, an example being a person born into a culture where demonic rites are practiced such as in Haiti with its Voodoo, or in India with its Hinduism and in certain sects of Islam such as *Wahhabism* where a death culture prevails and genital mutilation of children and decapitation of infidels is daily practice.

These people may already have generational or genetic demonic doors opened within their psyche from birth, with embedded demonic forces nascent in the womb, ready to exert and establish their presence later as the individual develops or is nurtured further by that unhealthy culture.

Similarly, babies whose mothers are addicts may also, through no fault of their own be the victims of a major spiritual setback before they are even out of the womb.

Opening a door to the spirit world is remarkably easy. Prayer to (the Christian) God opens the door to his Holy Spirit, whereas inaction in this respect can lead to increasing isolation from God and spiritual vulnerability.

Conversely, attempts to contact any spirit aside from God's Holy Spirit I affirm from experience is a foolhardy and dangerous undertaking. The most common way that possession occurs is through the act of communicating with spirits or *channelling* spirits either deliberately or accidentally.

CHAPTER 33.

Causes of Possession: Occult and Witchcraft

The Occult invites a Trojan horse of problems into a person's life, depositing a range of spiritual difficulties which can destroy mental health, happiness and even life itself.

There has always been a fascination with magic, folklore and the spirit world and particularly whether life exists after death. Ever since our race had its blessed origin in Eden, the desire to 'be as gods' is as much a temptation to modern man as it was to our ancient ancestors.

In the Old Testament we read of Jannes and Jambres, the magicians who contended with Moses and Aaron using witchcraft in the Book of Exodus 7 1-25; as well as King Saul consulting with the witch of Endor in the Book of Samuel to predict the outcome of a battle. In the New Testament we hear about Simon Magus, a sorcerer who converted to Christianity in Acts 8:9-11, as well as the prophetess in Acts 16:17-19 whose power was neutralised when the 'spirit' of divination was cast out of her by Paul the apostle.

Outside of the Scriptures there are countless occult practitioners too numerous to mention, however, the most notable are Nostradamus, the 16th century prophetic seer whose books have never been out of print, and Victorian occult luminaries including Arthur Conan D'Oyle, Edgar Allan Poe and Algernon Blackwood. More recently in the 20th century, Austin Osman Spare, Helena Petrovna Blavatsky and Aleister Crowley have been passed the baton. Crowley, the evil black magician and the favourite sorcerer of Rock stars was a cannibalistic paedophile whose occult teachings have been the backbone for Satanism and witchcraft throughout the modern world.

Images, concepts and symbols of the occult New Age movement and sorcery now permeate children's books, TV shows, cartoons and films, indoctrinating the minds of generations of youngsters.

From toddler shows featuring fairies and fantasy, to the lucrative *Disney Princess* genre with its endemic spell-casting and magical powers, you can't flick through TV channels without seeing extensive occult themes at play, particularly those targeting children in shows such as *Scooby*

Doo, Pokémon, Power Rangers, Ben10, Sabrina the Teenage Witch, Harry Potter and many more; all of which extol the power of magic and channelling.

The success of 'occult programming' disguised as light entertainment runs the gamut of TV schedules and movie-making. This is a dangerous beach-head strategy from which Satan can consolidate strongholds early on. By early teens, most children are highly versed in the A-Z of occult concepts from Amulets, Ankhs and Angels, to Wicca, Wizardry and the Zodiac with everything else in between including polytheism, altered states, sorceries and potions, science fiction, UFOs and aliens, tarot and telekinesis. This conditioning process is more advanced today than at any other time in history, effectively lubricated by complicit media.

Once the programming has been successful, the mind of a person is fertile ground for sowing more complex occult concepts or for direct possession by spirit forces. The list of danger areas is immense, especially for teens experimenting and showing-off within peer group environments.

I remember my interest in the occult began just after my 16th birthday. I had been prolific in reading all of Dennis Wheatley's Black Magic fiction books and was given another book, this time in the non-fiction genre about Black Magic from my brother-in-law, called *The Black Arts*, by Richard Cavendish. With a skull, candle and pestle and mortar on the cover it looked spooky enough, but from the content inside I realised it had been given out of ignorance on his part, brimming as it was with wildly inappropriate material for a 16 year old including white and black magic incantations, spell-casting and so on. There were tips on invoking spirits, love-spells and sex-spells which were of obvious interest to someone as highly sexed as I was as a teenager. I even recall uttering some of the spells with all seriousness – one of which was to attract the sexual interest of girls.

There was a whole section on tarot card reading and divination and this coincided with the purchase of a deck of tarot cards by my brother John who referenced the book to understand the meaning behind each of the main cards. My experimentation with the cards and magic spells was undertaken with a merry obliviousness about the spiritual dangers they posed. For pranks we would even load the tarot deck and deal what we deemed to be the scariest cards out in readings to friends: 'The Devil', 'The Hanged Man' and 'The Reaper', much to onlookers' amusement.

With hindsight I am convinced this period of occult experimentation was a foundational cornerstone for my mental illness, establishing some demonic beachhead, ready for the main psychotic/possession event two years later.

Ouija Boards

The sledgehammer of the occult toolbox; this infamous device is guilty of smashing the spiritual protection of millions of people, especially teens.

I did the Ouija Board on around five occasions, starting in 1980, doing the last one in summer 1983 just a short while before taking LSD.

The first time I experimented was in an old Northumbrian cottage in a small farmstead south west of Berwick upon Tweed, with my two brothers and two other friends of 15 years old. There was nothing dramatic to report, just a bit of a spooky atmosphere and a message spelling *PUGSHOT* which was puzzling.

The next time I used the board was at home in Marlow with my mum, brothers, sister and cousin who took the whole affair very seriously.

I remember designing the board with lots of astrological symbols, stars and patterns and had even written *GOOD* and *EVIL* boldly in the centre which was a most ill-advised action for a naïve 16 year old who had no idea about the power of evil spirits at this time. To this day I can't believe my mum, sister and cousin getting involved with this game so candidly, but they did, and seemed very serious about it.

The board was made of cardboard, and we had to adapt it as the glass didn't slide properly across the slightly ribbed surface. I reverted to simply cutting out letters, numbers, a *YES* and *NO* from sheets of A4 paper and I placed the squares of paper on a polished oak dining room table in a circle.

I remember a slight tingling sensation in my arms and hands as we received messages purporting to be from my father communicating his pet names to my mum and sister that only they had known about. That night my brother John said he heard the piano keys being plinked downstairs (my dad had been a keen, semi-professional pianist). Of course, I now realise this was simply the work of a familiar spirit – an evil spirit 'familiar' with my father during his life and was mimicking his presence from beyond the grave.

Nothing else exceptional happened. There was no dramatic slamming of doors or falling pictures which often accompany séances. However there were subtle changes I can retrospectively associate with the period immediately after using the board. I recall the whole atmosphere of the house changing markedly. It seemed to be a sad place to live after that. There was trouble in the home with one of my brothers acting out teenage angst and getting thrown out; my other brother and I started to smoke marijuana and there was a sense of lost innocence and generalised anxiety about the future.

Whether these factors were coincidental with teenage hormone changes or not I have no idea, but I also started to develop troubling obsessional compulsive problems which included a ridiculous obsession about touching things an even-number of times. If the even-number count didn't feel right or if I stumbled during the process I felt compelled to double-up the count, reaching maddening levels of touching and number-crunching. This started to affect normal living.

I also acquired another type of home-made superstition about brushing things with the back of my left hand if I'd previously touched it with my right. If I failed to do so I believed something terrible would happen to me or my family. Tiring and distracting, this OCD nonsense all came about after the Ouija episode. Had I inadvertently given access to some spirit that was causing the OCD? It's highly probable some spirit or spirits had taken up residence in me which would be central in facilitating easier access to other entities in the future. My brothers and my mother all seemed to be in a state of emotional decline. This was not imaginary.

I realise there are many frightening encounters documented about Ouija experimentation more dramatic than my experience; notably those gaining YouTube views and airtime on paranormal TV shows; however, melodrama is not ordinarily the modus operandi of Satan. His preference is usually subtlety and to effect damage beneath the radar of our perception. Like a saboteur sticking a tiny limpet mine on the side of a ship, a more typical outcome of using the Ouija (or any other occult dabbling) may go unnoticed for a long time until the vessel starts listing and sinking.

So many psychological disruptions such as the onset of OCD or generalised anxiety I am certain are caused by demonic interference with society blind to the spiritual origin of these problems. Only God knows the answer to how many diagnoses of bipolar disorder, psychopathy and the bizarre and undoubtedly demonic 'Tourette's Syndrome' have their root in occult influence or witchcraft.

Channelling

There are types of divination (seeking hidden knowledge about people or the future) that not only attract the attention of spirits, they are powered by them. Using pendulums; mapping ley-lines; tea-leaf or crystal-ball reading (scrying) are all forms of divination and there are many more. One of the most potent forms of divination is contacting spirits directly to foretell the future in the form of channelling them through a person, by freely opening oneself up to spirit possession.

It goes without saying that this method is a sure-fire way to get possessed by demons. This well promoted and popular occult discipline is so well known it should carry an 'As Seen on TV' starburst on it. Channelling practitioners believe they can communicate with spirits or angelic beings and other non-physical energies and entities including spirits of nature, dead people and even pets. The idea is that through channelling, contact with 'higher planes of existence' is possible, including contact with so-called extra-terrestrials.

Mediumship is the most common type of channelling which refers to communicating with spirit guides who act as go-betweens for conversing with loved ones who have passed away. Beyond basic mediumship, some channelling adepts also seek what they term higher knowledge for spiritual growth and for life guidance. This is crossover territory into mysticism and the study of 'Higher Knowledge' extends into various Eastern Philosophical traditions including Vedic and Brahmanic religious practices within Hinduism; Transcendental Meditation; Kundalini and Chakra Yoga; Hare Krishna; and Buddhist traditions. The Dalai Lama for example is a famous practitioner of Tibetan Buddhism which uses channelling as a means of connecting with spirit guides. The Dalai Lama himself has been filmed consulting channelled entities.

Automatic writing and verbal channelling (possession and writing or speaking through a human intermediary) are how channelled spirits communicate. Sometimes psychoactive drugs including cannabis; LSD (dextro-lysergic-acid-diethylamide); and DMT (dimethyltryptamine) are used to help lubricate spiritual communication. DMT will be discussed in its own right later.

God designed us to have a spiritual relationship with him and he therefore designed the human body with its vast and stunning complexity of nerves and sensory organs to be a receiver for spiritual wisdom and direct communication. Until 'The Fall' that is.

Since The Fall we have been cut off spiritually from our creator (a state of spiritual death), that is until Jesus made it possible once more for Man to have a living spiritual relationship with God through Jesus The Son, as one and only mediator between God and Man. (See Chapter 43 'How to be Saved').

1 Timothy 2:5
For there is one God, and one mediator between God and men, the man Christ Jesus.

However, even among the spiritually dead (everyone outside of Jesus Christ's salvation), the instrumentation for spiritual contact can still function, though it will not connect with God without Jesus. Our hardwired circuitry designed for communicating with God is used at our peril to communicate with other spirits because all other spiritual connections outside of God exist in the demonic realm. We are not meant to energise our spirituality unless it is enabled through God's Holy Spirit in a living faith and true relationship with God through Jesus.

Today, a false Luciferian spirituality encourages people to reach out to so-called other spirits of universal love and light without Jesus, using occult means. There are very powerful deceiving spirits who are able to transmit a range of feel-good messages and very pleasant sensations to the receptive mind and body in order to deceive individuals into false spirituality and false assurance of the hope of Heaven, *Nirvana*, *Paradise* or whatever your particular cultural system calls it.

It is a common theme for channelled spirits to parrot the phrases of universal love and truth, but always without Jesus, or saying that Jesus is just another ascended teacher or wise one, not God in the flesh.

Satan, whose preferred disguise is an angel of light deceives people into a false light and worship of a counterfeit god (himself) or demi-gods (his fallen angels).

2 Corinthians 11:14
And no marvel; for Satan himself is transformed into an angel of light.

Satan produces lying signs and wonders to convince unsaved people that they don't need saving from sin, and deceives them into believing they can exist independently outside of God's framework.

The volume of books and New Age philosophies which deal with the false light of generalised spirituality *without Jesus* is overwhelming. The old lie that Satan whispered to Eve (below) is as much at work today as it was in Eden:

Genesis 3:4-5
And the serpent said unto the woman, "Ye shall not surely die: For God doth know that in the day ye eat thereof, then your eyes shall be opened, and ye shall be as gods, knowing good and evil."

Any form of divination or channelling is extremely hazardous and to be shunned ruthlessly. Even a simple child's game of magic-wand spell-casting or wishing upon a star may have profound effects on a spiritual level. We may just find ourselves in the wrong place at the wrong time for a wandering demonic spirit to attach itself. Without true Godly discernment we do not know what is knocking on our own or children's spiritual doors in our various life stages, especially given the saturation of occult programming we are all bombarded with.

Access to the Holy Spirit comes when a person trusts in Jesus for salvation, going to Him in repentance and in faith for forgiveness of sins. (See Chapter 43 'How to Be Saved'). We must never attempt to speak with family members who are dead, and that goes for dead pets too, because we will only reach demonic counterfeits.

God's word tells us we are to pray to God the Father, directly, in Jesus' name or directly to our saviour, the Lord Jesus Christ.

John 13:13-14
And whatsoever ye shall ask in my name, that will I do, that the Father may be glorified in the Son. If ye shall ask any thing in my name, I will do it.

John 5:22-23
For the Father judgeth no man, but hath committed all judgement unto the Son. That all men should honour the Son, even as they honour the Father. He that honoureth not the Son honoureth not the Father which hath sent him.

We honour God the Father and Jesus Christ by praying to them. We can also pray to the Holy Spirit. All other prayer to anyone or anything else is Spiritism and idolatry and will be a magnet for entities.

Some Christian organisations including Roman Catholicism and Greek Orthodoxy are guilty of disobeying this clear biblical directive by praying to dead saints such as Mary. This is nothing more than spirit channelling with its many inherent dangers. I speak this warning in love to my brothers and sisters in these churches.

Divination: Fortune Telling and Tarot

Fairground attraction or girl's night out, most people see fortune-tellers, (psychics and clairvoyants as they prefer to be called) as providing nothing more than broad generalisations and 'predictable predictions' for light entertainment.

From tea-leaves to crystal-scrying, it's very straightforward to give a reading about a client's past, present and future since most people go to a psychic for specific life answers which trained body-language readers can easily pick up on. Fortune tellers know how to read visual cues and respond accordingly.

It's easy to foretell someone's future because they can't insist you are wrong even if you tell them they are going to the moon. If challenged about a reading, a clairvoyant simply advises that 'the moon' in this instance is symbolic of romance on a cruise ship, or a propensity to dream, or a romantic walk in the moonlight in an exotic location. Holiday destinations are a much-loved topic: "I see a place beginning with 'A' that has a strong pull for you". They wait for a reaction, or for you to fill in the gaps. You may respond with America, Albania, Antigua, Australia, Austria, Argentina, Andorra, Afghanistan etc.

Relationships too are a popular subject:

"Does someone called Steve or Dave mean anything to you? No? I'm a little cloudy here...Hmmm, let me focus...Ah, yes, I am definitely seeing an S in the name". And so it goes.

Whether or not this kind of Chinese Restaurant-fortune-cookie style of reading holds any significant spiritual hazard is only to be guessed at. From the viewpoint of filling a gullible person's head with false hopes or fears for the future is not a trifling matter especially if it leads a person to reckless lifestyle change through the lure of a false hope, or conversely, paralyses a person into inaction by consolidating a fear. However, there are many fortune-tellers who are able to communicate with an individual's familiar spirits. As mentioned earlier in the book, familiar spirits are those demonic entities that can attach themselves or be in close proximity to a person knowing intimate details about their life.

Tarot is another popular form of divination which relies on the fall of the cards to initiate a reading. Originally, both playing cards and tarot cards, originating in 15th century Northern Italy, were only used for card games in a pastime similar to Bridge. Only later were they used for divination with occult decks arriving in the late 18th century. The

1960s saw a revival of occult tarot which has developed beyond Hippy-interest into online websites, tutorials and consultations.

Many adepts of tarot divination are unaware of the spiritual dangers it poses and the extreme risk of opening doorways into the demonic realm. Even having a tarot deck in your home may cause spiritual problems for you or other family members.

Objects and Curios

Remember the folktale about the Genie of the Lamp? The word genie is derived from the Middle Eastern word *djinn* which is another term for a demon. Like Aladdin's lamp, the idea is that certain objects can act as demonic attractors or perhaps even house a demonic spirit, particularly those items with an occult history such as African masks and fetish statues; Chinese dragons; idol statues i.e. Buddhas, Mary goddesses and so-called 'saint' statues etc.

Some items are dedicated to demonic spirits and purchased in markets as holiday souvenirs with the buyer unaware they are bringing something malevolent into their home. Whether or not the spirits actually possess them is debatable, but it does seem plausible that they are attracted to the objects by the act of subconscious veneration and deliberate idol worship, as too many stories about ghosts and spirits suddenly being unleashed in a household after their placement are recorded to be dismissed as superstitious imagination.

A resurgence of ancient occult symbolism including hexagram and pentagram symbols and other mystical geometric motifs incorporated into contemporary designs for clothing, jewellery, decorative objects and tattoos is noteworthy. Any items designed to bring 'good luck' or to act as talismans must be avoided, including Egyptian ankhs (crosses with looped tops, an ancient fertility symbol); the broken-cross or 'peace' symbol; *Chais* (Hebrew characters spelling the word *life*); the cornuto hand sign with index and little fingers pointing up (a satanic horned sign representing the Goat of Mendes); along with a wide range of stars, wishbones, lucky coins, horseshoes etc. Again, it seems to be the act of attributing power to the symbols, a form of idolatry, which carries the most spiritual danger and not so much the symbols themselves, but it may be the case that wandering spirits will linger at an object of known occult or superstitious symbolism, so the risk isn't worth it.

In particular don't ignore the wide range of satanic music that may be in your home; especially the *Heavy Metal* and *Death Metal* genres which

149

are powerful methods of getting teenagers oppressed or possessed. There are many tragic cases of teenage suicides directly attributed to destructive messages in music, especially through bands such as *Black Sabbath, Twisted Sister, Slipknot, AC-DC, Iron Maiden* and *KISS* (which stands for *Knights in Satan's Service*). These wicked rock-star sell-outs are deliberately targeting your children to destroy their sanity and send them to Hell. (See Chapter 37 'Selling your Soul').

CHAPTER 34.

Causes of Possession: Drugs and Sorcery

Keeping the truth veiled is just as important to Satan and his demonic hordes as outright lying. There are so many deceptions and distractions in modern life to divert us from Jesus Christ, and they continue to grow.

You will recall that the key focus of this book was to highlight the dangers of drug use on the mind at a spiritual level, because drugging us is a key method to dumb us down spiritually, either by keeping us so fogged, tranquillised and spiritually ignorant that we never exercise our mental faculties sufficiently to even consider our fleeting life and our need for salvation, or by creating such mental anguish that we are driven to despair, suicide or chronic drug addiction to subdue depression symptoms, keeping us in bondage throughout our lifetime.

Demons and evil spirits thrive in dark and unhealthy environments. They despise light, natural order and wellbeing. Satan's modus operandi is to steal, kill and destroy, both physically and metaphorically.

A person weakened by illness or damaged by trauma and circumstances, can be more susceptible to mental illness and spiritual oppression. Add to this a cocktail of drugs - and I don't mean aspirin or a paracetamol or two, but strong grades of either street drugs or a cocktail of psychotropic medicines administered by your doctor and you have a perfect storm of vulnerability to spiritual oppression and even possession.

Modern Sorcery

The Greek word for sorcery in the Bible is *pharmakeia*. Generally our culture perceives sorcery as a category of entertainment associated with spell-casting and other occult practices such as witchcraft including astrology, shapeshifting, channelling and divination. Many of these activities are popularised in the occult and horror genres of TV and film: *Harry Potter; The Twilight Series; Sabrina the Teenage Witch; Charmed; Supernatural; Lucifer.*

Few realise the original meaning of *sorcery* was 'the mixing herbs and potions for spiritual purposes', especially to influence human actions and events or to enhance the practice of divination or spirit-channelling through inducing visions.

Sorcery, therefore in its truest sense is indeed the classic witches-around-the-cauldron idea from Macbeth and propagated through hundreds of children's fairy tales. Not only is sorcery dangerous in a physical sense with the inherent dangers of ingesting poisons within 'potions', but the spiritual dangers are much more hazardous.

While God sanctioned the use of herbs for healing (there are many examples of various plants used throughout Scripture; Aloes, Anise, Balm, Cassia, Hyssop, Frankincense, Myrrh and Saffron) God never sanctioned the use of herbs for anything other than physical healing and never for divination.

It could be argued that the first act of sorcery recorded was Eve eating the forbidden fruit in Genesis for she did it for selfish spiritual reasons after Satan convinced her it would give her enlightenment, suggesting she and Adam would 'be as gods' with the knowledge of good and evil. Eve and Adam both succumbed to the temptation. Whatever this fruit looked like or tasted like, God had clearly prohibited it for any purpose - food or medicine. There followed a devastating and soul-altering spiritual outcome which affected all mankind. Eve and Adam's rebellion brought sin and death into the world.

Sorcery will still be practiced in the end times. Spiritual Babylon, representing the false religious system of the last days, will deceive 'all nations' with *pharmakeia* or pharmaceutical drugs just before judgement comes.

Revelation 18:23
And the light of a candle shall shine no more at all in thee; and the voice of the bridegroom and of the bride shall be heard no more at all in thee: for thy merchants were the great men of the earth; **for by thy sorceries were all nations deceived.** *(emphasis mine).*

Sorcery today is still sorcery. Whether or not the pharmaceutical end-product is a herbal potion mixed in a bronze cup during the Dark Ages by an old hag or the outcome of modern pharmaceutical technology in a clinical laboratory; any drug or potion designed to have a spiritual effect on the user - and that includes all modern psychoactive medicines as well as street drugs – can fundamentally be categorised as sorcery. I know how extreme that sounds, but biblically speaking it is on the button.

The explosion of synthetic drug manufacture or modern *pharmakeia* is a little over a century old. Use of naturally occurring plants for medicine was all that was widely available up to the early 19th century until vaccines and anaesthetics were first developed trailblazing the 20th century exponential expansion of industrial chemistry and man-made drugs. These owed their existence to a burgeoning military-industrial complex founded on wartime weaponry research including explosives and poison gas. It is interesting to note that the same Mustard Gas used to kill on the battlefield was developed to be a prototype chemotherapy drug for cancer (Mustine) and many chemo drugs today are simply derivatives.

The 20th century was the century of mass-medication with antibiotics and vaccination at the vanguard. The introduction of fluoride into the water supply was another example. Adding fluoride, an industrial by-product into our water, completely violates the principle of informed consent. The dirty politics involved in the science and selling of fluoridation to a dumbed-down public is well documented for anyone wanting to research it thoroughly. I recommend The Fluoride Deception, a book based on ten years of research by BBC reporter Christopher Bryson on the history and dangers of water fluoridation.

Fluoride affects us physically and spiritually. In terms of acute toxicity it is more poisonous than lead, and just slightly less toxic than arsenic. While it is true that we can apply fluoride to our teeth to harden our tooth enamel, we do not need to swallow it for this effect. Indeed, the real reason for adding it to our water is to artificially tranquillise us. The first time mass fluoridation was mandated was in the 1930s by Hitler. He recognised fluoride was an effective mind-control agent which affects the frontal lobes of the brain and dulls the human flight or fight response. Accordingly, to pacify Jews and other inmates, high fluoride concentrations were added to the water supply on the trains and also to water within the concentration camps. If you wondered why the inmates never had the will to fight back in the face of certain death, fluoride is your answer. The key ingredient in Prozac is fluoride.

We live under a form of pharmaceutical tyranny that spends billions to bribe doctors and intimidate lawmakers. Today giant pharmaceutical companies lobby governments to outlaw natural remedies and supplements and push their option of man-made chemical substitutes upon us, many of which are simply low dose poisons derived from the petro-chemical industry or shabby synthetic versions of natural ingredients.

We watch the news about the dangers of street drugs, yet many of the psychotropic medicines you are prescribed from your doctor are even more powerful than those available from your local drug dealer. There is a trend among some unscrupulous doctors, who are financially rewarded for their compliance to the pharmaceutical mantra of "diagnose, drug, repeat" to be far too prescription-happy. Of course many good doctors are simply under so much pressure to see high volumes of patients that drugs are the path of least resistance to achieve their targets, however if you research addiction issues and social problems caused by prescription medications such as OxyContin® in the USA you will realise why doctors are an addict's preferred dealer of choice.

Most new drugs reaching our pharmacies are highly experimental with few long term statistics to prove their efficacy and safety over years of use. Chronic mental illness sufferers are too often convenient guinea pigs for profiteering physicians.

While I understand the torture of real depression and mental illness, many normal life problems and ordinary mood swings are unnecessarily inflated to the status of 'requiring treatment' through drug protocol.

New psychoactive drugs are very powerful and not only have many physical side effects, there are various psychological issues associated with their use, not least dependency. Such drugs are designed to act upon the central nervous system to alter brain function and produce temporary changes in mood and behaviour. There are many frightening side effects from personality changes to psychotic reactions i.e. spiritual as well as physical effects. The common psychoactive drugs are Amitriptyline®, Ativan®, Dalmane®, Elavil®, Endep®, Halcion®, Lectopam®, Mogadon®, Paxil®, Prozac®, Rivotril®, Serax®, Tranxene®, Valium®, Vanatrip®, Versed®, Xanax® and Zoloft®.

Look at the following warnings given to users of Amitriptyline® alone on www.drugs.com:

"Some young people have thoughts about suicide when first taking an antidepressant. Your doctor should check your progress at regular visits. Your family or other caregivers should also be alert to changes in your mood or symptoms.

"It is not known whether amitriptyline will harm an unborn baby. Tell your doctor if you are pregnant or plan to become pregnant while using this medication.

"Amitriptyline can pass into breast milk and may harm a nursing baby. You should not breast-feed while you are using amitriptyline.

"Amitriptyline is not approved for use by anyone younger than 12 years old."

Now, do you think that a drug that can trigger suicide and that may harm a baby as well as other many 'unknowns' should be allowed to market? Well, it is.

And here is the www.drugs.com caution on the general psychiatric effects of antidepressants found on the Prozac page.[5]

*"Antidepressants **may have a role in inducing worsening of depression** and the emergence of **suicidality in certain patients** during the early phases of treatment. An increased risk of suicidal thinking and behavior in children, adolescents, and young adults (aged 18 to 24 years) with major depressive disorder (MDD) and other psychiatric disorders has been reported with short-term use of antidepressant drugs."*

New York psychologist, David Kirschner PhD, also quotes some disturbing information in his article written for the September 2014 issue of the National Psychologist magazine in an article titled 'Mass shooters received only limited treatment'.[6]

These quotes include:

"As a forensic psychologist, I have tested/evaluated 30 teenage and young adult murderers, and almost all of them had been in some kind of 'treatment,' usually short term and psychoactive drug-oriented, before they killed."

"After each episode of school killings or other mass shootings, such as the Aurora, Colo., Batman movie murders and Tucson, Ariz., killing of six and wounding of Rep. Gabrielle Giffords and 12 others, there is a renewed public outcry for early identification and treatment of youths at risk for violence.

Sadly however, most of the young people who kill had been in 'treatment,' prior to the violence, albeit with less than successful results."

"Most of the young murderers I have personally examined had…been in 'treatment' and were using prescribed stimulant/amphetamine type drugs before and during the killing events. These medications did not prevent but instead contributed to the violence by disinhibiting normal, frontal cortex control mechanisms."

"Prior to the violent event, for which he is currently serving a life without parole sentence, Jeremy [Strolmeyer], an honor student with no history of violence, was misdiagnosed with attention deficit hyperactivity disorder (ADHD) and 'treated' with nothing more than a bottle of Dexedrine following a brief 20-minute 'cost-effective' psychiatric consultation."

Mass shootings make the headlines, but rarely is the fact that the killers were taking big-pharma's psychoactive drug-cocktails before or during their killing sprees ever alluded to on the news.

In some individuals these drugs are catalysts for violent and antisocial behaviour, particularly those who are already infested with a demon of violence or bloodlust through background and upbringing. Of course, the pharma companies would say that without their wonder drugs, these same mass shooters would have killed anyway or shot even more people.

When you look at the photographs of the 'Aurora' shooter, James Holmes when he was arrested it does not take much imagination to see the manic and demonic expression on the face of this sick individual. I would think this person had his demons sufficiently under control before taking his prescription drugs, but the drugs turbocharged his demons into action on that fateful day. I wonder how many suicides as well as murders can also be attributed to these psychoactive substances, legal or not? It is interesting to note that in the film *The Exorcist*, the young victim of possession, Regan, as well as dabbling with the Ouija board had also just had an injection at the hospital of the ADHD drug, Ritalin®. Was this a nod by the filmmakers perhaps to the catalyst effect of certain drugs in causing possession?

Modern medicine often calls mental illness a 'chemical imbalance' and tries to justify its treatment by using other chemicals to alter this imbalance. Patients accept with lamb-like innocence any diagnosis or prescription from a doctor, rarely even checking drug side-effects or natural alternatives.

We have been programmed into this compliant and misplaced trust in pharmaceuticals through a constant torrent of propaganda upheld by every mainstream media channel we are exposed to. From TV dramas showing the alleged success of chemotherapy and radiotherapy in curing cancer, to the barrage of pro-vaccine and pro-drug propaganda across all channels, we are in the grips of mind manipulation at an unprecedented level in the battle for our health. And we play an active role in our own destruction, demanding a drug for every ailment the modern world may throw at us, from feeling a bit low; suffering hormonal teenage angst or crying about a relationship breakdown. Western society with its skewed sense of entitlement for happiness 24/7 is complicit in its addictions, trusting the efficacy of anything with a child-proof cap.

What is particularly worrying is the manipulation of plant, animal and human DNA in modern medicine. The manipulation of DNA is very dangerous territory and whether or not the pragmatic intention is to heal, to make profits, or both; taking the approach that the end justifies the means is not an ethical one.

If you want to understand how frightening this technology has become, you should search out 'CRISPR gene editing technology' with its terrifying potential to create human/animal/plant hybrids and who knows what else? Manufacturing terrifying creatures like the monsters from the *Alien* or *Predator* sci-fi films is fast becoming reality (see Chapter 40).

Vaccines

Aside from gene editing, the vaccination industry is another huge experimental area within medicine where animal and plant DNA is injected directly into humans, bypassing the normal immune system protective firewalls of saliva, mucous membranes and stomach acid.

As well as being one of the largest money-making rackets foisted on a compliant public by big pharmaceutical companies backed by frenzied government support, I mention vaccines because I believe they also affect us on a spiritual level.

Corporate greed and clandestine activities overshadow the whole vaccine debate. When you have politicians sitting on the boards of pharmaceutical and healthcare companies you can't trust the government to be acting with an unbiased sense of welfare.

In February 2015, long before Covid, a Daily Mirror article revealed a host of UK politicians with strong links to healthcare firms including David Cameron and Health Secretary, Jeremy Hunt; Lib Dems Nick Clegg and Vince Cable.[7]

The Covid-19 situation has exposed even more apparent conflicts of interest in frontline politicians' connections with Big-Pharma including Sir Patrick Vallance, (Ex-president of GlaxoSmithKline) and Jonathan Van Tam, Deputy Chief Medical Officer for England. Patrick Vallance, the UK Government's chief scientific advisor and head of the 'Vaccine Taskforce' has £600,000 worth of shares in GSK, while Van Tam's connections include SmithKline Beecham, Aventis Pasteur MSD, and Roche. Van Tam wants to license Covid vaccines for children by the end of 2021 in spite of the fact that children are at nearly zero risk of contracting CV-19. What's more, Van Tam's colleague, Sir John Irving Bell chaired the UK Government's new test approvals group assessing virus diagnostics and has shares amounting to £773,000 in Roche. £13.5m of taxpayer's money was spent on the antibody tests that Public Health England stated were "unreliable".

Equally suspiciously, and not even mentioning his other pharmaceutical connections, Health Secretary, Matt Hancock awarded a contract to the tune of £5.5 million of taxpayer's money to a family friend for the provision of mobile testing units. The recipient, EMS Healthcare, is run by Iain Johnston – the former business partner of Shirley and Robert Carter, Hancock's mother and stepfather.

Let us not forget Chris Whitty, Chief Medical Officer (CMO) for England and the UK government's Chief Medical Adviser has powerful connections with The Bill & Melinda Gates Foundation, while Vaccine Deployment Minister, Nadhim Zahawi has family connections to 'Warren Medical Limited' in the healthcare sector. While little is known about the new medical company run by Zahawi's family, it is reasonable to assume the project may create a perceived conflict of interest.[8]

In addition to high-ranking politicians, at ground level we have hundreds of thousands of healthcare professionals benefiting financially from deliberately overlooking or brushing off adverse vaccine reactions.

Can doctors really be acting in the public interest when insurance companies pay huge bonuses based on the percentage of children who are fully vaccinated by age two? The American wellnessandequality.com website contains an article 'How Much Money Do Pediatricians Really Make From Vaccines?' revealing massive financial incentives for doctors to promote them.[9]

Do you and your children really require these potions for protection against disease? What the vaccine manufacturers fail to tell you is that the diseases their vaccines allegedly protect you from were already declining when vaccines were introduced. Even with limited resources you can search public records for charts that prove the sharp decline in diseases correlate to better hygiene and sanitation methods post-war with absolutely no link to vaccines.

This pattern continued until vaccines flooded clinics as a standard component of medicine from the 1950s. The same charts then show a sharp increase in the very diseases which were already on the decline. As vaccinations were propagated, so the diseases rose again and millions of precious children through the next seventy years have been given the infections that were already disappearing thanks to better hygiene, nutrition and sanitation.

Vaccines at best can claim the lowering of transmission rates however they didn't do anywhere near what public sanitation and nutrition improvements achieved for mortality rates, reducing death by an astonishing 90-99% depending on the disease. The vaccine manufacturers dishonestly latched onto the public health statistics falsely claiming it was their vaccinations that had done this.

The scam continues apace today with a slick PR machine regurgitating the benefits of *jabs* to a misinformed public and belittling those sensible enough to check the facts and refuse vaccines, insinuating these informed individuals are a menace to society.

How is it possible for an unvaccinated child to be a threat to someone who is vaccinated? If vaccines do what they are meant to i.e. 'work', then an unvaccinated person can be no threat at all. So why the fuss? To peddle more of the poisons.

I include vaccines because they are most certainly at the apex of modern-day sorcery in that they are neurotoxic concoctions containing animal or human DNA or both; a range of preservatives from aluminium to ethyl mercury and immune system adjuvants designed to trigger an immune response. The latter include squalene, detergents, mineral and plant oils.

Nut oils and egg albumin in vaccines are a proven reason for the rise in nut and egg allergies among vaccine recipients. 'Serum Sickness' was a known consequence of immunisations at the outset of their introduction. Indeed, the entire field of modern allergy has evolved from the study of Serum Sickness from early vaccination programmes. Various neurological disorders like encephalopathy, epilepsy, convulsions, and autism are also inextricably linked to vaccines. In 2017 an autistic character even arrived on the children's show, *Sesame Street* such is the need by the deeply fraudulent medical establishment to put a friendly face on the endemic state of vaccine-damage.

Some vaccinations have also been associated with onset of mental illness. In the US, Senator Rand Paul in an CNBC news interview in

February 2015 said he's heard of cases where vaccines lead to 'mental disorders' and argued that parents should be the ones to choose whether they vaccinate their children, not the government. Paul, a former ophthalmologist stated, "I've heard of many tragic cases of walking, talking normal children who wound up with profound mental disorders after vaccines."[10]

If you think my example of a vaccine being a toxic witches' brew is hard to swallow, the list below highlights some of the ingredients used in vaccinations aside from the 'diseases' themselves:

- aluminium hydroxide and aluminium phosphate

- ammonium sulphate

- animal tissues including pig blood, horse blood, rabbit brain, dog kidney, monkey kidney, chicken embryo, chicken egg, duck egg

- calf (bovine) serum and foetal (bovine) serum

- formaldehyde

- formalin

- gelatine

- glycerol

- human DNA from human diploid cells (originating from human aborted foetal tissue)

- monosodium glutamate (MSG)

- neomycin

- peanut oil

- phenoxyethanol (antifreeze)

- potassium diphosphate

- potassium monophosphate

- polyethylene glycol (PEG)

- polymyxin B

- polysorbate 20 and 80

- porcine (pig)

- pancreatic hydrolysate of casein

- residual MRC5 proteins

- sorbitol

- squalene

- thimerosal (mercury)

Now, do you think it a good idea to inject human or animal DNA into healthy adults, let alone eight-week-old infants whose tiny immune systems haven't had a chance to develop? Do you think that injecting aluminium and mercury compounds might damage brain cells, cause mental retardation, arrest a child's development or even cause cot death? The pharmaceutical companies claim all of these things are healthy to inject into tiny babies whereas their own research counteracts this.

In a colossal admission of liability The UK Department of Health was forced to reveal confidential documents outlining the details of MMR's initial approval in the 1980s, following a Freedom of Information Act (FOIA) request. The FOIA request was filed in response to the growing number of children afflicted with debilitating gut problems, brain problems and other symptoms believed to be associated with MMR, following their vaccination.

Revealed documents expose GlaxoSmithKline (GSK), the manufacturer of the MMR vaccine Pluserix®, as knowingly manufacturing vaccines that can cause serious complications in children, such as encephalitis and other conditions associated with autism. (Source: naturalnews.com)

"We have compensated cases in which children exhibited an encephalopathy, or general brain disease," admitted Tina Cheatham, Senior Advisor to the Administrator of the Health Resources and Services Administration of the U.S. Department of Health and Human Services (HHS). "Encephalopathy may be accompanied by a medical progression of an array of symptoms including autistic behavior, autism, or seizures."[11]

The American CDC (Center for Disease Control), Pediatrics, US government and Merck all admit MMR vaccine causes autism.[11]

This admission has huge repercussions, since encephalopathy following vaccination has been known to produce autism symptoms. GSK, the British government and various other players all kept this information secret, even after brave whistleblowers, such as Dr. William Thompson, came forward publicly with data linking the MMR vaccine to autism-related health outcomes.[11]

It is not just childhood vaccinations causing harm. Adult vaccinations can also trigger long-term illness and depression. Guillain-Barré syndrome causes various levels of paralysis and malaise as well as depression, and is a known side effect of flu vaccinations.

Famously, the BBC news correspondent, Malcolm Brabant developed severe psychosis after taking a Stamaril® inoculation against Yellow Fever. Brabant, who had been in and out of hospitals for years, wrote a book about his terrible experiences titled *Malcolm Is A Little Unwell*, described as a 'shocking narrative of his descent into madness'. In common with my own post-LSD psychosis, Mr Brabant also mentioned evil figures flying around the bedroom at night and his bed levitating. The illness caused him to lose his BBC job in Athens as doctors struggled to discover the right combination of medication to effect a cure.[12]

In the UK, excluding any child vaccination for Covid, a child's recommended vaccination schedule up to fourteen years old includes 71 vaccines (one injection may include six multiple shots, sometimes with different strains of the same virus). Vaccine overload is a problem in itself. Without strong parental pushback, young people will never escape the depredations of the pharmaceutical industry. Vaccines, in common with all drug interventions, have side effects, the likes of which often lead to more drug prescriptions to counteract the allergic reactions of the previous and so on, in a vicious cycle from cradle to grave; lining the pockets of a deeply corrupt system.

For diseases where no vaccine is available, profits are also assured as other drugs are employed. The anti-malaria drug, Lariam® for example, produced by Roche Pharmaceuticals, and also known as *Mefloquine*, continues to be used by The Ministry of Defence (MoD) which is accused of knowingly risking the mental health of its own soldiers after figures showed nearly 1,000 British servicemen and women have required psychiatric treatment after taking this discredited drug.[13] Psychosis, suicidal thoughts, depression and hallucinations are among the mental-health problems associated with it, eerily symptomatic of demonic oppression.

Other drugs responsible for mental illness include the countless hormone altering varieties of contraceptive pills, renowned for dramatic mood swings and a range of psychiatric problems including clinical depression. Additionally, protein pump inhibitors for reducing stomach acid; anti-convulsants; beta-blockers; cortico-steroids and the wide range of SSRIs given for multiple psychiatric disorders, deliver an evil candy-shop assortment of psychiatric risk throughout the average person's lifetime.

In summary, all drugs and vaccinations have side effects, some physical and many spiritual, both of which can be life destroying so it pays to thoroughly research every single treatment prescribed and make a concerted effort to seek out alternative remedies. I would stress this is more important now than ever given that global governments in cahoots with pharmaceutical interests are threatening to illegally mandate experimental emergency vaccines and gene therapies disguised as vaccines. Both have been authorised for use without the normal levels of rigorous testing and evaluation, skirting around the usual approval channels using the excuse of pandemic emergency for trial in the public domain. In my opinion, the most insidious element of the Covid vaccines is the use of aborted foetal cell lines in their creation, either through the testing regimen or through direct inclusion in the products themselves as in the case of the AstraZeneca Covid vaccines. Ingesting human DNA from a needle is simply cannibalism by injection. Do you believe there may be spiritual as well as physical side effects in 'consuming' a murdered baby? Do you believe a Holy God would condone this? Not only that, the mRNA and BioNtech vaccine interventions are RNA modifiers, and in spite of the assurances that this will not alter DNA, the manufacturers themselves are unsure of the short and long term side-effects of their own products.[14]

Beyond approved-for-use and authorised medications, the main drugs likely to cause spiritual problems, are the illegal psychedelic street-drugs:

Psychedelics and Hallucinogens; DMT; Nootropics etc.

These drugs are renowned for causing mental illness, but is it really a step too far or excessively controversial to view psychedelic and hallucinogenic drugs as facilitators for demonic possession?

Let's discover what the first person to take LSD - Albert Hofmann, the inventor of it had to say in 1943 when the drug was first synthesised.

In his autobiography, *LSD, My Problem Child*, Hofmann writes that after taking a large dose, he felt as if "a demon had invaded me, had taken possession of my mind, body and soul".[15]

Albert Hofmann experienced the hellish effects of LSD entirely by accident after inadvertently drinking water from a glass beaker contaminated with it from his lab. Around an hour later, he experienced a full 'bad acid trip' as he rode his bicycle home in Basle, Switzerland. (Hofmann also experienced other trips which were sublime in their nature which doubtless helped to confirm his belief in God and creation).

Hofmann famously stated, "When you study natural science and the miracles of creation, if you don't turn into a mystic, you are not a natural scientist. *Ye shalt know that I am in my Father, and ye in me, and I in you.* This promise constitutes the heart of my Christian beliefs and my call to natural-scientific research. We will attain to knowledge of the universe through the spirit of truth and thereby to understanding of our being one with the deepest, most comprehensive reality, God".[16]

In a letter in 1961, he compared his LSD discoveries to nuclear fission; just as fission threatens our fundamental physical integrity, he said, so do psychedelics "attack the spiritual center of the personality, the self". Psychedelics, Hofmann claimed, might "represent a forbidden transgression of limits".[17]

Psychedelic translated into English from the ancient Greek words psyche (soul) and deloun (make visible) literally means 'soul revealing', and psychedelic drugs are well known for their ability to activate receptors linked to schizophrenia, psychosis, and other psychotic conditions.

An eminent psychiatric scientist and scholar today is Charles Grob who has studied psychedelics. Grob's view is that a 'bad trip' is a psychedelic-heightened anxiety attack. He also observes that LSD users are prone to "anxiety symptoms resembling paranoid psychosis toward the latter part of the eight-to-twelve-hour experience".[18]

Grob's paper highlights case studies of adolescent patients undergoing bad trips. He describes physical symptoms such as "tachycardia, sweating [and] palpitations" alongside a potpourri of "psychological distress," including "varying degrees of anxiety, depression, ideas of reference, fear of losing one's mind, paranoid ideation and impaired judgment." Transient anxiety states are observed in "adolescent, novice users".[18]

As well as LSD, another drug particularly interesting to Grob with reference to its spiritual effects is DMT, or *dimethyltryptamine*. This drug is present in all living organisms in minute quantities and appears to be a chemical catalyst for mystical experience in relation to stimulation of the mysterious pineal gland in the centre of the brain.

DMT when ingested by smoke inhalation or orally via the South American herb, *Ayahuasca*, can provoke the most intense spiritual experiences. Like LSD these can range from the sublime to the terrifying. Amazingly, the DMT user-experience often presents like-for-like sensations among users where they relate common 'trip' scenarios, seeing the same landscapes and often communicating with the same entities; receiving the same messages as each other from the entities.

DMT therefore links to the alien-abduction phenomenon, since under the effects of the drug, users have described communicating with various types of spiritual creatures including reptilians and mantis-like insectoids as well as mystical angelic beings. Parallels to alien abduction stories include medical examination in a futuristic setting with the feeling that both mind and body are under scrutiny and are undergoing modification in some strange way.

Grob raises a frightening example of government-funded DMT clinical trials[19] conducted at the University of New Mexico by Rick Strassman, MD. During the project's five years, Strassman injected 60 volunteers with about 400 doses of DMT. He was expecting them to have beautiful, blissful experiences; while a slight majority did, others had horrible hallucinations of an uncannily similar nature, including "robotic monsters from another dimension trying to eat them". Even when the trip was over some were convinced it wasn't a hallucination.[19]

The above is markedly similar to the disturbing visions of demonic reptilian creatures in a dreary desert landscape I encountered during my LSD trip. A truly alarming possibility is that these places are real extra-dimensional locations. DMT experiments certainly lend strong credibility to the notion of Heaven and Hell being literal spiritual destinations – a very sobering prospect worthy of serious consideration for an unsaved individual. Even if the LSD or DMT visions are false visions implanted somehow by demonic suggestion, to the person experiencing them, they nevertheless feel so tangible that they might as well be real.

Accordingly, if by consequence of a person's deliberate refusal to turn to Jesus Christ in this life, they are locked into a hellish spiritual location upon death (such as The Outer Darkness mentioned in Matthew 8:12); even if it was a million-to-one possibility of this being the outcome, it would surely be enough of an inducement to make a person of even limited intellect immediately drop to their knees and pray for forgiveness. (If I wasn't saved already, I know what I would do).

As well as the more common psychedelics, in recent years, the emergence of a new range of mind-enhancing drug supplements known as nootropics (a Greek word meaning 'Towards the Mind') and hyper nootropics have arrived on the market, mostly available online. These are sub-hallucinogenic drugs designed as cognitive enhancers and are popular with students as they appear to improve memory, alertness and cognitive function, but they do have side effects. Depending on dose and personality types of users, episodes of psychosis have commonly been experienced and recorded.[20] Notably, because nootropics are available via unregulated vendors online there is a risk that other psychedelic concoctions are substituted for the advertised products.

The manufacture of such drugs and experimentation with them is a form of dangerous consciousness engineering, to create synthetic higher states of awareness. Use of psychedelics and nootropics is a risky undertaking. Whether a one-time only experiment, or over a longer term, psychoactive drugs and hallucinogens, even when taken under careful supervision in extremely controlled environments can be devastating to mental health.

Although I hear the stories of life-enhancing experiences for many users who have been brought to a undisputed acceptance of the truth of the spirit-world and belief in 'a god', I believe that even positive experiences are journeys into Albert Hofmann's *illicit territory*[17], and realms that sinful man is not meant to explore (at least not in a pre-resurrection state).

What's more, because of our fallen, sinful nature, these experiences make us easy targets for deceiving spirits, with a common outcome of a so-called *positive* mystical LSD or DMT experience fomenting an attitude of "I don't need Jesus, because I know what it's like to die and it was all love and peace in Nirvana".

All I can say is that once you experience a negative psychedelic event (such is the capricious nature of hallucinogens) the affirmation of the possibility of a literal or a spiritual hell, antithetical to a joyous heaven, is a sobering wake up call. In spite of the almost universal human desire for *Heaven* or *Nirvana* after death, trusting to get there through one's own volition, outside of the atonement and salvation offered by Jesus Christ, is in my opinion, a vain and foolish expectation.

Cannabis / Marijuana

Like alcohol (see next page) use of 'grass' or 'dope' has become socially acceptable for many. I smoked diverse types of cannabis over the years, experiencing various levels of intoxication and false enlightenment.

Marijuana is powerfully addictive and fickle. Some varieties deliver profoundly pleasurable sensations, mental creativity and insights, usually inspiring good humoured, lively conversation. Other types can send you into a moronic trance and lethargy, or worse, generate serious paranoia. Indeed, this is one of its most negative side effects. While it has excellent therapeutic uses for a range of physical illnesses when used as a medicine, if used solely and excessively for 'getting stoned', it is a drug of apathy, dulling the edge of ambition, making users excessively introverted, docile and extremely tired.

The mental health dangers of cannabis are well documented. Depending on the strain, cannabis has profound hallucinogenic effects, especially the so-called hybrid 'Skunk' varieties, which are so strong they create similar sensations to an LSD trip. I remember eating some powerful 'Skunk' one night in the form of a 'hash cake'. The cake was so strong I believed I actually saw the devil sitting in the chair opposite me. It was a terrifying experience because his face looked very dark brown and leathery with that classic pointy chin and devil horns poking from the forehead, smirking evilly at me. I know that sounds as ridiculous as the frog-like demons from Chapter 5, but I think demonic entities can take on mental forms that create most impact or fear in a person's mind.

Alcohol

Alcohol because of its legal status in most western countries and widespread cultural acceptance deserves to be separated out into a sub category of drug. It is of course a naturally occurring by-product of fermentation either from viticulture or brewing fruits, vegetables and other organic materials. For beer and strong liquors it is usually made from hops with barley or other corn additives with or without molasses or sugar.

Low alcohol consumption can have beneficial effects, but high doses are extremely detrimental physically and spiritually. I drink wine and occasionally beer, and I know the intoxicating effect that alcohol has in large doses. It can relax and cheer a person when taken in small to moderate quantities but can be highly anti-social and dangerous in large doses.

The Bible has many positive verses relating to the moderate use of alcohol as well as warnings against over consumption and drunkenness. The prolific references about winemaking and brewing are found throughout its pages and alcohol used in moderation for social gatherings and for medicine is clearly approved of both by Jesus in the wedding at Cana and the apostle Paul in his letter to Timothy 5:23 respectively.

Timothy 5:23
Drink no longer water, but use a little wine for thy stomach's sake and thine often infirmities.

However limits were set and intoxication where drunkenness resulted is warned about in Timothy 3:8 and Colossians 5:11. The Book of Proverbs warns about the many dangers of drunkenness from catalysing sexual promiscuity and violence as well as leading to poverty.

Today it can be argued that alcohol is a form of sorcery when it is a drug taken for 'the effect' and not for the sake of taste and refreshment or making water safe to drink which is what it was often used for.

I have seen various grades of demons at work in people under the influence of alcohol including myself. In my late teens and early twenties I was often a crazed drunkard in a bar or party setting, and dependent on the type of booze being guzzled I was variously in a range of drunken moods from looking for a dispute, to wanting sex, or simply being a loud, annoying, cynical, lustful and leering person sitting at the end of a bar talking arrogantly or aggressively. I affirm that spirits can take over a person who drinks to excess.

When people take drugs (such as alcohol) their bodies are spiritually more open to entities. Sometimes a drunk person talks or acts like someone else is talking through them and the next day they can't remember a thing they did. That's an example of a person getting possessed while they were drinking.

A person may have a dormant demonic spirit inside them that wakes up as alcohol flows, giving strength to the demon. It is why so many people appear out of character or changed for the worse when they drink.

Often a demon of drunkenness will stimulate reckless behaviour from tempting a person to dangerous stunts or taking risks with their own or other people's lives, perhaps through drink-driving, aggressive or destructive conduct, other drug taking and promiscuous sex.

A demonic spirit that is connected to a person through alcohol will always try and encourage others to drink too and will often become enraged when they don't. The demons animated by drunkenness will attract other demons including those with a predilection towards violence or lust. Which leads into the next magnet area for demonic infestation: sexual perversion and promiscuity.

CHAPTER 35.

Causes of Possession: Sexual Perversion & Promiscuity

What is sexual perversion and why are demonic spirits attracted to it?

The word perverted can be applied to anything that is unnatural, abnormal, degenerate or twisted, however it is a term that has become almost exclusively related to sexual behaviour.

Perverted conjures up an act or approach to sex that is either bizarre or ridiculous at one end of the scale to unhealthy; unhygienic; hurtful; degrading or cruel at the other.

There is no benefit in dredging through the warped and shocking range of sexual perversions that man is capable of, but perversion is essentially anything that goes against natural sexual health and particularly God's creative purposes i.e. birthing new life, and alludes to sexual activity that is fetishistic (including the viewing of pornography); physically injurious; painful; unhygienic; or repulsive.

The Bible describes various forms of sexual immorality from adultery, and premarital sex, to prostitution, bestiality and Sodomy. 1 Corinthians 6:9; Galatians 5:19; Colossians 3:5; Hebrews 13:4. Sodomy derives from the infamous biblical cities of Sodom and Gomorrah where sexual excess and especially homosexual man-with-man sexual activity was practiced and ultimately judged by God, described in Genesis, Chapter 18.

So what is healthy? The approach of animals towards sex is probably a good illustration of healthy because human society does not set a good example and probably never has.

When mammals or reptiles procreate they do it among their own species with a mate or mates within the confines of a herd or other delineated group for the purpose of nurturing offspring.

The essence of normal sexual activity for animals is therefore sex which leads to procreation. Among humans I would extend this to sex which affirms a loving bond with a spouse in a marriage.

The world has distorted the orthodox view of sex and has made sex accessible without the financial burden of childbirth, especially since the 1960s when the introduction of contraception and social changes made sex possible outside of a traditional family relationship. Contemporary 'hook up' culture has reduced sex to a series of physical sensations that can be experienced without commitment, with a range of partners without 'creating' children; and if they are created, they can be aborted and flushed away, or more sickeningly sold as additives for the food and pharmaceutical industries as a naturalnews.com article reveals.[21]

It is reasonable to expect spiritual consequences for sexual actions that rebel against God's creative intentions, even though they are culturally mandated. Like flies around a dung heap, demonic spirits are attracted towards anything that promotes unhealthy activities in opposition to God's design for healthy communities.

Here there will arise a challenge from the liberal-minded and moral relativists furiously demanding I withdraw statements that go against their narrative. I must simply affirm biblical truth, that rape; sex with animals; sex with children; homosexual sex and anal sex should all be classed as unhealthy or perverse because they are either very cruel acts undertaken to exert power and dominance over weaker individuals at one end of the spectrum; or unhygienic with social consequences (whether consenting or not) at the other. What's more, they are entirely un-creative and would never lead to childbirth which at its root is what God designed sex for, as well as being an ultimate physical and spiritual act of connection with a person of the opposite sex in marriage.

To this extent heterosexual sex with a range of partners for sexual gratification outside of marriage even if it should lead to childbirth also has social and spiritual consequences, since an environment of promiscuity with multiple partners does not create a nurturing and stable environment for children. I would argue that masturbation is against God's will if motivated by perverse desire or use of pornography which is exploitative to those involved in it and affects the mind of the individual viewing it with negative repercussions for wider society on a physical and spiritual level.

Before I hear reprimands of hypocrisy, I admit I am not guiltless and have had casual sex outside of the bond of marriage and viewed pornography frequently throughout adolescence and even occasionally in later life. This is fornication which is essentially selfish sex or sex that is undertaken purely for self-gratification. Fornication always has negative consequences.

My attitude to sex was socially-engineered in the *zeitgeist* of 1960s free-love culture. Brainwashed by feminists such as Betty Friedan and Germaine Greer whose concepts were notable throughout the 1960s to the 1990s, I was taught to reject the beauty of traditional femininity, with its ladylike modesty and its nurturing maternal values, qualities that had held civilisation and family together for centuries. Instead, I was trained to look upon women as sexual commodities to compete with as well as to acquire and dispense with when a new variety appealed. Most of the women I hooked up with were complicit in this behaviour; we had all been deceived. For further reading on how feminism and the New World Order have damaged men and women, *Cruel Hoax* by author Henry Makow Ph.D., is unrivalled.

Makow argues that while many feminist doctrines rightly addressed genuine grievances about unfairness, many swung the pendulum too far the other way, denying the physiological differences between the sexes and fostering many destructive ideas (for both men and women); identifying women as a combative group in opposition to men. Feminism also latched onto the lying premise of Aleister Crowley, the Satanist, arguing that a lack of restraint was freedom i.e. *"Do what thou wilt will be the whole of the law"*.

Such lack of restraint and fornication are areas many men and women (particularly those born in the last 60 years have found great difficulty in combating) simply because they have been given cultural approval turbocharged through the sexualisation of media and easy availability of pornography. This has caused a sky-rocketing divorce rate in addition to millions of children being aborted or born into care or single parent families, with all the attendant socio-economic problems and rising welfare bills needed to look after them. It is depressing and destructive behaviour.

In my own life I can clearly link obeying media-endorsed norms to sexual promiscuity, as well as to excessive drinking and cannabis smoking. These activities had serious spiritual consequences for me.

You see, as one demon enters a person, other demons can be assisted in gaining access. I gave the analogy of unlocking doors and unlatching windows to enter a house in Chapter 32. Evil spirits can gain easier entry into a person already infiltrated by a demonic tenant or two.

Matthew 12:43-45
When an impure spirit comes out of a person, it goes through arid places seeking rest and does not find it. Then it says, 'I will return to the house I left.' When it arrives, it finds the house unoccupied, swept clean and put in order.

Then it goes and takes with it seven other spirits more wicked than itself, and they go in and live there. And the final condition of that person is worse than the first. That is how it will be with this wicked generation.

A demonic entity inside a person will give its dark energy to that person often promoting sexual promiscuity, perverse sexual behaviour, addiction, recklessness or violence which in turn attract more demonic lodgers. Without deliverance, the person will eventually descend into chaotic living and complete immorality unless full spiritual deliverance through Jesus Christ is enabled. (See How to Be Saved, Chapter 43).

When God made us, he gave us a built-in 'firewall' called conscience to help protect us from making destructive decisions. Without this firewall a person can quickly make a mess of their life and the lives of others by rebellious choices that go against God's laws.

Over a period of time, as we commit the same sins more and more, our conscience becomes desensitised to our behaviour and eventually there is no guilt or shame about our bad choices so we end up trying to justify them. See how the alcoholic will joke about his drinking; hear how the fornicator boasts about his exploits or the time-hardened criminal will commit the same crime days after getting out of jail, blaming society for his own bad decisions.

Sodomy

I mentioned Sodomy at the beginning of this section. It is crucial to understand the dangers of practicing Sodomy from both a physical and spiritual viewpoint. Like heterosexual promiscuity, active homosexuality isn't an isolated sin, it is a defect of mind and character that will be accompanied by other sins.

Defending sexual sins is the new norm in a corrupt society. With regard to homosexuality there are vested interest groups who will grope around trying to justify its practice by demonstrating same-sex relationships in the animal kingdom. There are rare evidences of such, but these are always related to *surrogacy* in rearing a younger animal when a mate has died, or otherwise when intensive farming practices have unnaturally confined same-sex animals together causing attempts at procreation out of confusion and sexual frustration.

The Bible however is emphatic. Sodomy has seriously negative outcomes for individuals and wider society. Indeed in Old Testament times Sodomy was seen as so corrupting it was punishable by death. If practiced long enough, it leads to diseases of the body and mind and may even affect a person at a genetic level. God recognised the final outcome of letting Sodomy go unchecked, destroying Sodom and Gomorrah to halt the spread of dangerously unsanitary practices (at least temporarily) and to restrain spiritual corruption.

Sodomy is one of the most dependable ways a person can get themselves possessed by evil spirits. Among practitioners of witchcraft, the act of anal sex is believed to send a demonic spirit into someone. The evidence for this comes from practicing Satanists themselves who explain that Sodomy weakens the connection of the soul to the body so that demons can more easily infiltrate and attach themselves to a sodomised person. Once full of demons, the person is continually confused about moral choices due to the infiltration of the demons.

The Bible warns about the risks of having your mind darkened by Sodomy or even supporting such a position.

Romans 1:27-28
In the same way the men also abandoned natural relations with women and were inflamed with lust for one another. Men committed shameful acts with other men, and received in themselves the due penalty for their error. And even as they did not like to retain God in their knowledge, God gave them over to a reprobate mind, to do those things which are not convenient.

Ephesians 5:3-4 and 11-12
"But fornication, and all uncleanness, or covetousness, let it not be once named among you, as becometh saints; neither filthiness, nor foolish talking, nor jesting, which are not convenient.

"And have no fellowship with the unfruitful works of darkness, but rather reprove them. For it is a shame even to speak of those things which are done of them in secret."

It is a deliberate demonic insult to God's miracle of creation to use the anus rather than the vagina (i.e. passage to the womb) during sex. The demonic forces celebrate the fact that their hatred of God and Man is symbolically encapsulated in this un-creative, physically dangerous and unhygienic act.

This is not a rant against gays. Sodomy can apply to heterosexuals too. The gays I have met and worked with over the years have been very likeable people, most extremely caring and sensitive individuals. Homosexuals are no different to heterosexuals in their susceptibility to sinful sexual behaviour. What's more, there is much evidence to show that the pollutants in our water, air and food as well as pharmaceutical products are causing a rise in gender dysfunction at a genetic level. There is strong evidence that pharmaceutical products, vaccines and oestrogen-releasing chemicals and endocrine disruptors in the environment are affecting sexuality through altering the hormones and even the DNA of a person. Can any of us avoid being poisoned (even from within the womb) when pollutants are leaching into the whole ecosystem? However, that does not excuse our behaviour.

Heterosexual or homosexual, we are all prone to sexual promiscuity and God knows the difference between someone who actively pursues a life of remorseless excess, and those whose consciences still speak to them and who humbly reach out to Him for forgiveness, in spite of their ongoing sexual battles.

It is disgraceful that in some cultures gays are still persecuted, bullied, and refused jobs, but it is also a disgrace that anyone voicing reasonable opinions on sexual morality risk castigation from employers, their peers or hordes of emotionally infantile social justice warriors (SJWs) who preside raucously over every debate. Christian morality, once the flower of civilised society is now seen as divisive and is being brutally crushed by the neo-Nazis and Communists of Political Correctness.[22]

Diversity Consultants make careers from redefinition of sexual behaviours and positively discriminate against traditionalists, glorifying things that twenty years ago a healthy conscience would be too ashamed to discuss. The dark, gross and often violent side of sexual perversion and gender ideology is deliberately brushed aside by reformist lobby groups working alongside accomplices in our controlled mainstream media who roll out daily propaganda of *Sodomy-lite* for our re-education.

Society is browbeaten into accepting increasingly bizarre standards of immorality, fearful of accusations of 'intolerance' or 'hate' if it doesn't chant the progressive mantras. People who favour Gay Marriage are praised as fine, broadminded individuals, the litmus test for political correctness, while those who raise reasonable objections to this new elite-managed zeitgeist are condemned as detestable. In 2015, BBC radio presenter Iain Lee repeatedly attacked Christian views on homosexuality, calling them "obnoxious", "poisonous", "bigoted" and "homophobic".[23]

Lee, although criticised by the BBC for his comments and calling his language 'inappropriate', subsequently resigned, but this is a worrying incident in a resolute global media effort to marginalise those who stand up for traditional morality. It will eventually lead to a ban on the Bible as hate literature and will be used as an excuse to persecute Christians.

Fourth Wave Feminism is at the vanguard of the God-hating movement with a huge LGBT following consisting of male, female and transgender adherents extolling *Queer theory*, supporting gender fluidity and an anything goes hyper-sexualised philosophy with pro-abortion being a condition of affiliation. Profane and lewd behaviour amongst its adherents is worn as a badge of pride and the 'radical meets rebel' movement (encapsulated by the embarrassing antics of groups such as 'Pussy Riot') is undergirded by a Luciferian brand of multi-faith spirituality, especially Wiccan, demonstrating the lineage of witchcraft to contemporary feminism and perversity.

Recently in 2020, Feminist and LGBT commentators have baulked at the madness of the revolution their activism has ignited. One example is *Drag Queen Storytime* where transgender ideology is proselytised to kindergarten age schoolchildren as scantily clad drag artists read stories to them.[24] Feminist writer Meghan Murphy asks why parodies of gender stereotypes are acceptable in a way parodies of racial stereotypes are not. Murphy writes: "To me it seems equivalent to cultural appropriation or the way in which white people have mocked black people, Asian people, Indigenous people, and pretty much every other race/ethnicity that isn't theirs, under the guise of 'performance' or 'satire'."[24]

Filmmaker and gay rights activist Malcolm Clark tweeted: "The 'art form' often starts and mostly ends as a parody, often a grotesque one of women." Clark challenges the argument that seeing drag queens reading stories helps to liberate boys from traditional gender constraints. He asks: "What about the girls forced to meet a parody of women? Do their feelings not count?"[24]

Such 'transgender tension' is also oozing into sport. Feminists rail at the success of transgender sports-persons, as biological males who have transitioned into 'female' personas scoop gold medals and accolades once reserved for talented biological females.[25]

Gay or straight, sexual sin creates an environment ripe for demonic infestation. There seems to be a spiritual line that people cross, when they ignore the appeals of God to conscience and they reach a point where their souls become so darkened by dissolute behaviour and infiltrated by evil spirits that it becomes almost impossible for that person to turn to God in repentance. This is true of all sin, and only God knows when this line is traversed. A persistent practice of Sodomy will eventually harden a person's heart to such an extent they risk becoming spiritually unreachable as well as promoting inherent risks of depression and other psychiatric issues.

The fruits of heterosexual or homosexual Sodomy include diseases of the mind as well as body. Aside from sexually transmitted diseases (STDs), Sodomy feeds an inclination toward ever more bizarre and degrading sexual proclivities. In the last three decades, aberrant behaviours, historically viewed either as perverse or primitive are no longer viewed as such. Psycho-sexual syndromes such as Gender Identity disorder, transvestism, sado-masochism and the closely associated desire for extreme body modification and piercing are being normalised using mass media indoctrination. These are clearly spiritual issues, but unfortunately for the victims, various lobby groups benefit financially by promoting them as *alternative* behaviours, even disingenuously citing inequality as 'an injustice that must be righted' for the practitioners of such.

There is also a synergy between a sexually perverse lifestyle and addiction. A habitual practice of sexual immorality can kindle drug addiction and alcoholism leading to depression and other types of mental illness. Drugs and alcohol both inspire lust in a person while simultaneously dumbing down the conscience leading to an amoral existence. Rather than being approved as a lifestyle choice, society should be warning about the perils of a sexually promiscuous existence which leans towards marginalisation, loneliness, and despair.

Here are statistics from the LGBT Foundation[26] showing irrefutable links between the gay lifestyle and addiction problems / mental illness. Mental & Physical Health:

• LGB people are twice as likely as heterosexual people to have suicidal thoughts or to make suicide attempts.

• LGB people are two to three times more likely than heterosexual people to suffer from depression.

• Over half of gay young people deliberately harm themselves yet the NSPCC estimates that for young people in general it is between 1 in 15 and 1 in 10.

• 1 in 5 BME (black minority ethnic) lesbian and bisexual (LB) women have an eating disorder compared to 1 in 20 of the general population.

• 1 in 4 gay and bisexual (GB) men report being in fair or bad health compared to 1 in 6 men in general.

- A third of GB men who have accessed healthcare services in the last year have had a negative experience related to their sexual orientation.

- A quarter of GB men currently smoke compared to 22% of men in general.

- Across all age groups LGB people could be seven times more likely to take drugs.

- One in 12 LB women have been diagnosed with breast cancer compared to one in 20 of all women.

Statistics from the Health Protection Agency:

Drug & Alcohol

- Across all age groups LGB people are much more likely to use drugs: 35% of respondents had taken at least one substance (excluding alcohol) in the last month. This is likely to be 7 times higher compared to the general population.

- 34% of gay and bisexual males and 29% of lesbian and bisexual females reported binge drinking at least once or twice a week. This is likely to be more than twice as common in gay and bisexual males, and almost twice as common in lesbian, gay and bisexual females.

- Over a fifth of respondents scored as dependent on a substance, and a further quarter showed at least one indicator of dependency.

- While almost a third of respondents had sought information, advice or help about their substance use, significant barriers exist which are preventing many LGB people from accessing the support services they may need.[26]

Diversity Consultants may misleadingly attribute all the above issues to homophobia and marginalisation; and for some this may be true; however, it is deceitful to ignore the spiritual reasons behind such statistics.

Sexual promiscuity has spiritual side-effects and promiscuity particularly among gay men is renowned: A study by Bell and Weinberg (1978), published by the Kinsey Institute, and often called 'the most ambitious study of homosexuality ever attempted', showed that 28 percent of homosexual males had had sexual encounters with *one thousand* or more partners. Furthermore, 79 percent said more than half of their sex partners were strangers. Only 1 percent of the sexually active men had had fewer than five lifetime partners. The authors concede: "Little credence can be given to the supposition that homosexual men's 'promiscuity' has been overestimated" (p.82). "Almost half of the white homosexual males…said that they had had at least 500 different sexual partners during the course of their homosexual careers," (p. 85). A few years later, Pollak (1985) described sexual behaviour among gays as "an average several dozen partners a year" and "some hundreds in a lifetime" with "tremendous promiscuity."[27]

Sodomy energises a lifestyle of degeneracy and other life problems. How does a spirit of homosexuality enter a person originally? Only God knows, but such powerful entities often enter a person through traumatic childhood events including (and certainly not limited to) sexual abuse in childhood (especially anal sex); emotional rejection from one or both parents; dysfunctional upbringing (e.g. emotionally cold and distant father or domineering mother or vice versa); and rejection from members of the opposite sex. These are all likely door-openers to a multitude of different spirits including promiscuity and sexual immorality. These spirits may also manifest in depressive and manic symptoms and lead to further problems including drug and alcohol addiction.

The LGBT statistics do not affirm the gay lifestyle as a healthy one, and I would guess that the statistics for heterosexual promiscuity do not fare any better.

It is significant how God's rainbow symbol, used to announce the end of the judgement of the flood has been usurped as a gay emblem. In spite of the exoteric rationale behind the design, wrapping something as dysfunctional as Sodomy up with a rainbow flag and calling it empowerment is fraudulent.

If you are involved in Sodomy either from a heterosexual or homosexual viewpoint, God provides a way of escape through Jesus Christ. He understands the weakness of the flesh and all extenuating circumstances. He will nudge your conscience and draw you to Himself for forgiveness, love and healing. You may have found your conscience pricked on many occasions by your behaviour. Be warned however, God does not strive with an individual forever.

Whatever the sins of men may be, God has patience for a long time, with many appeals to conscience to turn from rebellious behaviour. If you override this Godly-drawing long enough you will eventually risk your conscience being hardened and that is when God gives you over to your selfish lusts in entirety; abandoning you to a degenerate mind-set that constantly fantasises about sex, and like a pig wallowing in its own excrement, engaging in everything your corrupted mind can think of.

But God values those who humbly acknowledge their weakness. His heart is for the destitute, the needy, and the lost sinner. Jesus spent his valuable time with sinners: the prostitutes, tax collectors, lepers, and society's rejects. That means there is hope for the worst of us. The apostle Paul writes:

2 Corinthians 12:9
"But he said to me, 'My grace is sufficient for you, for my power is made perfect in weakness.' Therefore I will boast all the more gladly of my weaknesses, so that the power of Christ may rest upon me."

God wants to transform us because he loves us. True growth and transformation do not rely on own strength but come when we declare our weakness and stop living in our own power. Make room for the Holy Spirit to fill and empower you.

God doesn't expect sinless perfection, it's an impossible goal this side of Heaven - he asks for our honesty and humility. We can boast of our weaknesses as Paul did and proclaim our need for God's grace. In doing so we receive power from on high; in acknowledging that we are weak, we gain the help of an Almighty, all-loving, ever-present God.

Stop finding your value and identity in what you do, and look to God as your strength. Allow his love, power, and help to be your source. God's strength is both able and available to you. (See How to be Saved, Chapter 43).

Paedophilia and Other Paraphilia

Because sexual immorality is no longer viewed as sin in this 'progressive' new world order we live in, it has led to a situation where almost every form of sexual expression is approved of as long as it takes place between consenting adults.

But how long until the boundaries of this are pushed toward *consenting children* with adults; or adults and children with animals?

Let's face it, legislation is quickly moving in that direction. There are powerful people who seem to want it that way. Evidence for paedophilia (see Chapter 35) and sex crimes at the top echelons of society is compelling: *Pizzagate* and *Pedogate* in the US; the *Dutroux*

Affair in Belgium; Savile, Edward Heath, Cyril Smith, and the *Westminster Child Abuse* cover up in the UK where incriminating documents handed to the then Home Secretary, Leon Brittan conveniently disappeared; all indicate something is rotten at the heart of the Establishment and suggests access to sexual exploitation of children with impunity is a perk of high office. Is it any wonder that government propaganda now educates us to view unhealthy things as good, and healthy choices as intolerant in a climate of increasing moral-relativism?

There are many nauseating and disgusting perversities which go against all natural inclinations and which clearly confirm deeply embedded demonic spirits in an individual. These include bestiality (sex with animals), necrophilia (sex with dead people) and cannibalistic sexual fetishes, all of which can be bracketed in the same spiritual league as paedophilia.

The unrepentant practice of child sexual abuse is an almost certain indicator of having crossed that metaphorical line with God. Paedophiles wield power over innocent victims for sexual pleasure in selfish and sadistic sexual acts. That is not to say paedophiles are beyond the forgiveness of God, but this vile group of people usually don't even think they're doing anything wrong. If they don't see their sin and their need for God's forgiveness, neither will they go to Him.

And what does God say about those who hurt and corrupt children?

Luke 17: 1-2
Then said he unto the disciples, It is impossible but that offences will come: but woe unto him, through whom they come!

It were better for him that a millstone were hanged about his neck, and he cast into the sea, than that he should offend one of these little ones.

Such despicable acts against the innocent must be at the apex of human depravity and it's why paedophiles like Jimmy Savile and his friends, the children's home child abusers; the compromised politicians and other hidden and protected members of the Establishment as well as those sexual cockroaches in the Church, notably many in the Roman Catholic priesthood and other denominations, are exposed and brought into the spotlight. A simple Google search for 'Establishment+Pedophiles' (American spelling will engender more effective search results) will open many doors the powers that be would like to keep firmly shut, especially where there is a clear Establishment connection to the religion of Satanism (or *Luciferianism* as they prefer to call it). See Chapter 37 and the section *'Selling your Soul and Generational Satanism'*.

It would be a dream for paedophiles of all socio-economic backgrounds to have their sexual degeneracy endorsed by gradually legalising it through a process of incremental steps, slowly undermining established sexual mores with the ultimate goal of abolishing the age of consent. Do you think that couldn't happen? Society thought homosexuality would never be legalised as late as the early 1960s. Through the process of incrementalism it is now celebrated.

A broad range of psycho-sexual paraphilia are now categorised under a blanket euphemism of 'sexual preferences' whereas for centuries they were clearly labelled as deviant. It would be very un-PC indeed to call these behaviours mental illness, and rarer indeed to suggest that there are actual demons behind the issues. Incredibly, even disgusting acts of necrophilia and paedophilia are being redefined by some groups as sexual preferences in an attempt to mitigate their vile nature.

I predict the current, or certainly the next generation will be the 'Everything Goes' generation who will take their turn in rewriting the statute book. Millennials have been so thoroughly immersed in the mantras of tolerance through the dumbed-down education system they are close to tolerating anything under the guise of *equality*. Many already view The Bible as hate text, and will certainly approve of the removal (by whatever means necessary) of those yucky Christian bullies who dare to uphold 'intolerant' and 'outmoded' moral principles.

God gives His clear warning about this:

Isaiah 5:20
"Woe unto them that call evil good, and good evil; that put darkness for light, and light for darkness; that put bitter for sweet, and sweet for bitter!"

CHAPTER 36.

Causes of Possession: Religion and Spirituality

I am a firm believer in freedom of speech and freedom of religious choice. No one should ever be persecuted for their religious choice or for evangelising their beliefs to others. As Evelyn Beatrice Hall said, *"I do not agree with what you have to say, but I'll defend to the death your right to say it."*

This is such an important principle. Your religion and your right to proselytise is your choice. It is a matter of conscience. I do not take offence when someone tries to persuade me of their religious or political preferences, nor should they be offended if I don't agree with them.

Believing this, I am exercising my right to warn you that religion and spirituality are key territories where demonic entities operate.

Religion is an area as dangerous as the Ouija board and witchcraft for the potential of demonic influence or possession depending on the religious entity being revered and worshipped. With demonic influence comes the risk of mental illness which can be experienced by a religion's adherents from mild to extreme. This is a controversial statement, but let me explain.

'Religion', or more specifically, 'false religion' is designed by Satan to divert people from the truth by setting up false light, half-truths or false teaching.

There are hundreds of world religions connecting not with God, but with demonic entities and deceiving spirits instead of God. These range broadly from tribal belief systems and nature worship, through to the massive pagan Islamic and Hindu religions and their offshoots. Many world religions have their roots in Egypt or Babylon, the cradle of human civilization and the place where false religions were created and spread by Satan and his fallen angels through their control over false prophets who evangelised false doctrines throughout population centres in the early civilised world.

The Hebrew Bible (*Tanakh*) teems with information about the many pagan tribes throughout Egypt, Canaan and Philistia; ranging from the powerful Pharaonic polytheistic beliefs to Babylonian Baal worship as well as Astarte goddess veneration and the worship by the Hebrews of Moloch with their terrifying rituals of child sacrifice.

Satan loves false religion. He desires global religious diversity because religion ensnares and enslaves minds. Not only do the varied world religions create confusion, strife and sometimes war through their competitive belief systems, Satan also seeks worship of himself and if he can't get it directly through Luciferian or Satanic followers he will get some satisfaction through setting up new religions and false worship to divert true worship away from the God of the Bible and onto idols like Allah, Vishnu, Kali, Buddha and a multitude of other gods and spirits.

Satan promotes this confusing pick-and-mix of faiths so that the average person is utterly confused when faced with which path is the true one. Satan has good reason to give us a *pot pourri* of religious choices. Why? Because 'religion' is not God's plan of salvation.

The world's religions are saturated with false teachings and false prophets who teach self-righteousness instead of relying on the righteousness of Jesus Christ. You see, it is 'relationship' with Jesus Christ and not 'religion' which is God's true plan of salvation. (See 'How to Be Saved', Chapter 43).

World religions have different ideas about who God is. Jehovah is not Allah, neither does Vishnu or Buddha have any connection to Jesus Christ. When the world uses the word 'God' to be the same spirit present in all the world religions this is blatantly untrue. Jehovah, the One Eternal God of the Bible, is not Allah of the Koran, or Vishnu the god of the Vedas. There are clear differences between them especially in terms of their morality and salvation theology.

That doesn't sound very inclusive does it? But remember, God is not politically correct; He is Eternal Truth personified in Jesus Christ. He doesn't care if His truth insults your beliefs. The following short list highlights some of the more popular false religions (there are many more) deceiving the world today.

Islam or Mohammedanism

The worship of Allah is the most common form of worship for 1.6 billion Muslims from the Pacific region of Asia; in India and Pakistan; to The Middle East and North and Sub-Saharan Africa.

In spite of what political correctness states, *Allah* is not another name for Jehovah (YHWH), the Eternal God and Father of Creation. Allah was a pre-Islamic deity, originally the Sumerian moon god called many different names including *Nanna, Suen* and *Asimbabbar*. His symbol was the crescent moon.

Of the 350 gods worshipped at the Kaaba in Mecca, Allah the Moon-god was chief deity. Mohammed, in establishing his own monotheistic religion for the Arabs preached that Allah was the same God that the Christians and Jews worshipped except that he had no son, and that Judas, not Jesus had been killed on the cross instead, contradicting the gospels.

The website https://biblicalfoundations.weebly.com/allah-in-history.html states that Muslims will find this information hard to digest, and that, "Archeology *(sic)* has found Allah. Allah existed as the Arabian moon god long before Muhammad ever introduced him to Arabs".[28]

Quotes given on the website include three following:

1. "Allah, the moon god, was married to the sun goddess. Together they produced three goddesses who were called 'the daughters of Allah'. These three goddesses were called *Al-Lat, Al-Uzza, and Manat*. The daughters of Allah, along with Allah and the sun goddess were viewed as 'high' gods. That is, they were viewed as being at the top of the pantheon of Arabian deities". (R. Morey, *The Islamic Invasion*, Eugene, Oregon, Harvest House Publishers, 1977, pp.50-51).

2. "But history establishes beyond the shadow of doubt that even the pagan Arabs, before Muhammad's time, knew their chief god by the name of Allah and even, in a sense, proclaimed his unity...Among the pagan Arabs this term denoted the chief god of their pantheon, the Kaaba, with its three hundred and sixty idols." - (The Muslim Doctrine of God, Samuel M. Zwemer 1905, p24-25).

3. "Historians like Vaqqidi have said Allah was actually the chief of the 360 gods [one for each day of the year] being worshipped in Arabia at the time Muhammad rose to prominence. Ibn Al-Kalbi gave 27 names of pre-Islamic deities... Interestingly, not many Muslims want to accept that Allah was already being worshipped at the Ka'ba in Mecca by Arab pagans before Muhammad came. Some Muslims become angry when they are confronted with this fact. But history is not on their side. Pre-Islamic literature has proved this." - (Who is This Allah?, G.J.O. Moshay, 1994, p138).[28]

Today the world sees two versions of Islam, a *lite* version and an extreme version. Islam-*lite* exists in both Sunni and Shia branches, but is essentially a watered-down cultural practice that includes visible outward prayer, regular visits to the mosque, and reading the Koran. Culturally the lite-version resides non-violently within other cultures surrounding it.

The vast majority of practising Muslims in the world fall into this moderate category. Most are very decent folk who are no more dumbed-down about God and the real spirit world than their neighbours of other faiths who also fit comfortably into that easy-going, get-on-and-get-by pattern that lends itself to an amiable society and cooperative existence between cultures. Extremist or Fundamentalist Islam however shows its true satanic colours in Sharia legalism, violence and bloodshed and is just as likely to persecute its own moderate members as *infidels* as it does members of other religions.

The fruits of a false religion at the very least include spiritual blindness and spiritual enslavement, but extremist Islam is so possessed by evil spirits it has become a death cult obsessed by paedophilia, torture and decapitation ripened within a culture of extreme misogyny. It explains why, at the Jihadist periphery of their religion, so many Muslims revel in bloodlust - you become what you worship.

Bloodlust is the most anti-societal form mental illness can take - violent psychopathy. How else can a person be empowered to undertake such horrific acts as terrorism, or genital mutilation on little girls, not to mention the propensity for paedophilia upon both sexes. *Wahhabi*-fanaticism ideology is present in modern Islamic Jihadism; you either convert or you die or pay the *jizya slave tax* – these are the savages of Islam, funded largely by Saudi Arabia, a country supported by complex US and European financial structures; who have been raping and pillaging in Libya, Iraq, Afghanistan, Syria and are looking to do the same thing in Europe, Russia and USA.

This is what Winston Churchill said about Islam:

"How dreadful are the curses which Mohammedanism lays on its votaries! Besides the fanatical frenzy, which is as dangerous in a man as hydrophobia in a dog, there is this fearful fatalistic apathy. The effects are apparent in many countries. Improvident habits, slovenly systems of agriculture, sluggish methods of commerce, and insecurity of property exist wherever the followers of the Prophet rule or live.

A degraded sensualism deprives this life of its grace and refinement; the next of its dignity and sanctity. The fact that in Mohammedan law every woman

186

must belong to some man as his absolute property, either as a child, a wife, or a concubine, must delay the final extinction of slavery until the faith of Islam has ceased to be a great power among men.

Individual Moslems may show splendid qualities, but the influence of the religion paralyses the social development of those who follow it."

—Sir Winston Spencer Churchill (The River War, first edition, Vol. II, pages 248-50 (London: Longmans, Green & Co., 1899).[29]

Eastern Mysticism

Eastern Mysticism is enveloped in a fog of demonic deceitfulness. Examples of the more well-known disciplines include *Buddhism, Confucianism, Hinduism, Jainism, Taoism, Shintoism, Sikhism, Theosophy, Transcendental Meditation, Hare Krishna, Yoga,* and *Zoroastrianism.* These account for the majority religious brands of occult spirituality originating in the Indian and Asian continents.

Eastern mystics say there is no personal God to communicate with and the essence of all existence is an impersonal life force. Therefore, prayer is not a part of the belief system, but rather, meditation so individuals can arrive at a personal awareness of how to advance to their next level of incarnation.

I was very familiar with such concepts as my dad's bookcase contained many books on philosophies and spirituality connected with Tibet and India. I recall trying out some of the chanting and breathing rituals and was left high-and-dry as to any spiritual benefit, probably due to impatience and lacking the discipline for the interminably boring hard work these monotonous exercises demanded to achieve so-called 'enlightenment'.

The world is generally kind towards Eastern Philosophy because it consists of a number of feel-good philosophies, which avoid pointing out that politically incorrect and unfashionable word *sin* that sounds so judgemental to the modern thinker. Unfortunately, sin is the big human problem and unless Jesus Christ deals with it finally, everything else you believe you have achieved in your spiritual life is worthless.

Acts 4:12
"Neither is there salvation in any other: for there is none other name under heaven given among men, whereby we must be saved."

(See How to Be Saved, Chapter 43)

My dad had experienced false enlightenment himself. He had become an adept at Yoga, meditation and various breathing exercises. After his frightening experience where he confronted something terrifying during a bout of *Kundalini* or 'Serpent Energy' meditation, he presumably realised that the philosophy he was dabbling in had opened him up to evil spirits. I believe this was the reason why he stopped his occult exploration, finally turning to Christianity in a final quest to understand the meaning of life. I wonder if my dad was responsible for unwittingly channelling the 'Hat Man' entity, which assaulted me. This demonic spirit came from somewhere; perhaps attracted through the practice of yoga, exploiting a spiritual gateway into our home.

Interestingly, *Kundalini Syndrome* is a distressing condition remarkably symptomatic of psychotic illness that yoga practitioners commonly experience. Alongside depression and dissociation, physical sensations including electrical energy; tingling and vibrations through the body; prickling on the skin, as well as headaches or pressure in the head are suspiciously present. With the obvious satanic connection to serpents, (the biblical term for Satan is 'that old serpent' - Revelation 20:2), I believe a spiritual or demonic cause is compelling and highlights the false light and real personality behind this meditative discipline.

What is for sure, my dad's *yogic* breathing exercises were no more than playing with spirituality without dealing with sin. They were a waste of his time. He died youngish at 55. Even if his breathing exercises had eked out a few more months for him, he would have died in his sins if he hadn't gone to Jesus.

Hinduism

Hinduism is the backbone of the Eastern mystic religions and needs a section of its own for the simple reason that, like Islam, so many people (nearly 1.1 billion) are influenced by its teachings. Hinduism includes a diversity of ideas on spirituality and traditions and can be more of a way of life or identity than a religion. Indeed Hinduism can be highly occultic at one extreme and atheistic at the other.

Orthodox Hinduism is arguably just as nefarious as Islamic fundamentalism, with the fruits of some of its traditions, especially the concept of *Karma*, manifesting widespread suffering.

That is not to say there are not some truths present in Hinduism, especially the idea of universal spiritual values such as social justice and peace, especially in Modern Hinduism, but it is also rife with contradictions. Child prostitution is rampant within the Orthodox Hindu culture and a harsh, frequently cruel and patriarchal societal structure with great female inequality exists, especially in India.

Hinduism has no central doctrinal authority and because of this the polytheistic Hindu worldview is confusing and bizarre. Just one visit to the impressively gaudy Hindu temples within India, Nepal, Bangladesh, and Indonesia will convince you of that. See the multi-limbed and multi-coloured pantheons displaying androgynous deities and Hindu saints, some with hybridised animal appendages and eye-popping grimaces; others indulging in gross sexual acts upon their towering psychedelic facades.

Like one of the scowling demons on its parapets, the Hindu world brims with fearful and fiendish gods with constant demands for homage and temple offerings to ensure good fortune. Hindu worship is governed by these demonic entities, with the idea that the smaller gods are different aspects of the same metaphysical *Brahman* and *Shakti* (energy). Many Hindu or Buddhist parents bring their children to their temples to offer their offspring as human sacrifices to demons for possession.

The extensive belief in karmic principles and reincarnation (into either animal or person) has spawned a caste system with extreme injustices, severe poverty and exhausting spiritual enslavement.

In the extremes of this superstitious world, cows are venerated, while people, including infants and babies, are left to die in filthy gutters in loveless degradation so that they can 'work out their karma' uninterrupted. There is lack of certainty about anything spiritual, leading an inquiring Hindu mind to either embrace atheism and humanism or to survive within the confines of the Hindu system immersed in religious OCD, leading to depression and often insanity. Demonic possession is well-known, evidenced by illiterate individuals being able to speak ancient forms of Sanskrit fluently during trances.

Judaism

Judaism's Hebrew Bible texts, The Tanakh, contain Moses' Torah and famously the first book of the Bible, *Genesis* which records the creation of the world, 'In the Beginning'. The Hebrew Abrahamic religion is not the oldest *written* religion in the world (Hinduism precedes it), but its narrative reaches back to the Creation, Eden and the ensuing pre-Flood world, so from that viewpoint it records the earliest historic descriptions of the world.

It is important to realise there are distinct branches of Judaism; the Torah-based Judaism of Moses affirmed by Jesus Christ, and the pagan, occult Babylonian system containing the Kabbalah and Talmudic doctrines of the Pharisees and The Sanhedrin - the Jewish Council which rejected the claim of Jesus that he was the prophesied Messiah.

The Pharisees accused Jewish followers of Jesus of blasphemy for asserting that Jesus was 'God made flesh'.

It could be argued that Torah-Judaism became Christianity whereas the Talmudic-branch hardened into the various Conservative, Orthodox and Reform Judaism branches which are today largely ethnic clubs. The Talmud contains some of the most extreme anti-Jesus sentiment and clear Jewish ethnic supremacist teachings.

Jesus singled out the persecutors of the early Christian Church by naming them 'The Synagogue of Satan'. These were people who called themselves Jews (the people of God), but who persecuted those who believed in Jesus the Messiah (the true people of God).

Revelation 3:9
"Behold, I will make them of the synagogue of Satan, who say they are Jews, and are not, but do lie; behold, I will make them to come and worship before your feet, and to know that I have loved you."

By rejecting the Jewish Messiah, they renounced their status as 'true' Jews, and it's why Jesus calls them liars.

There is a spiritual chasm between Judaism and Christianity that only Christ can bridge. Judaism (like Islam) denies the Christian belief that God can exist in three distinct persons, as Father, as the Holy Spirit and as Jesus the Man, yet still retain 'One God' status, even though Isaiah the Jewish prophet clearly taught this multi-unity concept about God:

Isaiah 9:6
*For unto us **a child is born**, unto us **a son is given**: And the government shall be upon his shoulder: And his name shall be called Wonderful, Counsellor, **The mighty God**, **The everlasting Father**, **The Prince of Peace**.*

The preaching of 'Christ crucified' and the divine Trinity continues to be a *stumbling block* to Jews and *foolishness* to many Gentiles.

1 Corinthians 1:23-25
But we preach Christ crucified, unto the Jews a stumbling block, and unto the Greeks foolishness, but to them which are called, both Jews and Greeks, Christ the power of God, and the wisdom of God. Because the foolishness of God is wiser than men; and the weakness of God is stronger than men.

1 Corinthians 1:21
For since in the wisdom of God, the world through its wisdom did not know Him, God was pleased through the foolishness of what was preached to save those who believe.

1 Corinthians 2:14
The natural man does not accept the things that come from the Spirit of God. For they are foolishness to him, and he cannot understand them, because they are spiritually discerned.

In spite of the spiritual blindness of many Jews, religious Jews nevertheless accept the idea of Satan and demonic forces, though Satan has a slightly different *modus operandi* for Jews, being an angelic 'tester' or 'hinderer' for man's loyalty to God's laws. In Jewish folklore, a *dybbuk* is a restless, usually malicious spirit believed to be able to haunt and even possess the living. Such demons can apparently possess people, animals and even objects.

In common with Gentiles, modern Jews are in danger of suffering from spiritual depression, demonically inspired in many cases. With atheism among Jews typically around 20%, many are in a state of atheistic despair, engulfed in materialistic nihilism, rejecting all religious and moral principles, in the belief that life is meaningless. That is tragic for a group of people whom God made stewards over the moral law through the Ten Commandments.

The spiritual forces of evil want to keep Jews and Gentiles disunited, focused in worldliness, atheism or religious traditions, with the aim of distracting them from their lost condition and diverting them from the truth.

2 Corinthians 4:4
"In whose case the god of this world (Satan) has blinded the minds of the unbelieving so that they might not see the light of the gospel of the glory of Christ, who is the image of God."

Possession comes in many guises and one of its subtler forms is a demonic spirit of religious divination whose purpose is to deceive others through false teaching or prophesy. The fruit of a false prophet is false teaching.

False prophets speak from their own mind or a mind under demonic influence, not by divine proclamation. The effect of false doctrine in the lives of men leads to a rejection of God's word, and rejection of biblical authority. It is no small thing.

Concerning the way of salvation, all false prophets will either deny the deity of Jesus Christ and will reject His work of salvation on the cross, or will say that Jesus' sacrifice is insufficient and you must add your own works to Christ's to ensure your salvation.

Christians are called to act as *salt and light* and guide people away from false worship into true relationship with God through Jesus. We are to speak the truth in love even if that means people get offended.

Jesus said that in the same way that we judge trees by their fruit, we should judge prophets also, not just by what they say, but also by what they do. If the fruit is good we recognise that a person is rooted in God, but if the fruit is rotten or evil then the spirit of that individual is rooted in evil.

Matthew 7:16
"Ye shall know them by their fruits. Do men gather grapes of thorns, or figs of thistles?"

When speaking to the hypocritical religious scribes and Pharisees Jesus said:

John 8:44
"Ye are of your father the devil, and the lusts of your father ye will do. He was a murderer from the beginning, and abode not in the truth, because there is no truth in him. When he speaketh a lie, he speaketh of his own: for he is a liar, and the father of it."

Israel had its false teachers and false prophets throughout the Old Testament and continues to have them today. Christianity also has its false teachers within mainstream Christianity as well as in various cults with a Christian veneer.

Pseudo-Christian Cults

Just because a person or a church describes itself as Christian does not mean that he, she or *it* is.

Christians throughout the world will have many cultural differences and methods of worship, but wherever they are located, the true church of Jesus Christ consists of people who have accepted God's gift of salvation and put their faith in Jesus Christ. This includes accepting Jesus' death on the cross as payment for their sins and His resurrection as proof of His power over death.

Within the New Testament there are no denominations, just a universal categorisation of people residing in different geographical settings all with their ethnic differences, but who nevertheless trust in Jesus Christ's once-and-for-all sacrifice at Calvary for salvation; with the Holy Spirit oxygenating their walk with God and using the Bible (The Word of God) as a roadmap.

This is the plain and true Christian faith which has always been the target of Satan since the early church. It is apparent that Satan's main method to destroy Christianity has been focused on undermining it from within, using false teachers who claim to speak for God but who are presenting a false gospel that is powerless to save, creating churches with a veneer of Christianity but no real substance.

2 Timothy 3:5
"Having a form of godliness, but denying the power thereof: from such turn away."

The Bible warns us not to believe any other doctrine, if it contradicts the doctrine received from God in the Scriptures, even if an angel were to deliver the teaching.

Galatians 1:6-10
"But even if we or an angel from heaven should preach a gospel other than the one we preached to you, let them be under God's curse! As we have already said, so now I say again: If anybody is preaching to you a gospel other than what you accepted, let them be under God's curse!"

A pseudo-Christian cult will consist of a leader (or group of leaders/ organisation) who, claim to be Christians but will distort and deny fundamental and distinctive doctrines of the Christian faith. These cults will idolise their church leader or the top church authority/hierarchy as the exclusive means of knowing 'truth' or giving answers to spiritual questions. There are lots of these cults in existence today including The Seventh Day Adventists, Jehovah's Witnesses, Christian Science Churches, The Church of Jesus Christ and Latter Day Saints (Mormon Church) and Unitarian Churches. The most notorious false teachers include the Watchtower Society; Joseph Smith; Harold Camping; Herbert W. Armstrong; and Ellen G White.

Pseudo-Christian cults will generally have an appearance of Christianity and will adhere to selected parts of the Bible for some of their teachings, but will always have an extra-biblical source or other book that is deemed to be of higher authority than the Bible when any spiritual questions arise that contradict the teachings of the 'cult'. For example; and I single out *three* of the biggest culprits:

Mormonism has The Book of Mormon (described in their own words as "Another Testament of Jesus Christ". Unlike biblical Christianity, Mormonism doesn't believe in original sin, i.e. the sin of Adam bringing the curse of death to every generation. Mormonism also dictates you must keep all the commandments and follow all its ordinances to both learn how to be gods and reach the highest level of heaven. This denies the fundamental Christian doctrine of unearned grace through faith.

Jehovah's Witnesses have their Watchtower books and teachings. They explicitly deny the deity of Christ and believe that salvation is impossible outside of the Watchtower. They are not allowed to question the Watchtower leadership and claim you need to read the Watchtower's magazines and other material in order to understand the Bible correctly without which you will "fall into darkness" – what they call reverting to normal Christianity.

The Roman Catholic Church, although teaching that the Bible is the Word of God, adds spurious apocryphal books to the Scriptures, and raises church tradition and the edicts of popes and councils (the words of men), to the same or greater level of authority than the Word of God. Its Catechism excuses any contradictions in its methodology and practices that are in opposition to God's Word such as prayers to the dead (channelling); and falsely places Mary, Jesus' mother as co-Redeemer with Jesus.

Furthermore, Roman Catholicism, although teaching that faith in Jesus Christ is necessary for salvation, denies the truth of the gospel by adding sacraments, good works, and Purgatory as additional requirements for forgiveness of sin and for eternal life.

Some people will say I am divisive for speaking out against these cults and especially the mighty Roman Catholic Church. Let me stress that I am not singling out individuals, but only the ecclesiastical organisations. The Greek Orthodox and Coptic churches as well as many Anglican churches can equally be criticised for works-based and even pagan practices.

According to writer Jeremy James:

"The Anglican Church is the official state religion or Established Church of England. Having been under the covert control of the ruling elite almost from its inception, it is the principal means by which true Christianity in England has been suppressed. Through its empty formalism and shallow doctrines, its seasonal ritual and genteel pageantry, it offers a comforting substitute for true Biblical Christianity. In order to keep the commoners and lower classes in

thrall, the nobility themselves profess to be Anglican and participate in certain annual services.

Behind the scenes, however, the ruling elite have for centuries been freemasons, atheists or Unitarians. They all reject the deity of Christ. The Anglican church has long been primarily a system of social control whereby the rich and powerful maintain their privileged positions and at the same time imbue the masses with the mindless patriotism that is needed to run an Empire." [30]

Having been born into Anglicanism, I have my suspicions that this overview paints an accurate picture. However, in spite of its many faults, it was foundational to my early spiritual growth, with its hymns, the Book of Common Prayer and the Creed.

No denomination is perfect and all have been inconsistent down the centuries. Encouragingly, I can affirm that within the countless Roman Catholic; Greek Orthodox; Coptic; and Anglican churches; and even the cults; there are millions of genuine seekers after truth, and true Bible-believing Christians within their ranks. I have been to Roman Catholic and Anglican churches that have preached the Word of God faithfully and effectively; yet at other locations have seen the very worst types of idolatry in play, keeping the congregation enslaved in dead and dismal ritualistic worship. In spite of the bad doctrinal baggage that plagues so many denominations, the simple gospel message still somehow shines through.

It appears to me that God has placed innumerable, genuine Christ-seekers within these imperfect systems so that in spite of their denomination's imperfections and historic and ongoing corruptions at least some semblance of Christianity is reaching people in places where otherwise the name of Jesus may never be spoken, such as in parts of the Middle East, Asia and South America.

It is impossible to ignore the ever-increasing list of Roman Catholic and Coptic martyrs, including women and children, who have bravely stood up against Jihadist savagery in the Middle East, or resisted Communism in China and North Korea, proclaiming their faith to the end with the threat of torture and death upon them. Is it really possible to take such a stand without the presence of genuine faith and the Holy Spirit residing in them? I doubt it. Remember, there is no Christian who has a perfect faith, or a perfect doctrinal position or any who can boast sinless perfection other than Jesus Christ himself.

Among other religions too, not every person who is deceived is misled through any fault of their own. Individuals are born into false worship because of geography, or tradition and cultural influence. God knows the hearts of men and knows the genuine seekers after truth in whatever religious system they find themselves. However, it is also important to preach the gospel and refute false teaching, so there must be a fair balance between holding your tongue for the sake of peace, and speaking out against false teaching when you find it.

In summary, within all Christian denominations you will see those with the genuine faith of Jesus filled by the Holy Spirit, and others who falsely believe they are saved by their religious works. Christians who believe the latter are barely different to any other believer in any of the countless worldly religions that rely on religious works to achieve spiritual status. Such false belief is powerfully under the control of religious demons.

So how do we know the difference between a spirit guiding from God and a spirit from Satan? The Bible is our guide.

1 John 4:1-3
"Beloved, do not believe every spirit, but test the spirits to see whether they are from God, for many false prophets have gone out into the world. By this you know the Spirit of God: every spirit that confesses that Jesus Christ has come in the flesh is from God, and every spirit that does not confess Jesus is not from God. This is the spirit of the antichrist, which you heard was coming and now is in the world already."

When people do not have the light of God's Word found in the Scriptures and the guidance of the Holy Spirit, they will walk in darkness fumbling for the truth. Life will be confused, meaningless and hopeless at worst, or at best, an exhausting spiritual journey up many promising looking blind alleys of half-truths that all lead to a dead end.

Proverbs 14:12
There is a way which seemeth right unto a man, but the end thereof are the ways of death.

It states in the Bible that there is only one mediator between God and man, and that is Jesus.

We are told to pray to God the Father in Jesus' name or to Jesus Christ. The Lord Jesus Christ is the compound redemptive name of Jehovah who is the God of Abraham, Isaac and Jacob and all the biblical prophets.

Praying within the context of any faith other than Christianity or Torah Judaism (*not* Babylonian Talmudic Judaism) is at best a waste of time, at worst a spiritually hazardous undertaking.

If prayer is not directed to the God of the Bible it will by default, be an incantation toward a dead idol or demonic entity inviting it to influence your life.

The Bible affirms the existence of the *triune*, three-in-one nature of God: the Christian *Trinity* where the One Holy God exists in three persons of God the Father/The Son/and The Holy Spirit (see page 184). It also states all the gods of other world religions are demonic or fallen-angelic idols.

Deuteronomy 32:17
"They sacrificed unto devils, not to God; to gods whom they knew not, to new gods that came newly up, whom your fathers feared not."

Psalm 96:5
"For all the gods of the nations are idols: but the LORD made the heavens."

1 Corinthians 10:20
"But I say, that the things which the Gentiles sacrifice, they sacrifice to devils, and not to God: and I would not that ye should have fellowship with devils."

A caveat here. It is entirely possible that a genuine seeker after truth in whatever religious tradition they find themselves may reach the One Eternal God in prayer by means of God's abounding grace. I believe that Jehovah of the Old Testament is God the Father, hence worshippers within Torah Judaism may still reach God in prayer thanks to God's ability to search the hearts of men and understand who is actively seeking truth.

A genuine seeker after the One Eternal God must surely engender the sympathy of God the Father. Jesus said in the Gospel of John that he would be a spiritual magnet to the souls of all men, teaching that a person must be specifically drawn to him by the Father.

John 6:44
"No man can come to me, except the Father which hath sent me draw him: and I will raise him up at the last day."

John 12:32
"And I, if I be lifted up from the earth, will draw all men unto me."

It therefore follows that through the power and grace of God, that all men will be *drawn* to Jesus Christ. Men are drawn by the moral power of the life and death and resurrection of Christ brought home to them by the Holy Spirit. A small example of God's *drawing* may be hearing a street preacher prick your conscience as you pass by, or noticing a Bible verse on a car bumper sticker as you sit in a traffic jam. A more powerful example of God's *drawing* might be a crisis in your life designed to compel you to seek comfort in the Scriptures, or induce you to visit a local church to meet the pastor for guidance. Because men have free will it is the rejection of this *drawing* that marks us out for judgement at the end of our life. We actively choose to go to Heaven by accepting Jesus, or we eternally perish by choosing to reject Him.

Unbelief in Jesus Christ is strongly tied to demonic influence and false teaching. Individuals that reject Jesus Christ as God in the flesh and deny the working of God's Grace through the person of Jesus, have no part with Him or His Holy Spirit and therefore are not under blessing, but under judgement.

John 15:23-25 (English Standard Version)
Whoever hates me hates my Father also. If I had not done among them the works that no one else did, they would not be guilty of sin, but now they have seen and hated both me and my Father. But the word that is written in their Law must be fulfilled: 'They hated me without a cause.'

All religions that reject Jesus Christ lie in the dominion and power of Satan and his fallen angels. This is why the Interfaith Movement is so misguided. While it is right to try to live peaceably with all men, it does not follow that we bow down to their idols by joining them in worship or fail to preach the gospel in case it offends. The Interfaith Movement is simply a precursor to the coming One World Religion under the Antichrist.

We must never tolerate evil and falsehood, but warn against it, speaking the truth. That is the mark of love to our fellow men; warning them about the consequences of false belief or unbelief. We must never persecute unbelief, but evangelise truth and love as personified in Jesus Christ. I speak to myself in condemnation of my own failure to deliver "The Good News" on many occasions, even when prompted by the Holy Spirit. An evil spirit of reticence has often cowed me when I should have spoken out.

Other Cults and Affiliations

There are many more cults too numerous to mention, but the most prominent include a range of divisive sects which destroy families. Notable among them is *Scientology*; renowned cult of Hollywood's elite which uses many advanced brainwashing techniques based around the science fiction ethos of the late author, L. Ron Hubbard. Scientology is more like a massive corporation or university dedicated to sophisticated financial scamming under the guise of lifestyle-enhancing counselling and meditation instruction.

Another giant of a cult is *The Unification Church* of Sun Myung Moon (The 'Moonies'). South Korea's personality cult is renowned for its giant group-marriage ceremonies while Sun Myung Moon is known for his verbal assaults against the orthodox Christian church.

Similarly hundreds of yoga-centric and transcendental meditation-based personality cults exist centred around a cult leader; many of whom are renowned for abusive activity and sexual coercion of women and children.

Depressingly, mass suicide cults continue to make headlines. The *Heaven's Gate* suicide cult took the lives of 39 members in 1997, ostensibly so they could join a spaceship following the Hale-Bopp Comet to a new life in space; while *The Order of the Solar Temple* responsible for 74 suicides promised members they were moving to Sirius. Most infamously in 1978, Jim Jones's *People's Temple* (a pseudo-Christian cult) compelled 900 of its own followers to drink cyanide or be shot.

Pseudo Christian cults as mentioned previously include the *Jehovah's Witnesses* and *The Church of Jesus Christ of Latter Day Saints* or Mormons, which do not adhere to the doctrinal integrity of biblical Christianity, but have large corporate headquarters extolling their own take on the Scriptures supported by their own literature and traditions. *Seventh Day Adventists* too, though comprising many genuine Christians, fall into the trap of exalting dead religious works with their rabid Pharisaic adherence to Jewish Sabbath-keeping.

Indeed, hundreds of pseudo-Christian cults exist worldwide, twisting the Scriptures usually to support a bizarre 'pet doctrine' by the cult leaders. Most notable in recent years have been *The Branch Davidian* doomsday cult of David Koresh; and *The Family* communal group founded by David 'Moses' Berg.

There is also a range of White Supremacist cults supporting racist doctrines, including the idea that Caucasians are the descendants of the ten 'lost' Tribes of Israel. These include the *Ku Klux Klan, Aryan Nations,* and *Christian Identity Church*. The Ku Klux Klan was infamous for evil cross-burning rituals and executions of Negroes during the 20th century, revealing a complete absence of Christian love.

Street gangs and gang culture are similarly centred on the threat of violence and are like religions to their members. Thousands of such cults exist worldwide, abounding with as much demonic influence as *spiritually* religious cults. They may have no explicit occult affiliations, but the relationship to violence, drugs, prostitution, and neighbourhood extortion is highly indicative of demonic control. Those gangs that do revel in overt satanic worship include the Mexican *Santa Muerte* death cult; and the Salvadorian MS-13 street gang operating in Houston, Texas. As reported by The Daily Mail, UK, the latter 'kidnapped, drugged and raped a 14-year-old Houston girl and murdered another to appease an insulted demon'.[31]

The psychopathically violent *Santa Muerte* death cult has a scythe-wielding Grim-Reaper demon as its miracle worker and is, according to a Houston Press article, the 'unofficial patron of many of Mexico's *narcos*, prostitutes, prisoners, poor, gays, transvestites and others on the margins of Mexico's Drug War-ravaged, poverty-stricken society...'[32]

Where moral breakdown, violence, drugs and prostitution are rife, demonic spiritual vultures circle for victims. These spiritual predators don't care how economically underprivileged or affluent a neighbourhood is; they can equally scavenge tasty spiritual carrion in rich communities too.

Wherever moral values are undermined there is a higher proportion of demonic activity. Even the most loving middle class homes may present a vacuum ready for demonic spirits to fill. In these days of increasing moral-relativism where Christianity is lukewarm at best, ignored or vilified at worst, demonic activity can present itself in many forms including a form of *godless spirituality* – a religion where anything goes and everything is believed or can be worshipped, as long as it isn't the real Jesus Christ of the Bible.

Angel Worship

Currently in vogue among New Age adherents is *adoration of* and *channelling of* angels. In the Bible, initiating dialogue with spirits (other than the Holy Spirit) is forbidden.

We read in the Bible that at God's command angelic beings sent from Him can initiate contact with people, but we are never to initiate contact with them through rituals or prayers. Communicating with any spirit outside of God's Holy Spirit is prohibited and that includes communicating with the spirits of dead relatives, 'saints' or animals.

We can of course communicate with God in prayer through the spiritual connection Christ's atonement enables, but we must never communicate by using angels or other 'spirits' as intermediaries. We can come to God the Father directly in prayer. The mediation of Jesus Christ empowers all our prayers and the Holy Spirit guides us to pray for things that are in God's will for our lives.

Even John the great Apostle himself was warned about being deceived into the worshipping of angels. A holy angel from God would *never* accept worship:

Revelation 19:10
"And I fell at his feet to worship him. And he said unto me, See thou do it not: I am thy fellowservant, and of thy brethren that have the testimony of Jesus: worship God: for the testimony of Jesus is the spirit of prophecy."

Revelation 22:8-9
"And I John saw these things, and heard them. And when I had heard and seen, I fell down to worship before the feet of the angel which shewed me these things."

"Then saith he unto me, See thou do it not: for I am thy fellowservant, and of thy brethren the prophets, and of them which keep the sayings of this book: worship God."

The worshipping of angels is therefore something only encouraged by 'fallen' angels. In the rare event that you should ever be confronted by an angel knowingly, this would be a great test as to their true allegiance.

The reason for the obsession with angels and angel-related mysticism seems to be the inability of rationalism and materialism to give answers and meaning to life. Without God, the futility of all of life's pursuits – education, career, relationships, finances, achievements - cannot be stressed strongly enough. A hundred years from now, all that is going to matter is the status of your soul and whether you are saved or not.

Man's heart is deceitful and angel worship has become a substitute for a real relationship with God through Jesus Christ.

Interest in the mystical and the supernatural pursued independently of God's revelation - the Bible - will lead you to a dead end, whatever the fallen angelic or demonic spirits and their human channelers or 'light workers' as some like to be termed, may tell you.

Increasingly the world is hearing feel-good messages from these fallen angels *(aka The Watchers)* and other so-called *alien* and *Extra Terrestrial-type entities* whose communications typically revolve around past incarnations or how us weak humans will be taken, with their help, to the next cycle of our Darwinian Evolution or 'Shift', expanding our consciousness into Oneness.

The lie transmitted by these deceiving spirits is that you can reach God independently by your own efforts, always without Jesus Christ. If Jesus is mentioned he is falsely represented as a feminised or hippy New Age Jesus – an Ascended Master, who travelled to Tibet to smoke weed and learn wise words from gurus, and he wasn't really the Son of God.

The Luciferian doctrine does not accept man's problem is separation from God through sin, instead we are told to believe that each of us has forgotten his or her own *divinity*. Therefore, the solution is to seek 'higher consciousness' through Shamanic meditation and discipline; breathing exercises; yoga; diet; crystals; chakras; channelling; spirit guides; goddess worship etc. to awaken 'the god in man'.

Satan's favourite feel-good message continues to be the old lie that we can 'be as gods' without dealing with sin; peddled through his New Age emissaries who are too cool, too hip and sophisticated to tie themselves to the narrow-minded thinking of Christianity.

Remember, Satan's favourite disguise is an angel of light. You have heard the phrase 'blinded by the light', well, there is *true* light and *false* light. The true light is Jesus Christ, and the false light that blinds a person to truth comes from Satan. Satan is trying to convince people that Jesus isn't the only way to reach God. To a dumbed-down world so used to tolerating everything, it sounds so much more rational and compassionate doesn't it?

Another feel-good lie is that Hell is a false creation of 'bigoted' and 'intolerant' Christianity. Why? Because if there is no Hell, then there is no need for individual accountability and therefore no reason to follow God's commandments and live within a moral framework.

I repeat again the infamous falsehood coined by the Satanist, Aleister Crowley: "Do what thou wilt will be the whole of the law", or, put another way, "If it feels good, do it!" The lie is, you can just live life and do whatever you want, trying to be happy for yourself, with no consequences.

The world is thus blinded by Satan's deceptions which sound very appealing to fallen man, but what does the Bible say?

Proverbs 14:12
There is a way which seemeth right unto a man, but the end thereof are the ways of death.

2 Corinthians 11:13-15
For such are false apostles, deceitful workers, transforming themselves into the apostles of Christ.

And no marvel; for Satan himself is transformed into an angel of light.

Therefore it is no great thing if his ministers also be transformed as the ministers of righteousness; whose end shall be according to their works.

Ephesians 4:17-19
This I say therefore, and testify in the Lord, that ye henceforth walk not as other Gentiles walk, in the vanity of their mind, having the understanding darkened, being alienated from the life of God through the ignorance that is in them, because of the blindness of their heart.

Satan is a masterful deceiver and it is why most horror film genres portray him as a dark, devilish being with horns, and his associates as frightening and powerful demons. That is what he wants you to think, because most of us are not drawn to darkness, but to light and people do not expect evil to look nice and wholesome. By appearing as a creature of light, people are more easily enticed to his lies; as a deep sea angler fish attracts plankton with illuminated bait. The adulation of angels is just another one of Satan's attractive deceptions to keep your eye off the true salvation, light and life offered by Jesus Christ alone.

CHAPTER 37.

Causes of Possession: Deliberate Invitation

Lucifer worship is an old religion that is booming. To most people the idea of "selling your soul to the devil" or potent demon is a fiction; the plot of a corny made-for-TV movie. The concept was famously mythologised in the *Faust* story with the notorious demon, Mephistopheles, a tale undoubtedly rooted in the Biblical narrative of Christ's 'Temptation on the Mount' when Satan offered him all the riches and adulation of the world as a reward for worship, which Jesus refused.

Matthew 4: 8-10 (NKJV translation)
Again, the devil took Him up on an exceedingly high mountain, and showed Him all the kingdoms of the world and their glory. And he said to Him, "All these things I will give You if You will fall down and worship me."

Then Jesus said to him, "Away with you, Satan! For it is written, 'You shall worship the Lord your God, and Him only you shall serve.'"

'Selling Your Soul' and Generational Satanism

Selling one's soul can be a very real transaction as the Bible account confirms, and today, a host of famous celebrities, politicians, scientists and many people at the top of their professions have admitted they have literally traded their soul in return for riches and fame in this life. Such individuals are careless and indifferent to the warnings of God, not appreciating the high risk of mental illness, addiction and exposure to depression and misery it entails in this life alone, not to mention damnation in the next if they don't turn and repent.

Sadly, the deal doesn't just affect them; the rest of us too have to live with the consequences of their greed and self-interest.

A high proportion of celebrities and cultural icons are tools to promote unbiblical doctrines such as atheism and Evolution theory as well as sexual promiscuity, drug taking, violence and general depravity.

Soul-selling Satanists are behind Hollywood and the glitzy world of international show business and entertainment as well as Deep State politics, high finance, and the scientific 'technocracy'. Highly influential, these individuals deliberately support evil; their dark materials disseminated through art, music, entertainment, news and education. Such programming is designed to cast down our minds and divert us from the hope of the gospel message, encouraging us to doubt God and instead believe that this present life is all there is.

The process of selling one's soul can be very straightforward. Indeed to some degree, we are all sell-outs to Satan when we willingly do something against conscience and therefore against God who programmes *conscience* into our psychological blueprint like an automated piece of software for self-correction. However, there are distinct occult routes and defined rituals where a person can offer him or herself to Satan for direct possession by demonic spirits for worldly rewards.

These range from as simple a transaction as making mental assent to doing a deal with a demonic entity after pursuing such an arrangement i.e. through supplication to a demonic spirit or entity requesting such a deal; or in high-level witchcraft a deal may be brokered through another party (high priest or priestess) acting as intermediary for a particular demonic spirit.

You exchange all your ethics and moral code in return for wealth, sex, power, influence etc. The trade-off means you give allegiance to Satan by agreeing to do his will throughout the duration of your fleeting human lifetime in return for money or fulfilment of carnal desires, or both.

And Satan has the power to provide them through the people and organisations he operates within including media; music and television; politics; science; finance and banking; and military-industrial structures. At the highest levels, all institutions are undergirded by various secret societies including Freemasonic and Illuminati Orders, Jesuit Orders, Hermetic brotherhoods, Jewish mystic and Gnostic groups and many more, giving credibility to the phrase, "It's not what you know; it's who you know."

CHAPTER 38.

Causes of Possession: Programming

Programming through use of propaganda is putting an idea inside someone's mind (political, scientific, religious or otherwise) to control his or her thinking. It is a type of possession.

Mass media, especially radio and television have been the most powerful methods of dispersing programming in recent history, with the promotion of various ideologies, from scientific opinion and political dogma to cultural systems and religious creeds including atheism, all designed to trigger a certain response in their target audience. This programming has enabled a tiny minority of people to lead whole populations into tacit approval of wars, group persecutions (holocausts and pogroms), and today, promotion of mass medication using fear of disease as the catalyst.

Political brainwashing post-First World War was responsible for many hellish dictatorships from Stalin's Russia; Hitler's Germany; Mussolini's Italy; Mao's China; Pol Pot's Cambodia; Pinochet's Chile and many more.

The unquestioning allegiance to Communism, Nazism or Fascism - all of which are *collectivist* ideologies where individualism is crushed by an all-powerful State apparatus, is a form of ideological possession. The brainwashed individual is both dependent on the system he belongs to as well as simultaneously fearing it.

Today's postmodern world is a giant collectivist programming apparatus that uses fear in conjunction with technology to brainwash and control individuals. Postmodern programming has created an inversion of morality and introduced many upside-down values, stemming from the spread of its neo-Marxist dogma. In this decadent environment, healthy attitudes are viewed as 'intolerant' and an evil thing like abortion is euphemistically called *Pro-Choice* rather than baby murder. Most recently powerful medical propaganda funded by globalist pharmaceutical interests has been used to garner support for mask wearing and vaccine mandates. If you thought you were immune to propaganda, ask yourself if, five years ago you'd ever believe you'd be wearing a mask in a supermarket or willingly rushing out to have The State inject you and your children in a clinical-trial.

As soon as you wake up to the fact you are being programmed, it is fascinating to see how subtly the propaganda is dished out. I watch the nightly news primarily to work out what propaganda they are trying to feed us dumbed-down 'sheeple people' and I will do the opposite of what is being suggested if it doesn't line up with God's word.

Programming is most powerful when it contains small truths wrapped around a bigger lie, and is usually disguised as entertainment. The cult of celebrity displays symbolism of devil worship and Illuminati control. The Illuminati is the highest and most secretive branch of Freemasonry also known as Luciferianism (Lucifer worship); a euphemism for worship of Satan.

British Freemasonry usually refers to Satan as Helios or Apollo, the sun god of Greek mythology and the organisation teaches using parables from Hermeticism and Alchemy, concealing its Luciferian secrets from its lower rank-and-file by using false explanations of its symbols to mislead. Many decent charitable men (and women) are members of this powerful occult tradition without realising who they are really bowing their knee to. For a broad overview as to how the world is really structured (with its 'powers and principalities') and why people end up selling their souls and getting possessed, I strongly recommend the books of Canadian author, Henry Makow Ph.D. on the Illuminati who does an excellent job exposing many dark institutions.

Contemporary 'celebrity' sell-outs to Satan or active blasphemers of God include pop and media stars like Beyoncé, Rihanna, Madonna, Britney Spears, Taylor Swift, Miley Cyrus, Lady Gaga, Prince (deceased), Kanye West, Will Farrell, Brad Pitt, Meryl Streep, George Clooney, Bruce Willis, Barry Manilow, Jon Malkovich, Sir Ian McKellen, Ted Turner and many, many more.

Historically, the most famous sell-outs who corrupted society in exchange for money and fame are The Beatles and The Rolling Stones who were jointly tasked with promoting drug use (especially psychedelics) as well as Eastern religious philosophies and occultism instead of Christianity. John Lennon was an active blasphemer of Jesus Christ in his book, 'John Lennon in His Own Write', while Mick Jagger claims Anton LaVey, the founder of the Church of Satan and author of the Satanic Bible, helped inspire The Rolling Stones' music. The albums titled, "Their Satanic Majesties Request", and "Sympathy for the Devil" clearly reveal their true allegiance.

Sixties icon Bob Dylan too famously admitted he made a bargain with "the chief commander on this earth and the world we can't see" in an interview with Ed Bradley, aired on the 60 Minutes programme in 2004.

It is difficult for me to feel anything but anger and righteous indignation toward these cultural prostitutes, many of whom have literally had a satanic anointing; who target the minds of our precious children. Nevertheless, even people this corrupt can be saved and I have a duty as a Christian to call them out for their sins, but to guide them toward Jesus Christ who can nullify any contracts they have made. Their souls were never theirs to sell in the first place.

When you realise how such a tiny yet influential group of people is responsible for so much of society's vice and sleaze it makes no sense that they are idolised. However, that is testimony to how spiritually bankrupt the world is when Jesus Christ is side-lined.

You and I have all been conned by popstars and celebrities who promote a counter-culture of sex, drugs and rock and roll; rebellion against parents; multiculturalism; the gay agenda; all wrapped up in clichés of peace, love and freedom, not realising the real agenda is to sow hatred for Jesus Christ and subvert traditional Christian values which are the true foundation for a healthy, prosperous, peaceful and loving society.

Wes Penre, author of website Illuminati-News describes the situation eloquently:

"Whether or not we believe in a Biblical Hell, those musicians emit low vibrations of evil and destruction, which are forced upon our youth by the music industry. One does not have to be a genius to understand what effect this has on young people's minds and their way of seeing things. Music is VERY powerful, and used in a wrong way it can change a whole generation in a way that may have catastrophic consequences. With morals and ethics gone, what remains is anarchy and chaos - the desired state the Illuminati wants the world to be in before the takeover. By making rebels out of our teenagers and have them go against their parents, the Illuminati is trying to dissolve the Family Unit, which is a very strong bond. As long as families stick together and the parents teach their children morals and ethics, the Elite will have a very hard time to control us. And they know it!"[33]

The programming continues with each successive generation brainwashed into accepting increasingly degenerate values as being 'cool' and healthy. Daily we are swallowing a sugar-coated poison-pill delivering a covert globalist and transhumanist agenda, leading to a cashless society via the digitisation of money and total satanic control through the eventual Mark of the Beast. Yes, really.

Most accept this satanic programming as normal and even celebrate it. The true and unrecognised mental illness of today is how people can wallow in a 24/7 haze of synthetic applause, canned laughter, gender dysfunction, sexual perversity, junk food and pill-popping, and find it all so...joyful. And woe-betide anyone who speaks out against it, they are just so un-cool and intolerant as those gorgeous, witty, sexy celebrities are paid to tell us.

People are dumbed-down through listening to propaganda peddled by mainstream media from the BBC to CNN, to Fox News Network, CBS and Russia Today. Mainstream media sets the narrative while smaller news organisations simply parrot the same agenda from approved sources and everyone laps it up, and that includes the majority of professing Christians.

There are certainly deliberate efforts by many media companies and Hollywood in particular to deliver nihilistic messages of despair to their audiences or otherwise incrementally push the boundaries of decency and taste so that increasing satanic influence can be brought to bear on an unsuspecting public.

I say unsuspecting, but some brave voices saw what was happening decades ago and attempted to stem the flow of violence, sexual perversion, and irreverent language that now defines much entertainment today.

Mary Whitehouse was a renowned English TV critic and saw what was happening when the UK had just 3 channels to worry about! She was ridiculed for being an old-fashioned prude but understood exactly how incrementalism would end up.

Today the 9pm 'watershed' has been breached and the flood of programme genres from horror to porn is available via 24/7 streaming. Soon, there will be pornography available for children (with a Parental Guidance label attached to make it alright of course) because that is what incrementalism does. It pushes the boundaries, calls it daring and brave and makes arrogant statements like "Isn't it marvellous that we can discuss such and such perversion or controversial lifestyle so openly". This is satanic deception designed to corrupt children spiritually and usher in the coming Man of Sin. People are being primed to literally worship Satan. Does that sound crazy?

Explain then the recent trend on television engendering sympathy for fallen angels and the Devil in films like *Hellboy*, or in TV series such as *Lucifer*, or *Charmed* where there are good and bad demons. Such conditioning is sending deceptive messages to control and shape our thinking. If you instil in a child's brain that demons can be quite cool as is the current trend; the truth that they are really trying to make your life miserable, kill you and take you to Hell becomes a little blurred, especially when combined with the ridiculous lie that Hell is a cool party venue bouncing with fun and freedom, when in fact it's a suffocating place of horror, monotonous despair, madness and regret.

Self-Harming Behaviours

Satanic programming has been responsible for many self-harming behaviours among children and teens. Media extolling the virtues of skinny models and celebrities who push impossible ideals of beauty on to impressionable young people has catalysed a rise in mental disorders ranging from low self-esteem to 'cutting' and body dysmorphia as well as eating disorders.

The rise of tattoos and piercings in just one decade is testimony to the insidious power of this propaganda. In the 1990s, tattoos on women were practically unheard of, but now it's rare to find a man or woman under the age of 40 without one. Allow me to be even more controversial and state that the act of tattooing, however fashionable it is currently, may indicate a demonic presence at work, particularly if the individual displays a desire for morbid occult or demonic illustration, or has tattoos or piercings in the genital area.

Extreme body-piercing and body-modification *clearly* confirms demonic possession. A quick 'Google Images' search of the term 'extreme body modification' should convince even the most hardened sceptic of the destructive demonic power behind such actions. You will often find that a person engaged in such activity will have many other demons too, especially spirits of sexual promiscuity, addiction, depression and suicide.

"But that's intolerant hate speech!" I hear the cries. No it's not. It's the truth. The origins of self-injury were learned by the Jews in Egypt where it was common practice for the pagans to make cuts and gashes on their face, arms, and legs when someone died. The cutting symbolised respect for the dead and an offering to demons of death. God forbid the practice:

Deuteronomy 14:1
"You are the children of the Lord your God; you shall not cut yourselves nor shave the front of your head for the dead."

Leviticus 19:28
"You shall not make any cuttings in your flesh for the dead, nor tattoo any marks on you: I am the Lord."

These Scriptures link to the New Testament and the possessed man in Mark 5 who sat night and day crying out and cutting himself with stones (see Chapter 31). The demon-possessed man in the Bible had a range of spirits that would certainly have included spirits of suicide, (note how the herd of pigs ran over a cliff immediately after the legion of demons possessed them).

Eating Disorders

Cutting can also be associated with eating disorders (bulimia and anorexia) as well as psychiatric problems (such as anxiety and bipolar).

Most people who cut or self-mutilate usually explain they are trying to 'get rid of something on the inside'. This may be subconscious awareness of an evil spirit within which gives them the idea that purging through blood loss will let the pain or spirit escape. This is of course a demonic lie and is designed to cause suffering as well as to cultivate greater degrees of mutilation (when the pain doesn't go away with a little cut); desensitising them to pain and acclimatising them to thoughts of suicide. It is interesting to note the importance of blood to demons. Spiritually, blood is the life essence of a person, and in shedding blood, demons are getting a person to self-sacrifice themselves to them; making a mockery of how Jesus Christ shed his blood as a sacrifice for the sins of mankind.

Anorexia and bulimia are all about purging something from within, either starving it into submission or vomiting it out. The Lena Zavaroni scenario (see Chapter 19) is an all too typical tale of teenage angst developing into a full blown mental disorder with fingerprints of the demonic all over it.

Growing exponentially among teenage girls (and increasingly boys) such eating disorders have complex psychological foundations with multiple contributory causes, including cultural, hereditary and family influences. Many also display clear demonic influence, especially so when the eating disorder is long term and has caused an individual to be sectioned or hospitalised.

Disturbingly, in the last decade or so and clearly influenced by the growth of online forums and social media, bizarre forms of anorexia and bulimia have evolved where sufferers are taking a clear sense of pride in their affliction with an intense element of competition manifesting among them, examples of which may include challenges as to who can lose the most weight most quickly etc. This disease-idolisation has given a warped sense of purpose to sufferers who are promoting the afflictions as lifestyle choices with devotees even affectionately nicknaming anorexia 'Ana' and bulimia 'Mia' supported by multiple *Ana* and *Mia* websites proselytising the starvation lifestyle with religious fervour, bringing *Ana* and *Mia* worshippers together for online chats; celebrating bingeing and purging techniques; sharing skeletal photos and even disgusting videos of vomiting with close ups of toilet bowl remnants.

It is the same kind of sick clique-mentality and warped sense of superiority shown by drug addicts or cult members. Many people with eating disorders and the related mental illness of body dysmorphia are beginning to display similar psychological profiles to those of mind-controlled suicide cults or street gangs who promote reckless behaviour as a condition of affiliation.

People get angry about attributing demons to these kinds of psychosocial syndromes because they will prefer to opt for societal influences and even genetic links to explain mind-control away. These of course will play their part, however, a demonic cause is a compelling argument. Associated emotions of sadness, loneliness, emptiness and depression alongside the eating disorder or body-dysmorphic condition confirms the spiritual nature of these conditions. Eating disorders don't 'do' happiness, fun and laughter, just misery, fear or a persistent desire for death, all unmistakable demonic fingerprints.

The Bible even recognised the spiritual component of eating disorders:

Psalm 107: 17-21 *(NIV translation)*
*Some became fools through their rebellious ways and suffered affliction because of their iniquities. **They loathed all food and drew near the gates of death**. Then they cried to the Lord in their trouble, and he saved them from their distress. He sent out his word and healed them; he rescued them from the grave.*

Chapter 39.

Causes of Possession: Trauma and Shock

Psychological shock and trauma can also facilitate entry of demonic spirits. I do not understand the dynamics of this, but it appears to be so. The correlation between mental illness and the aftermath of shock and trauma is clear.

Post Traumatic Spectrum Disorder (PTSD) is characterised by chronic and generalised anxiety along with other psychological problems swinging pendulum-like through a spectrum of categories including PTSD in combination with psychosis; PTSD with depression, or anxiety and panic, or dissociation; or PTSD with OCD and so on.

PTSD symptoms are dependent upon the age, gender, genetics, and background of each person. Some patients may exhibit symptoms from mild nervousness to sheer terror while others are prone to aggressive outbursts and uncharacteristically violent behaviour. A common post-battlefield illness, PTSD may also arise after a period of chronic fear including childhood trauma, an abusive relationship, injury or accident.

Having experienced intense psychological fear during my LSD bad trip, I can vouch that trauma is a doorway through which demons can pass. How this occurs is unclear, however, I have a hunch that when the brain experiences huge levels of negative mental stimulation it emits a form of electro-magnetic energy that attracts negative entities within the plasma-energy field that interlaces the world around us and within us.

As previously said, I believe the substance of 'spirit' may be a form of electromagnetic plasma energy that will one day be understood scientifically, related to the science of positrons, neutrons, dark matter, antimatter and their interactions. This is admittedly the realm of quantum physics and I realise my understanding of the complexities of it are very limited, however it is certainly not unscientific to talk about spirit in terms of electromagnetic physics. I am sure it is much more complicated than that and I apologise if I am being inadvertently irreverent in describing this mysterious component of God's creation in such terms.

As a form of sentient plasma, spiritual energies could influence how we think or act. An evil spirit for example, may hijack a healthy person's thinking and influence brain activity, negatively effecting mood or behaviour, from oppressing a person to outright possessing someone.

It follows that God's Holy Spirit can influence us too in a positive manner, possessing us for our benefit and edification. It is interesting to note that the tongues of fire visibly experienced during Pentecost seem to be a form of plasma-energy; a rare observable manifestation of the Holy Spirit:

Acts 2: 3 *(NIV translation)*
*They saw **what seemed to be tongues of fire** that separated and came to rest on each of them.*

Plasma is the fourth state of matter and the least understood, quite simply because it is sometimes visible, sometimes not, manifesting as either light, heat or energy. It is where science meets the abstract.

I realise that to most people, including many Christians, I sound like an eccentric talking, but perhaps rational science is on the threshold of vindicating such *irrational* notions, which leads aptly into the next chapter.

CHAPTER 40.

Causes of Possession: Technology

In today's interconnected world there is a range of technology which I believe makes it easier for demonic spiritual forces to affect us spiritually and physically.

It is a reasonable assumption to consider the idea that demonic spirits, which may consist of a form of plasma-energy or operate within this environment, might also generate electromagnetic forces and radiating frequencies detectable by the brain under particular conditions, so-called *negative energies*.

Interestingly, electro-magnetic energy is observed using radioactive isotopes during brain scans undertaken to view brain activity. This advance in psychiatry asserts the brain shows clear patterns for certain types of mental illness from bipolar, to schizophrenia, to depression, perhaps anorexia and OCD.

If science claims the brain's electrical output can paint a picture of mental illness, it is also reasonable to consider the possibility that symptomatic patterns shown on these scans may be generated directly or indirectly by the presence of sentient plasma entities. The same goes for epilepsy. While many epileptic conditions will be physiological, there will be others with a spiritual basis.

It seems plausible that entities may gain power and thrive in environments that discharge negative energy. A demonic intelligence will feed off the energy created by negativity and fear, simultaneously promulgating negative thoughts within a person to generate an energy-feeding source.

Is this why poltergeist phenomena or hauntings and manifestations seem to increase in intensity as fear-energy in a household rises? Evil does seem to entrench or attract more evil once a spiritual beachhead for it is established.

God does not work outside of science, he created all science. He knows everything about the subatomic structure of the universe and the miraculous working of the human body – infinitely and completely above any worldly scientific knowledge.

The brain was originally designed to be a receiver of spiritual truth and God knows about the neural mechanisms, hormones, chemical interactions and electrical circuitry that influence spiritual experiences better than any psychiatrist does. It is reasonable to expect that fallen angels are also aware of the biology and neurological functions of mankind and are able to influence the psychiatry and physiology of their enemy (made in God's image and likeness) using hordes of demonic helpers.

Electromagnetic and Microwave Radiation

Science itself measures electromagnetic waves in the brain modulated by our thought processes, and as such when parts of the brain are stimulated after an accident or during a brain operation or deliberately by electromagnetism, the brain can experience spiritual side-effects.

Extremely Low Frequency microwave or ELF technology is described in various U. S. Defense Department publications, including one entitled, 'The Electromagnetic Spectrum and Low Intensity Conflict,' by Captain Paul E. Tyler, Medical Commandant, U. S. Navy, which is included in a collection entitled, 'Low Intensity Conflict and Modern Technology Edict,' by Lt. Col David G. Dean, USAF.[34]

The paper was delivered in 1984 and the collection published in 1986 by Air University Press, Maxwell Air Force Base, Alabama. Pulse microwave devices can deliver audible signals directly to a person while remaining undetectable to anyone else. The technology is very simple and can be built by using an ordinary police radar gun. The microwave beam generated by the device is modulated at audio frequencies and can broadcast messages directly into the brain.[34]

Parts of the brain can also be stimulated to create elation or even depression in a person, for example it is a fact that the *supramarginal gyrus* and *posterior cingulate* in the brain are linked to depressive mood. It does indeed seem that spiritual things exist within the bounds of explainable physics, it's just beyond science (i.e. paranormal) to understand all the finer details yet.

In his book, *Neuropsychological Bases of God Beliefs*, Michael A. Persinger, Ph.D., hypothesises that the personal religious experience of God can be a result of electro-magnetic stimulation of the temporal lobes of the brain. He states, *"The power of the God Experience shames any known therapy. With a single burst in the temporal lobe, people find structure and meaning in seconds. With it comes the personal conviction of truth and the sense of self-selection"* [35]

As such, a reader of Persinger might believe those who express faith in God or other spiritual events are delusional because it is only brain chemistry or electrical stimulation that causes the person's experience. This is certainly Persinger's inference, but correlation does not imply causation. Electromagnetism may indeed stimulate a form of religious experience, but that does not negate the existence of God.

It is dangerous territory to conclude that belief in God is somewhat psychotic and requires medical intervention. *Ergo*, a non-conformity of opinion, say in politics, or medicine, could be viewed by vested interest groups as *illness* when it is simply a different viewpoint. When science rationalises hypotheses around Darwinian evolutionary theory as many in the field of psychiatry do, the danger of medical fascism becomes a perilous possibility.

Conversely, I believe it is entirely logical and healthy to view the brain as having been designed by God in all its chemical and electrical complexity to experience Him when correctly stimulated in normal function. The brain was thus intricately designed to control both physiological as well as spiritual functions and be both a transmitter and receiver of mystical knowledge, probably connected to the physics of plasma energy and electrical frequencies as discussed previously.

In my opinion, belief in God should be viewed as a quality of normal and healthy brain function. Unfortunately, it has been stifled, chiefly from hereditary epigenetic factors going all the way back to the first men and women and onwards through every successive generation. So, how has this spiritual death happened?

With the Fall of Mankind, the spiritual component of brain function has died through being disconnected, or severed from God. Sinful or 'unholy' human beings can only connect to unclean spirits, and cannot be connected to a Holy God, at least, not without a spiritual filtration or purification system in play. It's why we need Jesus Christ as mediator between God and Man before we can receive the Holy Spirit.

1 Timothy 2:5
For there is one God, and one mediator between God and men, the man Christ Jesus.

In our modern world, the spiritual *death* of normal brain function is further exacerbated by environmental factors including, but not limited to, vaccine brain injury in early childhood caused by mercury and other neurotoxins; toxic food additives such as aspartame and phenylalanine; pesticides and agri-pharma chemical spraying; fluoride in the water (see Chapter 34); pharmaceutical drugs; high frequency EM radiation, notably 5G radiation and of course and most importantly, hostile demonic forces.

The spiritual brain in the 'unsaved' individual is only able to connect to demonic 'unholy' entities at their particular frequency. Some of these entities may even call themselves God and give deceptive messages to the receiver such as in the channelled writings of authors Neale Donald Walsch in his *Conversations with God* book; and Helen Schucman in her book, *A Course In Miracles*.

Oprah Winfrey's favourite spiritual poster-boy, Eckhart Tolle, although apparently not channelling spirits to write his books, also expounds some common deceptive and demonic ideologies.

1. Tolle claims God and man are one (pantheism), whereas Christianity affirms that God is distinct from man, that He created man.

2. Tolle asserts the Buddhist belief that the human self is an illusion, whereas Christianity affirms the existence of the self, but understands it is corrupted by sin.

3. Tolle believes death and the physical body are illusions (Buddhism), whereas Christianity affirms both are real.

4. Tolle believes that Jesus is not uniquely God, since everyone is God, whereas Christianity denies that everyone is God, and claims that Jesus is the unique human manifestation of God.

Tolle may not have set out to deliberately deceive, but he is an example of how sinful man can readily *connect spiritually* with deceptive demonic entities. Such connections also often manifest in visions or communications from so-called spirit-guides, light beings or angels, in messages subtly contradicting what God has already revealed in Scripture (see *Angel Worship*, Chapter 36). Such entities can also take on forms including ghostly apparitions, orbs, poltergeists, or aliens, all of which are what The Bible describes as 'unclean' or unholy spirits.

The ability to see visions occurs more frequently when someone is physically exhausted, or taking certain drugs or during hypnagogic sleep (the transitional state from wakefulness to sleep) also known as 'sleep paralysis' (see Chapter 20), when it seems the brain circuitry is more able to tap into these frequencies. Similarly, common reports of near-death experiences on the operating table also coincide with slowing or failing bodily functions – physical death.

Spiritual death or spiritual disconnection from God is an inherited characteristic of fallen humanity. Adam and Eve originally had a living, and active spiritual connection with God before their sin broke the circuit.

It is clear however that this spiritual aspect of a man's intellect can be revived - made alive by Jesus Christ when we go to him for salvation. (See Chapter 43, How to Be Saved).

All of our needs as sinners are fully provided for in Jesus Christ who completely paid our sin debt on the cross at Calvary. Through believing in him we become identified with his death, burial and resurrection. He died to set us free from spiritual death, truly being the mediator between God and Man and bridging the severed spiritual circuitry, enabling the Christian to access the Holy Spirit.

Salvation and spiritual *life* through faith in Jesus Christ is God's free gift to Fallen Man.

The moment we get saved, God removes the penalty of sin from us and we have a spiritual union with Christ who provides that vital, eternal spiritual filtration allowing us to connect with Holy God and receive the Holy Spirit.

It doesn't mean that we will be sinless in this life, but we immediately enter a process of spiritual sanctification where Jesus builds and strengthens our faith, gradually perfecting us from within, making us more holy as we walk with him. It is a lifelong process that continues to the day we die. We will not be entirely free from our sinful nature until that moment we pass into glory, however we are assured of forgiveness of sins and salvation from the moment we trust in him.

Whatever size our faith is when we first accept Jesus, the Christian will tell you that reading God's word develops it and makes it stronger. The parable of 'the mustard seed of faith' once planted, growing into a giant tree is certainly something mature Christians recognise. A tiny little faith is sufficient to bring you into the merciful arms of God.

Luke 13:19
(On faith) *It is like a mustard seed, which a man took and planted in his garden. It grew and became a tree, and the birds perched in its branches.*

It also appears that the spiritual circuitry of the brain once enlivened can be further stimulated into greater insights when the physical body is less indulged and given to prayer and fasting. During these periods, spiritual breakthroughs are galvanised more speedily and divine truth experienced more intensely during or in the soon aftermath of a fasting episode as connectedness with The Holy Spirit and disconnectedness from the pull of the flesh and the world is promoted.

To have the brain operating as a healthy, organic electrical circuit with connection to the Godhead is a most desirable position. It makes sense therefore that Satan would aim to stifle that possibility with worldly distractions, spiritual deception and direct mental assault.

More than ever before, electromagnetic factors are significant irritants of brain circuitry. People living near radio, TV and mobile phone masts, as well as those living in proximity to powerful electric cables above or below ground can be adversely affected physically as well as mentally by electromagnetic outputs. The Apple iPhone and iPad and other hand-held smartphones and tablets transmitting and receiving microwave radiation are known destroyers of micro-cellular health and have been linked to unprecedented levels of sterility in men and women.[36] With the arrival of 5G and 6G technology, there is even greater threat of an unknown quantity.

According to an article by Martin L. Pall, Professor Emeritus of Biochemistry and Basic Medical Sciences, Washington State University, certain frequencies can directly influence the micro-cellular structure and biochemistry of our brains and can be a significant component of mood alteration, even bringing about mental illness. Microwave frequency electromagnetic fields (EMFs) produce widespread neuropsychiatric effects including depression.[37]

Even low electromagnetic frequencies over a long duration can affect the brain. At higher levels, in laboratory conditions specific hallucinations have been induced in people exposed to them, with subjects complaining of feelings of despair and paranoia, and sometimes overwhelming terror with a sensation of something malevolent watching them or being close to them. To use 5G and 6G as a covert weaponised form of mind control would not be beyond the conscience of a tyrannical government, and a small step from its current proven use in crowd dispersal and military applications.

Could electromagnetic fields be door openers to demonic entities and spiritual forces? It seems a strong possibility that they may find it easier to attack or infiltrate us when we are under electromagnetic assault.

Genetic Engineering

The revolution in genetic engineering with advanced genome editing is allowing scientists to reprogram the genes of any living creature quickly and easily. From glow-in-the-dark mice to hybrid humans, the technology is being developed allegedly to promote longer life and better health, but what are the spiritual implications?

I believe that *transhumanism* genetics are manipulating our DNA and 'dehumanising' our genome so that we are easier to possess, control and destroy. Is a fallen angelic and human hybridisation programme again underway as it was in Genesis 6? It seems plausible.

Jesus even warned us:

Luke 17:26–27
"And as it was in the days of Noah, so shall it be also in the days of the Son of man."

The obvious meaning of the above verse is that immediately preceding his second advent, the world would be just as rebellious, wicked and ripe for judgement as when Noah was alive, but are we also to imply Jesus meant other similarities too such as the return of the Nephilim? I can't be certain, but it's clear the timeline of the arrival of the Nephilim resulted very quickly with The Flood. What I do know is that mixing foreign DNA with human DNA is a highly dangerous science.

What will the spiritual effect on men be if they are contaminated with animal or plant DNA, or perhaps even genetic material extracted from Nephilim? If it is the case and similar events in history are repeating, will we see giants roaming the earth again alongside other freakish crossbreeds? With the CRISPR genome-editing programme moving at light speed across continents, we will know soon enough.

The first human-monkey chimera was developed in April 2021 (at least the first they have admitted to) in a Chinese and American scientific collaboration. Allegedly for growing human organs for transplant, this is horrifying use of technology overstepping the boundaries of ethical scientific research with terrifying implications for mankind.[38]

CERN

In another example of dangerous technology being developed, ostensibly to uncover the hidden secrets of life and matter, experiments undertaken by scientists operating the particle accelerator at CERN in

Switzerland clearly infer there is common ground between real science and the stuff of the paranormal in much of their dialogue.

CERN's Large Hadron Collider is designed to unglue the mystery of matter in the universe. Here the daily focus is breaking through the sub-atomic veil between light and dark matter in pursuit of *The God Particle*, or Higgs' Boson; that mysterious particle which gives all things physical their mass.

The whole CERN set up is designed to affirm highly complex, abstract theories and to reveal hidden or 'occult knowledge'. It appears that science is revisiting alchemical knowledge from 500 years ago, with all the tools of modern technology at their disposal.

If you don't believe this modern technology has occult roots, simply look at the symbolism the CERN organisation uses to represent its research. The blatant '666' within the logo; the Shiva statue, or Hindu Goddess of Destruction standing outside the CERN facility; the very name CERN, similar to *Cernunno*, the Celtic depiction of the 'horned god' of death and rebirth; and the weird 'Symmetry' contemporary dance video choreographed within the collider facility and displayed on their website. The video depicts light and darkness and alludes to well-known occult themes such as *yin and yan*, 'as above, so below', freemasonic chessboard symbolism, and most disturbing of all, men reaching out towards dark entities through a veil. Coincidental?

Recently in 2016, a mock ritual human sacrifice took place at CERN with black robed scientists pretending to stab a terrified woman (reported by The Guardian newspaper). This was allegedly a prank.[39] But to what end?

CERN technology has been developed by a scientific occult-priesthood or *technocracy* who at the highest level are in direct contact with the powers and principalities governing our worldly spiritual dimension under Satan's rule.

Ephesians 6:12
For we wrestle not against flesh and blood, but against principalities, against powers, **against the rulers of the darkness of this world, against spiritual wickedness in high places**. (emphasis mine).

These cosmic powers literally give guidance and technical instruction to this occult-priesthood as they communicate with them and other elite members of the Establishment through channelling and satanic rituals. The occult knowledge is kept hidden from lower ranking scientists and individuals who operate in compartmentalised units of research, never being given access to the big picture their leaders at the top of the knowledge-pyramid are privy to.

It seems to me that fallen angelic intelligences, in their rabid craving to destroy Mankind - the jewel of God's creation - are influencing and rewarding the leaders of our world to guide us down a pathway of deception and destruction so that they, the fallen angels, might gain spiritual energies through feeding off our fears; traumatised emotions; sickness; stress; and death, with the ultimate prize of taking us to eternal damnation alongside them.

The covert aim of CERN's occult priesthood is to open portals to other dimensions. This intention has subtly been admitted to alongside the easier-to-swallow cover story that it's all about discovering the origins of matter; a narrative the general public can understand. Few realise the potential application of the collider technology may be to unlock a door for a satanic army of demonic spirits to break through physically into our earthly plane from its current location, using some form of plasma-tunnel.

Have I been watching too many *Star Trek* episodes to suggest this crazy scenario? Perhaps, but please humour me for a few more pages because Hollywood's main role is to introduce concepts and implement agendas incrementally to a dumbed-down public.

What will happen if these powerful entities break through into our dimension? Will this be the New Age Movement's long-awaited 'Disclosure' of extra-terrestrials who will announce themselves to the world and say they were our creators and have come to save us? Perhaps the Large Hadron Collider will be the means whereby the bottomless pit in Revelation is opened up:

Revelation 9: 1-3
"Then the fifth angel sounded: And I saw a star fallen from heaven to the earth. To him was given the key to the bottomless pit. And he opened the bottomless pit, and smoke arose out of the pit like the smoke of a great furnace. So the sun and the air were darkened because of the smoke of the pit. Then out of the smoke locusts came upon the earth. And to them was given power, as the scorpions of the earth have power."

Luke 21:26
"Men's hearts failing them for fear, and for looking after those things which are coming on the earth: for the powers of heaven shall be shaken."

Again, this is conjecture, but the possibility of such an event is no longer in the realms of science fiction.

After all, the world is being programmed to think of Jesus Christ, the Saviour of the World as nothing more than a kindly, somewhat emaciated teacher in a toga and sandals, while fictional Superhero comic book hybrids (typically generated by merging human flesh with alien or animal DNA) are being raised up in our collective psyche as the alternative 'save the world' heroes.

Note how superheroes don outfits to appeal to the flesh, highlighting their power and impressive musculature: *Batman, Spiderman, Wolverine, Wonder Woman, Supergirl, Batgirl, The Fantastic Four, X-Men, Avengers, Captain America, Hellboy*; from cereal packets to the big and small screen, the extra-terrestrial and transhumanist conditioning is everywhere.

Hollywood and media giants are acclimatising us to accept a number of scenarios which promote the arrival of ETs and the hypothesis that an alien creator-race seeded the planet using Evolution dynamics to make us.

Why would Hollywood and mass media expend so much effort and money on this message, hammering it home so consistently and emphatically for the last fifty years or more?

The answer is a disturbing one, but one which lines up with Jesus Christ's warnings to Christians to be sober and clear-minded so they can avoid being tricked into accepting a coming deception so compelling that without the direction of the Holy Spirit, even God's most elect servants would be deceived by it.

Matthew 24:24
*For there shall arise false Christs, and false prophets, **and shall shew great signs and wonders; insomuch that, if it were possible, they shall deceive the very elect.***

CHAPTER 41.

Causes of Possession: The UFO and Alien Deception

Despair lies at the heart of mental illness, founded on the delusion that 'life is pointless' and 'there is no hope'. Without hope we are spiritually dead even as we live.

The current interest in UFOs and aliens is the world's attempt at finding hope and answers about life, death and the universe without mention of Jesus Christ crucified, or if a form of 'god' is referenced it is a mystical spirit or higher state of being we can channel without repentance or acknowledging our sins – the so called *Christ-consciousness* of Eastern Mysticism.

We are being assaulted with deception from every angle: Political deception (mainstream news/propaganda); economic deception (fractional reserve banking, stock market manipulation); medical deception (drugs and vaccines); spiritual deception (cults and idolatry and New Age doctrines) and so on. UFOs and aliens fall into the latter category.

The last four generations have grown up with concepts of interplanetary travel and the notion of other intelligent alien life-forms in space. Embedded in the common psyche is the idea of *evil* or *benevolent* aliens visiting earth in space ships, desiring world domination or world peace respectively.

This is the mind set I grew up with and passionately defended. I recall arguing zealously about the certainty of the 'Ancient Astronaut Theory' promulgated by Erich Von Daniken; that Earth's ancient civilisations were developed through the intervention of space beings who built Atlantis and Egypt. Such ideas were supported by accounts from the ancient Sumerian civilisation, who talk about the 'Anunnaki' - gods who came down from the skies and who had the form of serpents.

The idea that world affairs were interfered with by beings from a heavenly realm is clear from Genesis 6:4, however, the Bible describes what these visitors really are, and they are not our classic ETs or aliens.

These interfering beings were the fallen angels who had sexual relations with human women, giving birth to a race of giants known as the *Nephilim,* eventually corrupting nearly all flesh on the face of the earth (DNA mixing).

It's Just a Theory...

A vital component of the contemporary extra-terrestrial/alien framework is Charles Darwin's *The Theory of Evolution.*

For 150 years, generations of children have been powerfully re-educated into accepting Darwinian-style Evolution taking place over millions of years. Darwin was right about *microevolution* and Natural Selection - the ability within a species of animal and also humans to subconsciously select particularly helpful genes to adapt to their surrounding environment. Adaptation does not mean *evolution.* You see, microevolution is a God-designed attribute of his Creation providing optimum survival chances within species. By contrast, the contemporary definition of Evolution supposes that life *evolves* through species mutating over millions of years. There is absolutely no compelling evidence for this in spite of what we are taught.

The Creation record is a key target for Satan and I was also taken in by Evolution Theory until quite recently.

In spite of believing in a creator God, I had thought God had used Evolution to create life on earth, not realising it was a flawed theory, discredited even more so today among many leading secular as well as Christian scientists. It is interesting to note that Darwin was a plagiarist and evolution was an idea that had been around for half a century before Darwin began his work. His own grandfather pushed the theory in England, and overseas many others including Goethe had discussed life forms evolving. Darwin however wanted all the glory for himself, so he tried to dismiss other contenders out of the story including Erasmus Darwin, his grandfather, denying he'd had any influence on him.

I am amazed our educators can still justify indoctrinating children with Evolution as fact when so much evidence exists to contradict it. But Evolution falls into that propaganda initiative of "If you make a statement strong enough and repeat it often enough, you may be able to convince yourself and others that it is true".

Of course there is no joy, wonder or meaning to life if nature is a soulless, self-creating happenstance. It would make existence futile. However, if you look at Creation as the 'Art of God' and realise there is a loving and infinite design to it all, it becomes a wondrous thing to contemplate.

The Creation model is certainly as scientific as the Evolution model, but the subject of Creation is never honestly debated. It seems the Establishment are terrified people will hear the opposing argument and decide for themselves after hearing all the facts. We are actively discouraged from discussing Creation in our rabidly secular public education system (especially in Europe) because the evidence for it is so compelling and the science so strong it puts the Theory of Evolution to shame.

Such is the propaganda drive to compel belief in Darwinian theory, I had thought Christians were a bit eccentric or even backward for believing the biblical story of Creation until quite recently, not fully understanding the compelling scientific evidence for Creation from cosmology, thermodynamics, palaeontology, biology, mathematics, geology, and other sciences. I had been duped by pretty pictures of *evolving* branches of different species moving from the sea, to the swamp, to the jungle, to the city; all from someone's imagination without the required scientific *observation* necessary to reach such conclusions.

Indeed, there are only very few examples of dubious intermediate life forms in the fossil record and these are highly speculative, whereas much of the fossil record shows all life arriving simultaneously with distinct species present in the same forms as they exist today.

Sedimentary rock layers also show clear evidence of cataclysmic flooding with rapid formation of layers and buried plant and animal fossils across vast areas, often high above sea level. Some fossilised trees penetrate supposed millions of years of horizontal rock strata vertically which is a clear impossibility if the sediments are laid down over millions of years. Only a global flood in which the ocean waters flooded over the continents could have done this.

Historic fossil and documentary evidence also survives showing humanoid giants existed, some up to 36 feet tall with complete skeletons, proving the biblical narrative from Genesis 6. It is alleged that key institutions including The Smithsonian Institute in the USA and The British Museum in London have been complicit in covering this information up to promulgate the Evolution narrative over Creation, but that's beside the point; the Bible tells us that giants existed and I believe God, not men.

More recently Evolution Theory has been superseded by the Intelligent Design Theory which at least supposes a creative architect, though it is no less deceptive than Evolution, given that it proposes life was created by an alien super race using Intelligent Design in harmony with Darwinian Evolution i.e. aliens are our creators, not God. This of course still begs the inconvenient question for the Darwinians, 'Who created the aliens who created us?'

Space Brothers?

As discussed at the end of Chapter 40, it is my conviction that the *Aliens from Outer Space in Flying Saucers* hypothesis is a huge satanic programming strategy - an incremental drip feed of disinformation designed to promote the Ancient Astronaut Theory over the biblical Creation story.

Thanks to sci-fi shows like *Star Trek, Stargate, The X-Files* etc., generations of people have been, and continue to be programmed into believing that good aliens are typically handsome Nordic males and beautifully proportioned Nordic females with great hair; exuding mystical wisdom and interplanetary love, while the evil aliens are either freakish reptilian monstrosities or impish Martian creatures with big heads and almond shaped eyes. Hollywood has repeated this idea so many times now that you get the idea we are being set up for something...

..And I believe we are.

In The Book of Daniel and The Book of Revelation, the Bible warns how the world will unite under the power of a final religious system that worships the Antichrist. Whom this brutal, evil beast of a dictator will be and what precise form his system will take is still uncertain, but the Antichrist will be a man possessed by the essence and character of Satan.

How will religious unity be achieved among all the world's squabbling belief systems and cultures? It would have to be a convincing story for Islam to unite with Judaism, or Roman Catholicism to unite with Hinduism, unless of course the 'proof' came from an apparently wondrous, jaw-dropping, extra-terrestrial source.

It is almost universally accepted by the New Age Movement that extra-terrestrial *Disclosure* will take place imminently. The New Age storyboard goes something like this:

Benevolent aliens will land, perhaps on the Whitehouse lawn, just before we destroy ourselves in another world war and they will help us stupid, hostile human beings reach the next step of our Evolution through a spiritual awakening where we can either adapt and join them or die.

There follows a possible deception scenario that is not inconceivable given the time, effort and investment that the *Illuminati* and evil Hollywood has expended throughout the last century on programming us with the good *vs* bad alien visitation idea.

The plot below is hypothetical of course, and the whole event may be surprisingly different, but such a scenario is worthy of consideration nevertheless.

Mark Twain famously quoted, "A thing long expected takes the form of the unexpected when at last it comes".

Acknowledging this, let me be very clear, I am speculating here to wake people out of their mental rut so they might consider Christ's warnings about the Great Deception in Matthew 24 as being highly relevant to the days and times unfolding. Okay?

Therefore my 'speculative' Great Deception event may present itself as a fake extra-terrestrial or alien visitation; fake because the aliens that reveal themselves will really be fallen angels and demons, not space beings as such, but interdimensional spiritual entities.

The big lie will be that we are their special 'science project' and they've been watching us develop for centuries and have been very disappointed in our progress; our wars; our greed; our pollution, and they've had to come back to help us move on to the next phase of our evolution so we can become as sophisticated as them - like gods!

Will this old satanic lie from Eden once again be offered to tempt mankind away from the true light of Jesus Christ? It's certainly possible.

Perhaps they will inform us that our wayward governments have been working hand-in-glove with the evil grey aliens since *Roswell* to develop technologies of war and that these grey aliens and their reptilian masters are the real enemy (and don't they look just like demons). Of course the handsome and beautiful Nordic-type extra-terrestrial visitors will pretend to be our true interplanetary friends.

A key part of the deception will be that all the world religions, while containing some truth, have got it all wrong, *especially* Christianity.

They will try and convince the world that the Bible has been misinterpreted and that Jesus isn't God in the flesh, but just a mystic who attained *Christ-consciousness* through spiritual discipline and that now he's really just like one of them; an Ascended Spiritual Master.

Supporting such messages will be the False Prophet, a very religious figure; a bit like a satanic version of John the Baptist, preparing the way for the final world ruler. This False Prophet will swing into action alongside all these other amazing events, signs and wonders, with his key message for everyone to 'worship' the Antichrist.

All the false religions including apostate Christianity will believe the lie and give worship to the false Messiah who will be a man possessed by Satan. According to Scripture it appears he will be a man who can prove Jewish lineage and the title 'Antichrist' also means he will be 'opposed' to the real Jesus Christ, who will be His enemy, though he himself will be a fake Christ, an imitation Jesus, posing as the real Messiah of Israel.

The Antichrist will speak persuasive words such as promising world peace, safety, justice, prosperity and freedom for all. There will be just one requirement to enjoy the benefits of his 'system' and that will be to take a mark in the right hand or in the forehead, symbolising total allegiance and worship.

Satan's *Mark of the Beast* will be both a distinctive physical mark labelling everyone who accepts his (the Antichrist's) rule over them, as well as a spiritual marker of allegiance that will be visible in the non-physical dimension. It will probably be a type of tattoo or RFID implant, or maybe a mixture of both. This special mark we may be told will be conditional for evolving into the new, enlightened golden age of mankind. It won't be promoted as the 'Mark of the Beast', but will almost certainly have some *cool* spiritual name and symbol which will represent 666 either numerically or symbolically.

(Since writing this chapter, the events surrounding the Covid-19 alleged pandemic and the introduction of experimental mRNA vaccines have opened the door to the possibility that the eventual Mark of The Beast may be a kind of vaccine-passport that permits the holder to function normally in society. It is interesting to note that the "Bill & Melinda Gates Foundation" has been involved in funding proof-of-vaccination research in collaboration with Rice University, Houston, resulting in the creation of a so-called 'Quantum Dot Tattoo' that uses soluble microneedles containing fluorescing invisible ink known as *Luciferase*.[40] Could this be the prototype for the eventual Mark? It could tick the box for the requirement that the 'Name of the Beast' will be a component of the Mark, and what easier way to implement it than in conjunction with a vaccine?).

This false messiah's arrival is anticipated by the Jews; the Muslims (Imam Mahdi); the Buddhists (Maitreya); the Hindus (Kalki); the Zoroastrians (Saoshyant); and the Confucians (the 'True Man'). All of these religious groups will look to the Antichrist as a world peace bringer and he will deceive all the earth apart from a remnant of Christians.

As mentioned in Chapter 20, there is even technology available today called 'Voice of God' or 'Voice to Skull Technology' that can project real voices and music into a person's head using microwaves, so the whole deception could be fantastically believable, especially if everyone on the planet was to receive a message in their own native tongue from a seemingly supernatural, disembodied source.

Any true Christians* remaining in the world at this point will insist that the whole thing is a massive fraud and will either go into hiding or be rounded up and killed as they will be hindering this next phase of 'evolution' and apparent world peace for the rest of mankind. Christians will be viewed as dangerous enemies of the state and will be vilified for sowing the seeds of doubt in the minds of the masses who won't want their belief system challenged.

*There is much debate as to whether the Rapture of the Church will happen before, during or after the Tribulation period predicted in the Bible. I have heard compelling arguments supporting each position, but whatever happens, the Tribulation period will start when the Man of Sin (Antichrist) begins his 7 year reign. The Great Tribulation starts at the mid-point of Antichrist's reign. If the Rapture happens before this period, then people remaining on the earth will still have the opportunity for salvation by believing on Jesus Christ and repenting of their sins, as long as they refuse the Mark of the Beast. If however the Mark of the Beast is taken there will be no possibility of turning back to Jesus, it will be certain damnation for all who receive the Mark.

All who refuse the Mark certainly won't be able to buy or sell anything, as they will not be capable of trading the digitised version of money conditional on taking it. It is possible that the Mark of the Beast will also be hardwired with altered DNA and properties that include immunity from diseases such as cancer, heart disease and even aging. Remember, I am speculating here, but this could be the big sweetener, the final temptation for Mankind.

During the bloody turmoil of the Great Tribulation, the Antichrist will quickly reveal his true satanic colours. Unfortunately, it will be too late for anyone who has taken the Mark of the Beast to change their course of action and repent because they will have been changed permanently at both a physical and spiritual level.

The Antichrist may even lie about the real Second Coming of Jesus Christ and make people think that Jesus and the good angels are actually evil aliens coming from another galaxy, and humanity has a duty to defeat them.

In whatever manner these events unfold, the Bible verses clearly warn us that unless you are protected by God's indwelling Holy Spirit you will willingly succumb to Satan's lies:

2 Thessalonians 2:8-12
"And then shall that Wicked be revealed, whom the Lord shall consume with the spirit of his mouth, and shall destroy with the brightness of his coming:

*Even him, whose coming is after the working of Satan with **all power and signs and lying wonders**,*

*And with all deceivableness of unrighteousness in them that perish; because **they received not the love of the truth**, that they might be saved.*

*And for this cause **God shall send them strong delusion, that they should believe a lie:***

That they all might be damned who believed not the truth, but had pleasure in unrighteousness."

God will therefore send a strong delusion to the unrepentant who choose not to believe the Gospel of Christ and who take delight in mocking and rejecting Him.

It also states in Revelation 9:6,
And in those days shall men seek death, and shall not find it; and shall desire to die, and death shall flee from them.

This is again speculation, but the desire for death may well be the problem with animal or even fallen angelic DNA merging with human DNA, administered as a component of the Mark of the Beast. Some of the Covid vaccinations currently being distributed contain genetic modification technology, with some including cell line information harvested from aborted babies, chimpanzees, mice and who knows what else? If a vaccine was created with fallen angelic DNA or something that turns men 'inhuman' in a spiritual sense like the *Nephilim* hybrids, it might confer an irreversible spiritual seal on its recipients impossible to repent of. Perhaps that is why God's wrath is kindled so mercilessly after the Mark of the Beast is taken. It is clear in

God's word there is no hope for anyone after they take the Mark. Just like before The Flood, all human flesh will be corrupted apart from a remnant (the true Body of Christ, born-again Christians).

Revelation 14:9-11
And the third angel followed them, saying with a loud voice, If any man worship the beast and his image, and receive his mark in his forehead, or in his hand,

The same shall drink of the wine of the wrath of God, which is poured out without mixture into the cup of his indignation; and he shall be tormented with fire and brimstone in the presence of the holy angels, and in the presence of the Lamb:

And the smoke of their torment ascendeth up for ever and ever: and they have no rest day nor night, who worship the beast and his image, and whosoever receiveth the mark of his name.

There are some who think the book of Revelation is an early Christian hoax that doesn't tie in with the rest of Scripture. I don't agree with this. I think the reason for rejection of Revelation is that people don't like the idea of judgement. I also think that of all the books in the Bible, the Book of Revelation is the most hated by Satan because it reminds him of what is going to happen to him when Christ returns.

Let me reiterate this narrative is my own speculative idea on how *The Great Deception* may pan out based on an amalgamation of various other Christian commentators' opinions. It may not happen at all like this and I would not want to be guilty of predicting timelines or what Satan's lying signs and wonders may be, but it seems to me and many others around the world that such a scenario is not implausible and could correspond with the events foretold in Matthew 24 and in Revelation.

It is astonishing just how many things seem to be gearing up exactly in line with the prophesies of Jesus Christ in Matthew 24: False Christs will arise, deceiving many; we will "hear of wars and rumours of wars"; and there will be an increase of "famines, and pestilences, and earthquakes, in diverse places". The Book of Revelation predicts global government, global commerce and the rise of a One World Religion under Antichrist. These are all things that appear to be getting very close, especially now that vaccine passport programme implementation is gradually escalating into a "no-jab, no-job, no-shopping" form of State coercion.

Everyone needs to wake up to the prophesied truth that events may occur any day now to deceive and tempt people into rejecting Jesus Christ and worshipping Satan instead.

After my LSD experience when I saw, with my mind's eye, those dormant, frog-like demonic creatures exuding evil, I changed my mind about so-called ETs or extra-terrestrials, though technically the fallen angels are extra-terrestrials as they are not from the Earth, but they are also intra-dimensional. The LSD had opened up some spiritual doorway or portal to another place of existence and shockingly I saw those creatures not as aliens in the Hollywood sense at all, but instinctively viewed them as the devils or fallen angels of the Bible, or at least some form of demonic reptilian entities. The sense of spiritual evil was a giveaway and shared common ground with countless millions of reports about alien abductions.

It is interesting to note that when John the Prophet saw the evil spirits in Revelation he also described them as "like frogs". If John was describing something akin to a demonic reptilian entity (and I mean if) he had no contemporary reference to lean on, like depictions of aliens on TV, he just had to describe what he saw using the nearest reference point available to him.

Revelation 16:13
*"And I saw three unclean spirits **like frogs** come out of the mouth of the dragon, and out of the mouth of the beast, and out of the mouth of the false prophet."*

Today there exists a subculture of individuals obsessively interested in the subject of UFOs and aliens, some of whom I believe are under strong demonic influence. This unhealthy mania is usually aligned with philosophies and religiosity from the New Age movement. Individuals within such groups would not be classed as mentally ill, (eccentric perhaps), but nevertheless are clearly being deceived and manipulated by spiritual forces.

Commonly, many of these same individuals complain about past or ongoing alien abduction experiences. They might also suffer various types of poltergeist type activity, haunting phenomena and sleep paralysis in their homes. Since the 1960s the alien abduction experience has risen dramatically with some surveys suggesting as many as 4% of the general population have been abducted.[41]

It's nothing new. Paranormal abductions have been going on for centuries. During the Middle Ages, there were numerous stories of people seized by terrifying goblins or *faeries* in their sleep, hence the expression "away with the fairies". All these historic abductions are usually terrifying, often painful, and also blatantly deceptive.

It seems these demonic visitors take on forms relevant to prevailing cultural beliefs and geographical location. Commonly the visitors have been old hags; sometimes Roman Catholic iconographic depictions of saints or the Virgin Mary; occasionally a vampire-like man or woman; at other times, shadow people like the Hat Man; and very commonly today, grey aliens or other types of ET. Abductions can also be stopped instantly by calling on the name of Jesus. That's a fact.[42]

Attempting to communicate with alien intelligences, nature spirits, or extra-terrestrials is nothing more than channelling demonic spirits. There are even books available that promise to put you in touch with these so-called *aliens* using a mixture of incantations and training the mind to make telepathic connections. Many people are also using drugs to expedite this with many astonishing commonalities of experience, particularly among DMT-users who share hallucinations often matching another person's encounter in precise detail. These chiefly relate to descriptions of the 'aliens' and conversations with spirit beings who dispense philosophies aligned with the Luciferian doctrine of 'global spirituality' without Jesus Christ - a New Age 'counterfeit gospel'.

It is no coincidence such deceptive messages match the doctrines of the *Interfaith Movement* peddled by many of the world's leading religious figures past and present including Desmond Tutu, the Dalai Lama, Sun Myung Moon, various popes, and many government-approved churches and global spiritual foundations. These messages essentially echo the mantras of the super-rich elite and their pawns, including financier of the *United Religions Initiative,* George Soros and various New Age authors including Eckhart Tolle; Deepak Chopra; Rick Warren; Neale Donald Walsch; and New Age dogma-pushing celebrities such as Oprah Winfrey; Shirley Maclaine; Will Smith; Tom Cruise and many more.

The spiritual pillar of globalisation and the New World Order is under construction and will culminate in a One World Religion under Satan. Does that sound crazy? I emphasise if you are a Christian you have a duty to seek out the truth in all things. The love of the truth is a vital part of being a Christian and that includes truth as it applies generally, whether in your home; at work; in the domain of economics; politics; science and medicine.

Christians should seek knowledge in all things and discover more truth. We are not to be lazy or ignorant sheep, simply believing the talking heads on the nightly news and politicians. They have an agenda, which is controlling your mind and manipulating your body, especially what they want to inject into you. It is your duty as a Christian to investigate and to question what you are told in the light of Scripture. It is easier to be a lazy fish and swim with the current, gulping down the propaganda from so-called *scholars* and *experts* on TV and in newspapers; textbooks and lecture halls, than to really think about things for yourself in the light of God's word.

You need to be knowledgeable about prophetic Scriptures and use your intelligence - not to develop single-minded rigid ideas, but to be open and flexible enough to understand the times we are living in from a biblical perspective.

What would happen in your church if alleged aliens from another galaxy or dimension suddenly strolled up to the world's microphones announcing your religion is a sham and that they are the real creators of the planet?

Most Christians would not have an answer and without an understanding of what both Satan and modern technology are capable of, their faith would crumble. The Bible cautions us to seek the truth because ignorance leads to error.

Hosea 4:6
"My people are destroyed for lack of knowledge: because thou hast rejected knowledge, I will also reject thee, that thou shalt be no priest to me: seeing thou hast forgotten the law of thy God, I will also forget thy children."

Matthew 22:29
*Jesus answered and said unto them, "Ye do err, **not knowing the Scriptures, nor the power of God**." (Emphasis mine).*

2 Corinthians 2:11
"Lest Satan should get an advantage of us: for we are not ignorant of his devices."

We are in the midst of a tumultuous spiritual battle with most Christians as deeply ignorant of the days and times we are living in as the rest of the world; completely unaware of what is going on behind the scenes; preferring to ridicule those who are warning them and labelling them as conspiracy loons, extremists or worse.

Christians need to revisit the Scriptures about the *End of Days* and not ignore the prophecies of Daniel, Revelation and Matthew 24. Believers should have a sense of urgency in opposing false teaching, which also includes deliberate exclusion or sanitisation of God's word in case it offends.

The corporate church, i.e. the government-mandated version of church that only 'preaches happy' and now encourages its congregations to line up for experimental gene therapies and vaccines (most of which have been created directly or indirectly from aborted baby cell-lines), needs to shake itself away from its slumber and get to preaching the complete word of God.

CHAPTER 42.

Concluding Thoughts

We are living in a time of unprecedented deception and a period where many spiritual gateways or portals have been opened, causing countless people to be possessed or oppressed by demonic forces probably more than any other time in history.

I hypothesise that people are more susceptible to possession because of the spiritual softening-up they have received from an onslaught of factors; from street-drug and psychiatric drug interventions which I believe can facilitate it; along with an increasing array of demonic concepts and occult doctrines delivered into our homes via mass media in greater concentrations than ever before and now turbo-charged through new technology platforms. The boundaries of decency continue to be eroded.

The result of this has been a rapid moral decline creating an 'anything-goes' permissiveness where centuries-old ethical certainties have been inverted to such an extent that things previous generations recognised as vile, shameful and unhealthy for society are now seen as good and beneficial. Spiritual evil is no longer cloaking itself.

As such, I propose that a very high proportion of mental illness is caused by demonic possession, especially where the disorder leans towards self-harm and suicidal inclinations (eating disorders, cutting; depressive psychosis, bipolar, schizophrenia etc.).

Why do I believe so many of these afflictions are demonic? Because they create a truly negative self-focus in a person. This self-focus ruminates continuously upon its own anxiety, misery, hopelessness and fear. It is essentially the most destructive form of *selfishness* possible where individuals are so tortured, crippled and entirely preoccupied by mental anguish that they can neither do anything useful for others or anything effective for themselves. The creativity of life is sapped, happiness devastated and suicide becomes a great temptation; a satanic scheme for sure.

If an individual should like to do something positive for the world, then mental illness throws an immense spanner in the works. Furthermore, wherever mental illness strikes, the damaging impact on others is colossal. Whoever it is—a mother or father; sister or brother; spouse, friend or neighbour—the repercussions of mental illness are surely as profound as the most debilitating physical infirmity. However, where physical infirmity is largely predictable, even routine, mental illness is a chaotic roller coaster.

The psychiatric establishment will grope around the edges for solutions if it continues to ignore the 500kg gorilla in the room with 'spiritual problem' written all over it. These spiritual issues will manifest physiologically, affecting the whole endocrine and hormone system and most psychiatrists will rationalise a materialistic solution, throwing drugs at the problem; however, if you really want to know your enemy and see who you are truly fighting, only spiritual goggles will stop you floundering in the dark. Only Jesus Christ can defeat our demonic adversaries.

Wake up people! Dark days are upon us and most of us are too focused on prosperity, hypnotised by television, and tranquillised to care.

We have fluoride in our water and inoculations are making all of us, especially our children, sick. Food additives and drugs poison our minds and bodies daily and new manmade diseases assault our immune systems with pharmaceutical companies actually modifying the genetic sequences of viruses and patenting them for profit. Other evil corporations like Monsanto are genetically modifying natural seed-lines, and creating patented *Terminator* seeds, which are sterile.[43]

Daily our governments controlled by the hidden hand of the Deep State lie to us about what is best. They steal our savings, assets and our pension funds through currency manipulation and market crashes and they create false-flag terrorist events to generate bogeymen like Osama Bin Laden and Kim Jong-un as justification for non-stop wars to feed the Military Industrial and Central Banking Complex.

Now 4G and 5G microwave radiation is permeating our environment on a huge scale, adding to neurological malfunction and a brain tumour epidemic exacerbated by telecommunication masts, mobile phones, smart-meters and an escalating *Internet of Things*. Now the *Covid* debacle has created the perfect opportunity for totalitarianism as our leaders coerce or even force vaccinations if we want to go to school or have a job, even though they know vaccines are altering our DNA and killing us.

Our lives are being micro-managed at every level and our brains (especially the minds of our precious children) are immersed in occult programming 24/7, misleading and destroying us on a spiritual basis.

Try and mention this toxic New World Order to friends, family, and fellow Christians and by and large you get a backlash, or at best a humoured disdain. All I can say is there is a big shock coming to those who prefer ignorance over truth. There will be those of us who are spiritually prepared and those who are not.

Proverbs 22:3
A prudent man forseeth the evil and hideth himself, but the simple pass on and are punished.

Part Three – *Salvation, Deliverance and Healing*

CHAPTER 43.

How to Be Saved

There are many complex issues and negative themes discussed in this book, and a sensitive reader, particularly one suffering from mental illness, will be desperate by now to hear some words of encouragement and hope.

Thankfully, there is a counterbalance and a great hope, not just for those suffering from the ravages of psychosis and their friends and families, but for everyone.

This is the most important part of this book. The good news!

Whatever your life is like now; rich or poor; famous or anonymous; beautiful or ugly; young or old; healthy or sick; the most important and vital mission of your life is 'salvation'. A hundred years from now, the only thing of importance will be whether or not your soul was saved.

The question is, why do you even need to get saved?

If you are a typical middle class individual residing in the West you probably think of yourself as a 'good person' who loves their family, friends, neighbours; gives occasionally to charities when asked, and is an all-round honourable and thoughtful person. If that pretty much sums you up, well done; by worldly standards you are certainly much nicer than the murderers, rapists, terrorists, child traffickers, drug dealers and thieves who are so common in the world today.

But do you know what Jesus calls people who think they are good, even if they are a lot better than others? He calls them *self-righteous*.

According to the Merriam-Webster Dictionary 'righteous' means, *'Acting in accord with divine or moral law: free from guilt or sin'*.

Do you act like this and are you free from guilt or sin? Really?

Self-righteousness is not just a huge claim for a person to make, it's an impossible claim. In fact the only person who ever lived who could claim to be completely *self-righteous* is Jesus Christ. No one else in history can claim the standard of being free from sin.

Romans 3:23
For all have sinned, and come short of the glory of God.

The trouble with sin it separates us from a relationship and closeness to a Holy God, our creator. Sin is rebellion against God and His divine laws.

So where did Man's sin come from? The Book of Genesis in the Bible tells us it originated in the Garden of Eden.

Man was the crown of God's creation; God created Man in his own image; however, when Adam and Eve were tempted by the first rebellious sinner ever – Satan - they disobeyed God's commandment not to eat the fruit of the tree in the centre of the garden, and they lost their right to eat of the *tree of life* which would have enabled them to live forever. Instead they were thrown out of Eden and prevented from continuing the loving relationship they had previously enjoyed with God.

Genesis 3:3
But of the fruit of the tree which is in the midst of the garden, God hath said, Ye shall not eat of it, neither shall ye touch it, lest ye die.

Their uprising against God's commands (sin) conferred a spiritual death on Adam and Eve and all of their descendants (that's us). Their original sin made it impossible for Man to continue in God's holy presence. This was known as 'The Fall' and set humanity on a disaster course which continues to this day.

Author Michel Quoist puts it so eloquently in his book, 'Christ is Alive' where is explains that sin is not just the breaking of a set of rules; it is the refusal to love:

"Sin is the refusal to recognise and acknowledge God as the supreme end of each man and all men and of the world. It is the refusal to render homage to God. It is the building of a god for oneself in place of God, by thinking only of oneself, by taking for oneself alone what belongs to other men and to God. It is making oneself the centre of creation, and thereby displacing mankind and the universe and causing imbalance and disorientation in the world."

"Because God's plan is a plan of love, which can be realised only through love, man's refusal to participate in that plan 'offends' God in his very being – which is love. Sin is the non-requital of God's love.

"Since Jesus Christ united humanity and divinity within himself, and since through him God has united himself to all humanity by taking mankind to

himself in its totality, the rejection of one member of the body of humanity implies the rejection of the Head."

1 John 4:20
Anyone who says, "I love God," and hates his brother, is a liar.

So how does anyone get out of this mess? The truth is, you can't – at least not by yourself. As an individual, you are powerless to be good enough or to love other people enough to earn your way out of the Hell-ward predicament you are in. You could be one of the kindest, most loving and caring people by the world's standard, but your own good works would never make you righteous or holy enough to enter into Heaven and back to a perfect relationship with God.

You see, only someone who is *perfectly righteous* can enter Heaven. That means someone who has lived their life having never killed, stolen, committed adultery, lied, cheated, desired something belonging to someone else, or even whispered or thought a cruel or foolish word.

If you have done any of these things, you are not wholly righteous and Heaven will be closed to you. In fact (and worse still) you will have no other destination to go to other than 'the resurrection of damnation' (John 5:29) which is a period in Hell upon dying, before being taken to the final judgement, which for the unrepentant and unsaved results in eternal damnation in the Lake of Fire.

That seems a very raw deal doesn't it?

And yes, it certainly would be a raw deal if God didn't provide us with an escape route; another way of cancelling out our wrongdoings and evil deeds (sins). He did this through Jesus Christ.

Matthew 1:23
Behold, a virgin shall be with child, and shall bring forth a son, and they shall call his name Emmanuel, which being interpreted is, God with us.

Romans 6:23
For the wages of sin is death; but the gift of God is eternal life through Jesus Christ our Lord.

John 3:16
For God so loved the world, that he gave his only begotten Son, that whosoever believeth in him should not perish, but have everlasting life.

As the Son of Holy God, Jesus was the second 'Adam'. Although Jesus, Adam and Eve were all born without sin, Adam and Eve (our ancestral parents) failed to keep God's divine law requiring obedience in love towards Him. Jesus however didn't fail. He lived a life of complete love towards both God and Man up to his undeserved physical death.

Innocent Jesus had to die for us, as there was no other way to eradicate the effect of sin except by Christ's precious blood.

Hebrews 9:22
In fact, the law requires that nearly everything be cleansed with blood, and without the shedding of blood there is no forgiveness.

This shedding of innocent blood was the means by which the penalty for sin was paid; a perfect man's life had been sacrificed for the lives of all who have sinned. The Jews foreshadowed the death of the Messiah in the slaughter of the Passover lamb as a sacrifice for sin, however the prophet Isaiah tells us that God was sickened by these sacrifices (Isaiah 1:11) and described how the Messiah would provide perfect sacrificial redemption (Isaiah 53).

Jesus' crucifixion was a perfect and voluntary sacrifice proving his love for God and Man through his willingness to die like this; paying the penalty for the sins of the world with his own blood. The Messiah's sacrifice provides complete redemption and it is why Jesus is also known as *The Lamb of God*. God hated animal and human sacrifice so much he came in a human form to put an end to it Himself, once and for all, so no longer was any more bloody sacrifice needed.

There is no sin in perfect love. By living a completely obedient, sinless life, Jesus became the first man ever to live and die without sin attributed to him. Jesus was therefore the first man born that didn't deserve death, and because of this, death could not wield any power over him and he was able to rise up from the dead and live forever.

When speaking about his life Jesus said:

John 10:18
"No man taketh it from me, but I lay it down of myself. I have power to lay it down, and I have power to take it again. This commandment have I received of my Father."

Jesus lives! For this reason he is able to 'credit righteousness' to anyone who comes to him and receives him. This is the Gospel, which means the 'good news' about Jesus Christ.

A very contemporary way to understand the good news and the power of Jesus' sacrifice is by imagining every single person to be an organic computer infected with a deadly computer virus (sin) that will cause the computer to continuously malfunction (living in rebellion against God), eventually leading to complete failure (natural death), never to be switched on again (spiritual death).

Jesus however who is the Saviour God and the sole origin of salvation can provide each one of us with a FREE anti-virus software program (His righteousness) to ensure that when we are switched off (physical death) we can be rebooted, (life after death), fully free from the sin virus, as long as we come to him (faith) during our physical life to have his righteousness installed in us (i.e. while we are still alive and functioning, before we get switched off).

How do we come to him and receive this metaphorical antivirus software? How does Jesus credit his righteousness into us faulty human computers?

As mentioned in Chapter 35, Jesus taught that a person must be specifically drawn to him by the Father.

John 6:44
"No man can come to me, except the Father which hath sent me draw him: and I will raise him up at the last day."

John 12:32
"And I, if I be lifted up from the earth, will draw all men unto me."

Without God's direct intervention, the unsaved human soul will remain spiritually dead.

So how can you know God is drawing or calling you? He starts by opening your mind to a basic understanding of the Scriptures and your need to repent. A strong sign is when you reach a point in your life where you sense the weight of your sin, feeling guilty and ashamed; fearful of death and hopeless about the future. You see the need to change and live a life that is in accordance with the Scriptures, but you find it impossible to get out of the sinful rut you are immersed in.

If you find yourself in this position it means God is beginning to work with you, making you conscious of your sin and giving you a desire for cleansing and forgiveness so you can make a fresh start. He has begun to reveal His grace to you.

The next step is up to you. You need to respond to God's invitation for forgiveness and receive the gift of eternal life. How do you do this? By believing (faith) that Jesus Christ will restore you if you come to him and receive it. **But to receive this free gift, you must come to him.** Only then will you be saved and move from spiritual death to eternal life.

John 1:12
But as many as received him, to them gave he power to become the sons of God, even to them that believe on his name.

John 10:28
"And I give unto them eternal life; and they shall never perish, neither shall any man pluck them out of my hand."

Acts 10:43
To him give all the prophets witness, that through his name whosoever believeth in him shall receive remission (forgiveness) of sins.

Matthew 11:28-30
Jesus says, "Come unto me, all ye that labour and are heavy laden, and I will give you rest."

All the people who will come to Jesus are promised eternal life. The only reason a man or woman will end up eternally separated from God is by deliberately rejecting God's offer of salvation and not coming to him.

God doesn't want anyone to end up in Hell. Hell is a place created by God for the punishment of Satan and the fallen angels. These wicked creatures have no mercy, are completely consumed by hate and if they could they would see to it that every man, woman and child suffer agony forever if they could pull it off. That is why God has created Hell, to separate these wicked spiritual forces from his redeemed creation in a place where they can no longer hurt us.

The trouble is, by ignoring God's offer of salvation, you have no other spiritual destination possible other than the place reserved for Satan and his demons which currently have a spiritual hold on you. This is *not* God's desire for you.

2 Peter 3:9
The Lord is not slack concerning his promise, as some men count slackness; but is longsuffering to us-ward, not willing that any should perish, but that all should come to repentance.

Matthew 25:41
Then shall he say also unto them on the left hand, Depart from me, ye cursed, into everlasting fire, prepared for the devil and his angels.

The only way to remove Satan's hold on you is to come to Jesus. Salvation has been provided; it now must be accepted. This means believing that Jesus is Lord and has been raised from the dead. You should confess this belief in prayer and to other people.

Romans 10:9
"For if you confess with your mouth that Jesus is Lord and believe in your heart that God raised him from the dead, you will be saved."

Romans 10:13
"For whoever will call upon the name of the Lord shall be saved"

All it takes for a person to go to Heaven is simple surrender of their heart. It's why the thief on the cross next to Jesus, although he lived his life in rebellion toward God and his commandments, was nevertheless redeemed when he humbled himself and asked Christ to remember him when he came into His kingdom. Jesus said to him, "Today you will be with me in Paradise" (Luke 23:43).

All authority in Heaven and on Earth is given to Jesus. Are you willing to make him the ruler of your life? If you understand that you are a sinner, and you believe that Jesus Christ is able to save you from the penalty of your sins, you are ready to receive God's gift of salvation.

The Sinner's Prayer

Here is a suggested prayer you can pray:

"Heavenly Father, I know that I have broken your laws and my sins have separated me from you. I am truly sorry, and now I want to turn away from my past sinful life toward you. Please forgive me.

I believe that your son, Jesus Christ died, taking on the penalty for my sins, was resurrected from the dead and is alive, and hears my prayer. I invite Jesus to become the Lord of my life, to rule and reign in my heart. Please send your Holy Spirit to help me to obey You, and to do Your will in my life. In Jesus' name I pray, Amen."

Prayer is the simplest way of exercising faith which is necessary for God to save you. If you have faith enough to pray this simple prayer and invite God to come into your life and save you, He will.

Did you have faith enough to pray this? Then you really have received Jesus today. Welcome to God's family.

Christ has delivered you from the kingdom of darkness, and no demon or anything else can separate you from the eternal and everlasting love of God. You notice I use the term God and Jesus interchangeably. That is because they are both God. God arranged it so that he would come in human form in the sinless person of Jesus, called Immanuel (God *with* us); while God the Holy Spirit is God *in* us.

Jesus wants you to learn how to live in obedience to him. Are you willing to read his word in the Bible and meet with other believers to learn what he taught? Jesus promises that as we do these things we will grow closer to him as we follow up on our commitment. God has a master plan for you in this life and the next, and He will completely transform you.

- Tell someone else about your new faith in Christ.

- Spend time with God each day. Don't fret if you can't spend a long period of time, just develop a daily habit of praying to Him and reading his word in the Bible. Ask God to increase your faith and your understanding of his word.

- Seek fellowship with other followers of Jesus. A group of believing friends will answer your questions and support you and there are many online ministries operating today so you can always chat in a forum if physical fellowship is not possible.

- Find a local church where you can worship God.

- Get baptised as commanded by Christ.

Acts 2:38
"Repent, and let every one of you be baptised in the name of Jesus Christ for the remission of sins; and you shall receive the gift of the Holy Spirit."

Titus 3:5
"He saved us, not on the basis of deeds which we have done in righteousness, but according to His mercy, by the washing of regeneration and renewing by the Holy Spirit."

Ephesians 2:8-9
"For by grace you have been saved through faith; and that not of yourselves, it is the gift of God."

John 6:47
"Truly, truly I say to you, he who believes has eternal life."

Salvation is a FREE gift. When someone gives us a gift, we don't contribute anything to it. We just take it in the spirit it was offered. You must now be willing to get off your throne and let Jesus Christ be Lord of your life. If you do He will guide you into all truth and use you for His eternal purposes.

The Lord promises that anyone who comes to Him will *never* be turned away. No exclusions. That means drug addicts, alcoholics, prostitutes, homosexuals, murderers, women who've had abortions or men who have approved of them; Jesus says everyone qualifies to come to Him from the worst murderous dictator to the vilest terrorist.

Remember: It's only those who won't come to him that won't be saved.

The Bible confirms that unrepentant sinners will never come to the Lord.

John 5:40
"And ye will not come to me, that ye might have life."

Jesus didn't say "Ye cannot come"; but rather, "Ye will not come." The Scriptures clearly explain why they wouldn't come to Jesus to be saved.

John 3:20
"For every one that doeth evil hateth the light, neither cometh to the light, lest his deeds should be reproved."

Therefore, if a person sincerely comes to Jesus to be saved, even if they still have much sin in their life, Christ will save them as He promised. The very fact that they are coming to Christ to be saved is clear evidence of some degree of repentance in their heart. What is repentance? It means 'a change of mind', and recognising we are sinners in need of God's help.

Belief does not stand alone. Faith also means acting upon what Jesus taught and while God doesn't expect sinless perfection, true faith will be evidenced by a sincere attempt to lead a life pleasing to Jesus. Expect many failures, but keep getting back up and confess sin when it occurs.

John 14:21
"He that hath my commandments, and keepeth them, he it is that loveth me: and he that loveth me shall be loved of my Father, and I will love him, and will manifest myself to him."

The Holy Spirit will not enter anyone who is not 'born again', which simply means placing your faith in Jesus Christ. Then, you can know that Jesus is in you and you have His power and His victory.

There are many outstanding online resources which affirm the truth of salvation through Jesus Christ alone and how to be saved. Here is a selection available at the time of writing:

https://Bible.org/article/gods-plan-salvation
https://www.contendingfortruth.com
https://lifehopeandtruth.com/change/christian-conversion/god-

calling/
https://revelationsofjesuschrist.com/
https://www.exministries.com

CHAPTER 44.

Spiritual Refreshment

I said in the introduction of this book that if you are a mental illness sufferer there are life-enhancing things you can do to bring you to a place where your strength, joy and sense of happiness is restored.

First of all however, let me emphasise that if your mental illness has a demonic root to it rather than a physiological basis, it is impossible you will achieve a 'self-help' return to mental health without God's intervention.

That is why reading and acting on the previous chapter 'How to Be Saved' must be the key step you take before trying to begin a journey back to sanity in your own strength, because you cannot remove demonic spirits through your own power. They either have to leave themselves (not likely) or the Holy Spirit has to shift them. This is called 'deliverance'.

Deliverance

Once you have approached God in prayer and trusted in Jesus for salvation, only then can you expect deliverance. Deliverance is being made free from the bondage and penalty of sin, death and judgement. It is also deliverance from the demonic spirits possessing you, but that does not include deliverance from the bad habits that may have got you possessed or oppressed in the first place and it does not mean that we will not be attacked spiritually. Jesus and the disciples contended with Satan on many occasions. However, we can be delivered from their influence in our lives by using two weapons God has given us - the shield of faith as a defensive weapon and the offensive weapon of the Word of God, parts of our spiritual armour with which we battle the demonic powers of the world and the spiritual forces of evil. Other items of our spiritual arsenal include 'the breastplate of righteousness' and 'the helmet of salvation'.

Ephesians 6:12-17
For we wrestle not against flesh and blood, but against principalities, against

powers, against the rulers of the darkness of this world, against spiritual wickedness in high places.

*Wherefore take unto you **the whole armour of God**, that ye may be able to withstand in the evil day, and having done all, to stand.*

Stand therefore, having your loins girt about with truth, and having on the breastplate of righteousness; And your feet shod with the preparation of the gospel of peace; Above all, taking the shield of faith, wherewith ye shall be able to quench all the fiery darts of the wicked. And take the helmet of salvation, and the sword of the Spirit, which is the word of God.

As well as reading your Bible daily, it is very important for new Christians to have the support and prayerful help of other Christians. Joining a local church or Christian fellowship that places the Bible at the core of its fellowship and as a main resource for preaching and teaching is very important. A 'church' is not a structure or building but rather a body of believers who should believe that the Bible is the inspired and inerrant word of God and is the final authority on every church matter.

You may also find you need additional help from secular groups such as addiction counsellors if you have problems with drugs or alcohol addiction.

Believers can overcome their struggles with their past, old habits and addictions, because "everyone born of God overcomes the world" (1 John 5:4).

Expect results. God *promises* to help those who seek him and to give to those who ask him.

Matthew 7:7-8
"Ask, and it shall be given you; seek, and ye shall find; knock, and it shall be opened unto you: For every one that asketh receiveth; and he that seeketh findeth; and to him that knocketh it shall be opened."

I pray that with God's help you will find relief and rapid spiritual healing. If you said the prayer in the previous chapter there is no doubt that you have become a child of God in spite of any concern you may have to the contrary. Don't trust your feelings, trust God's promises.

If you have committed yourself to God's healing power by receiving Jesus Christ; inviting him to come in and change your life and acting upon what he teaches; you have just made the most important decision of your existence. There is no other step more important than the one you have just taken. Now that *is* a positive thought.

CHAPTER 45.

The Future is Bright

Positive thinking can be impossible if you have a crippling mental illness. There are many self-help gurus out there who haven't experienced the 'removal of hope' that say, depressive psychosis or schizophrenia elicits. Just getting out of bed and having a shower can feel like moving a mountain, never mind being told by some well-toned fitness fanatic you should 'snap out of it' and improve your mood by detoxing with a cleansing herbal tea while meditating on living in the present moment. That is easier said than done for even a healthy, functioning human being, never mind someone who is bipolar or schizophrenic and feeling suicidal.

Having experienced the grinding torture of mental illness, and knowing what I know now, I have listed some more helpful suggestions to assist and energise your journey back to spiritual vigour in the next chapter. These are steps which helped me move forward and which I am sure will also help you too.

Healing is a process that will vary from person to person. Your journey to mental health will certainly be different to mine, perhaps of different duration and with diverse experiences. We are all unique, with varied life histories, backgrounds and environments, and we all have different demons to expel, both metaphorically and literally.

But drawing close to God, filling our lives with him, and living through faith is the most effective way to make the environment intolerable or highly uncomfortable for a demonic presence to remain in or around you. Thankfully you are not relying on your own strength in the fight for deliverance, as you now have God on your side.

If you have invited Jesus into your life, God is now your Father and you are a child of God by adoption; however, although demons no longer have ownership of you, they can still attempt to undermine you, derail your commitment and cause difficulties.

One of the main ways Satan tries to derail your commitment is by throwing condemnation at you each time you sin. This is especially crushing after you have made a sincere commitment to Jesus Christ. Satan tries to convince you that Jesus won't forgive you for falling back into sin (again), but the bible tells us instead that Jesus Christ always hears and forgives a repentant sinner. Every time we slip up or backslide we go to God in prayer to ask for forgiveness. God knows our weaknesses.

1 John 1:9
If we confess our sins, he is faithful and just to forgive us our sins, and to cleanse us from all unrighteousness.

God does not promise a problem-free life, but he does promise that a life lived for him will be worth it, using all your problems to help you grow spiritually. God is not some kind of stern headmaster with a cane in his hand waiting to whack you every time you slip up, rather he wants everything you do in life to come from a heart filled with a true understanding of his loving-kindness.

Jesus Christ wants to take you as you are and transform you. He's going to take all your talents and make you into the person he designed you to be and he really has a great plan for your life.

Jeremiah 29:11
"For I know the plans I have for you," declares the LORD, "plans to prosper you and not to harm you, plans to give you hope and a future."

1 John 4:4
"Ye are of God, little children, and have overcome them (Satan and his demons): because greater is he that is in you (the Holy Spirit), than he that is in the world (Satan)."

CHAPTER 46.

15 Pieces of Advice for the Mentally Ill

There will be times when you are feeling less positive and demotivated (we are people living in a fallen, imperfect world), so here are some general pieces of advice I wish someone had given me when I was mentally ill, to help you on your journey; practical ones relating to your physical health; and spiritual ones to help you grow in faith.

1.   Remind yourself you will feel normal again

Fearful days with mental illness can be so bad you think you'll never get better. But you will. I can remember thinking I would never experience even humdrum normality again, never mind happiness, but that thought was just a demonic lie planted in my head.

When I did experience happiness again I recalled the time I wanted to kill myself and was so relieved I'd persevered through the darkness.

Imagine a bulb overwintering in deep soil in a wretchedly cold garden, up to its neck in blackness. That bulb does not recognise how close it is to bursting gloriously into the sunlight on the surface as it struggles upward. As all gardeners know, the blackest soils make better blooms. Without suffering no one grows. Even the most crippling depression once overcome has great value because experiencing deep darkness makes the light appear much brighter.

An important thing to note too is that happiness, while being a desirable component of life must not be expected all the time. Life is designed by God to have its challenges and ups and downs. Challenges and difficulties make us grow spiritually and are to be anticipated as an attribute of existence.

2.   Wean yourself off / reduce your medication

If you are taking psychiatric drugs as part of your treatment these can often prolong psychiatric problems. Prescription medications can keep you in a zombie-like state of inertia, neither getting any better or any worse. You must reduce prescription drugs in consultation with your GP or hospital; do not undertake it yourself, and please find out about the many dietary and alternative herbal remedies available for your condition.

Don't let your doctor brow-beat you into long-term drug use. Many doctors are quite ignorant about alternative treatments. You know you need to come off those medications at some point; you weren't designed by God to be a drug addict even if your pills are sourced from friendly and well-meaning people in white coats.

3.   Reduce the booze and stop the drugs

I understand the comfort of cigarette smoking and having a beer or a glass of wine when you are anxious and nervous. However, if you are using illegal street drugs such as cannabis, 'legal highs', opiates or psychedelics, you must stop now. Not only is this lifestyle physically damaging it is spiritually toxic and may wreck any hope of mental health improvement.

After getting saved I still smoked and drank for many years after coming to Jesus. It's difficult but not impossible to stop bad habits instantly, I know people who have, but it took me three or four attempts to stop smoking and as far as drinking beer and wine, I try to moderate this, but recognise I am still a work in progress.

Many mentally ill people need help overcoming physical addiction to medications, alcohol and street drugs too. Often the hardest part is removing yourself from the source of addiction, for example, other addicts who could tempt you back into the lifestyle, or in the case of an eating disorder illness, removing yourself from the 'triggers' of online materials or friendships that could seduce you back into anorexia or bulimia.

The drinking buddies and people you hang out with who still take drugs or who are still fixated by their eating disorder will be very unhappy you have started to turn your life around.

In the case of someone whose life has been moulded by an OCD entity, or an eating disorder spirit such as 'Ana' or 'Mia' you may also need the help of a skilled therapist to manage any lingering and habit-hardened negative thought processes. Support is very important.

Some good friends and family members too can also be infested with demons and will not want to see you filled with the light of God or to see the old you change. As you become filled with light and truth you become a mirror that reflects badly on them and makes the demons inside them fearful. Expect demonic spirits residing in people to mock or cynically deride the 'new you', calling you 'square' or a hypocrite is the usual method to try and undermine you.

Be aware that some counselling therapies designed to help overcome addiction can occasionally be guilty of prolonging it by keeping you focused on the habit, or giving you that sense of unity and belonging with other people in the counselling group who may inadvertently pull you back into destructive habits. This is not always the case however, and right judgement must be applied to each situation. Often a clean break from others and making new non-addict friends will be the only option.

4.   Be careful what you read, watch on TV or listen to

There are countless books, TV programmes and media channels that are depressing and downbeat; avoid them.

Sci-fi shows and fantasy genres certainly made my dismal moods dramatically worse during the darkest days of my illness, although you personally may find they don't. I did however, respond positively to watching sports or light-hearted quiz shows, which may not have improved my mood, but certainly didn't make it any worse. Most of all avoid the *horror* genre in books, TV or films and gaming. Horror is spiritually damaging in nature and feeds the mind with darkness rather than light.

Similarly, there are also many shows on the paranormal on television which contain frightening imagery as well as misleading messages; often promoting the false belief that exorcisms must always be undertaken by a Roman Catholic priest; an intervention which typically fails suggesting Jesus isn't powerful enough; only to be followed up by the successful intercession of a New Age healer or psychic who sympathetically communicates with the spirits or uses 'white witchcraft' such as *smudging with sage* to cleanse the home. White witchcraft and spirit communication will energise spirits rather than remove them because black and white witchcraft both share the same satanic root.

Pornography in all its forms must also be shunned. This addiction is as spiritually dangerous as drug abuse because porn, like drugs, feeds the pleasure receptors in the brain releasing dopamine. Dopamine receptors quickly become accustomed to a dopamine 'high' and will desire ever increasing concentrations, demanding more and more intense experiences, eventually leading a person into a life of depravity. People who have worked in the pornography industry such as Shelley Lubben,

258

now a born-again Christian and anti-pornography activist, describes the Porn Industry as "The Devil's Final Frontier", because it is only about money and evil.[44]

Music choices too are critical, as they can seriously affect your mood and attract negative entities. *Heavy Metal* and *Death Metal* genres are the worst types of music possible for a mental illness sufferer, but don't be deceived by mainstream pop music either; most pop songs have subliminal messages that promote drug taking, sexual promiscuity and even suicide, such are the satanic ethics of the music-industry, so be careful.

That said, much music can be therapeutic. Listening to the radio, particularly to light-hearted radio chat shows can be great company if you are lonely and an excellent distraction from despairing self-focus and rumination.

5.   Shun loneliness, but avoid noisy crowds

Isolation isn't healthy, but neither are harsh, noisy places packed with anonymous strangers where the atmosphere can feel threatening or intimidating. Rather, seek out good, gentle company as much as you can, whether that is with family, neighbours or friends; perhaps in a local coffee shop, or community centre.

I realise if you are young, the temptation to head to bars and clubs will be strong, but the din of pubs and nightclubs can exacerbate your condition as well as being expensive and will not provide the ambience you need for easy conversation or meditation. Again, you may respond to noisier stimuli better than I did, so to each their own.

6.   Join a Community Church / Christian Fellowship Group

No man is an island, and each of us needs the backing of the wider community. I truly value my Christian friends and the wider Christian outreach community, who effectively support and pray for one other, providing long term spiritual guidance and pastoral support.

Find a Christian church and present yourself to them, with all of your problems. Authentic Christians will want to help you and you will very likely find some who have experienced similar problems to your own so you will have support and common ground immediately. If you are a bit shy, just phone the church pastor or vicar in the first instance to introduce yourself or you could even take a friend to the initial service. It is very important to have a Christian support network around you who can pray for your healing and who can answer questions and doubts you may have about your spiritual journey.

7. Read your Bible daily

Escape into the comfort of the Scriptures. You will be refreshed and sustained by reading God's word.

I had a small Gideon's Bible from school and this was amazing because it included a Guidance in Life or 'Helps' section in the front which pointed me to pages relating to the issues I was dealing with on a particular day, for example: 'Afraid of the future' directed me to *Psalm 23 or Matthew 6: 25-34,* or 'Faith is Weak' would take me to *1 Thessalonians 3; or John 6.*

God's word has incredible power. That little Bible turbo-charged my spiritual growth and increased my faith daily.

The Lord has incredible patience to lead you through the process of trusting him. God knows that experiencing all that the Christian life is intended to give requires great faith. Jesus said, *"Blessed are those who have not seen and yet have believed"* (John 20:29). If you find yourself fearful, worried, or doubting, it is all right. Just don't stay there! Search out God's promises *"casting all your anxieties on him, because he cares for you"* (1 Peter 5:7).

8. Pray

Find a quiet time to pray to God and tell him exactly how you are feeling. Ask him for his help and be patient, knowing he has heard your requests.

You may find periods where your faith is at a low point, when things aren't happening as fast as you would like them to, but God does things according to his timetable, knowing that his future for you is wonderful.

It doesn't matter how eloquently you pray, just be sincere; God knows what you need even before you ask him, and the Holy Spirit promises to intercede for us when we can't find the words:

Romans 8:26
Likewise the Spirit also helpeth our infirmities: for we know not what we should pray for as we ought: but the Spirit itself maketh intercession for us with groanings which cannot be uttered.

9. Eat healthily

You are body, mind and spirit. Eating healthily especially boosting depleted vitamin C and vitamin D levels can help you physically and mentally.

Fill your body with great nutrition and your mind will respond. Foods high in omega-3 fatty acids, such as salmon, herring, sardines and mackerel), seaweed, chicken fed on flaxseed; and walnuts, have been shown to reduce symptoms of schizophrenia, depression, ADHD and other disorders.

Foods rich in magnesium such as almonds, spinach, pumpkin seeds and dark chocolate can help with anxiety and depression. You can search many further suggestions online about diets specifically for depression and anxiety with explanations on how certain foods and nutrients can help improve your mood. A much better option than prescription drugs.

10.   Exercise

I can't emphasise enough how helpful a good workout can be for improving your mood. If you think of your body as a planet, you need fresh water, sunlight, a balanced ecology and a clean and healthy 'atmosphere' for it to thrive.

All exercise is good, but outdoor exercise is better. Fresh air is so important and taking in the world around you rather than self-focusing is something you really should do.

Sunlight hitting the back of the retina can stimulate lots of happy chemicals in the brain while exercise helps you manage anxiety and get much needed oxygen pumping through your veins. Activity also stimulates brain chemicals that help nerve cell growth and boosts neurotransmitters such as serotonin that influence mood and produce a stress-reducing hormone called ANP which helps the brain respond to stress and anxiety effectively.

Try and push yourself to go outdoors daily whatever the weather; appreciating each season, the trees, flowers, birds, insects; the different skies, clouds and shades of light. You will end up meeting and talking to new people and making new friends in the most unlikely places.

A change of scenery is a great tonic especially on a sunny day with its refreshing natural beauty and birdsong. Whether it's a brisk walk or a five mile run, you will discover many positive effects, exploring new perspectives away from yourself and your worries.

God's creation contains astonishing beauty, with daily miracles we take completely for granted such as the birth of a baby, the scent of a rose, the beauty of trees and flowers, the fruitfulness of the earth, the wonder of the animal kingdom and the changing seasons, to mention just a few.

Nature is particularly pleasant outside the winter months (dreary winters in the UK can be particularly depressing), so when the sun is shining you need to make the most of the opportunity to enjoy the natural world around you.

Anything pleasant that can connect your mind and soul with the truth and beauty of God's wonderful flora and fauna will benefit you. Demonic spirits hate God's creation and will do everything possible to destroy it.

Demons do not like metaphorical light (exposure), and I am also persuaded they have a huge aversion to physical light too. Although they can still operate during the day, they do not appear to be as powerful as during the hours of darkness.

11.   Clean up

Cleaning up is exercise with benefits. This may be mundane, but tidying the house, DIY, gardening or painting & decorating have many advantages, not least because they all improve your surroundings which can give you a great sense of achievement. Anything that gets you out of your bed and starts muscles moving and blood pumping will pay dividends. Once you get started, you're on a roll...

Having a junk clear-out can be a great tonic too. A clutter-free environment can significantly improve your mood, especially if there is a financial boost through selling old unwanted items on eBay or at the local car boot sale. Tackle a job at a time, and measure the mood-enhancing results.

If you have a sense of purpose in your life even if it is one task a day, it can be a positive distraction from your anxieties.

If you can muster the confidence, start a new project, or simply go and volunteer to do something useful like helping a neighbour or spending time working in a charity shop or community centre, or simply do a random act of kindness. You never know what might result from it.

I know that unemployment is a terrible blow and is often a trigger for mental illness, but sometimes, just doing anything, even without getting paid can bring you an increased level of self-esteem, like cooking a dinner or baking a cake. Why not add fruit or berry-picking to one of your walks and try your hand at jam making?

Other great activities include cycling, fishing, camping, birdwatching, gardening, and art-related activities such as sculpture, model making, and painting. There are many local art and creative groups as well as gardening and allotment clubs for people with little money which can also help you develop new friendships.

If I'm making this sound easy, forgive me. It's not; you really have to force yourself to take action because the alternative - inactivity - is much worse.

12.   Take a break and get a new perspective

A change of scenery can be highly effective therapy, especially if you feel your environment is locking you into a state of depression. I realise that holidays and vacations can be expensive, but you don't have to spend fortunes, especially with great value 'Airbnb' accommodation and even less expensive camping opportunities.

If you are lonely or finances are in disarray, there are various budget coach trips advertised in local papers that are very popular for people wanting to meet and make new friends. Some of the deals are amazing. There are also hardship and mental illness charities which may be able to provide you with financial assistance.

I assure you that there are many people caught up in the trap of making millions in the City or who are so encumbered by the demands of their career they have a far poorer existence than someone with little money, but who has the time and the imagination to appreciate the true riches available for free, simply by having close family relationships, community friendships and contemplating Gods' wonderful creation.

As Christians, we live in the world, but that doesn't mean becoming 'worldly'. God wants you to reject the vanity of this temporary world system with all its greed, selfishness, lusts, desire to show off and pride of life. If you cling onto these things as though that's all there is, you will constantly be worrying about how much you have; measuring success by comparing your life with others and you will never be satisfied. Your life does not consist in the abundance of your possessions or how many holidays you go on, or things you've ticked off a bucket list. True riches are knowing you are a loved child of God who is soon to experience all the infinite joys of Heaven in all their wondrous variety, eternally.

13.   Listen to SermonAudio.com and other online resources

Websites hadn't been invented when I was suffering mental illness back in 1983/4, but latterly I found www.sermonaudio.com to be an amazing online resource for biblical sermons and a fount of strength and spiritual comfort. You can search the sermons by subject, Bible passage, preacher and church. This resource is free and you can stream or download uplifting teachings on video or podcast to listen to whenever you need some spiritual guidance. I particularly recommend you hear or read the sermons of Victorian preacher, Charles Haddon Spurgeon.

I personally subscribe to a daily email from a ministry called First15, an online Christian resource helping people set aside fifteen minutes a day in a quiet time of Bible reading and prayer. It is an excellent devotional resource that relates Scripture to daily life with reflection, prayer, musical worship and a daily call to action. To get devotionals sent to your inbox you can sign up on www.first15.org. For something meatier, try www.contendingfortruth.com.

14.   Talking

Communicating how you feel to a trusted friend or family member can help you cope. As you wean yourself off medications, most of us find talking about our progress and problems highly beneficial. If you have found the support of a local community group or church then that is a great place to meet others for company and encouragement.

There are also many psychotherapy treatments available, such as Cognitive Behavioural Therapy (CBT) and Neuro Linguistic Programming (NLP). Such treatments can be far more effective long-term than drug treatments for managing psychiatric problems. However, you will have noticed there is an unprecedented intolerance of Christianity in the world today and if you start talking about the truth of real demons in one of these sessions they'll probably roll their eyes and say your belief in Christianity is part of your problem. I would think that finding a Christian psychotherapist will be a significant challenge in itself.

Be warned, there are many therapies that are highly 'New Age' and can attract spiritual entities, these include transcendental meditation, Reiki and Kundalini Yoga. Avoid. These also tend to focus on the self with the message of 'nothing can bring you peace but yourself' and 'trust in yourself' or 'love yourself' with the attitude that it's all dependent on you; how well you breathe, or focus, or 'let go', and so on. Remember, it's not all dependent on you when you trust in Jesus Christ.

Charles Spurgeon, the great English preacher said, "Walk with God, and you cannot mistake the road; you have infallible wisdom to direct you, permanent love to comfort you, and eternal power to defend you."

Beware of the many people who will do their utmost to undermine your faith. These are often well meaning people and you need to be on your guard against such spiritual negativity especially when it comes from the mouths of unsaved friends and family members who are 'trying to help'. I had discouragement in my early Christian walk from members of my own family blinded by TV programming believing the lie that being a Christian was tantamount to belonging to a dangerous cult.

15.   Manage despairing thoughts

Don't ever toy with suicidal thoughts.

God never directs people to suicide, only demons do. Suicide is a permanent and demonic answer to a temporary problem.

If you are tempted to suicide, you need to pray to God for strength and guidance to help you handle the immediate crisis as well as find someone physical to talk to. If you have managed to find the support of a local community group or church, you need to seek them out immediately or if it is in the middle of the night and you are isolated, please phone the Samaritans: 116 123 (UK) 116 123 (ROI). If you are reading this in another country be sure to write down the telephone numbers that apply to you.

Suicide is NEVER an option. Ever.

CHAPTER 47.

Words of Wisdom for Recovery

Here are some encouraging Bible verses and words of wisdom from other sources to keep you on track with your recovery:

Bible verses:

Matthew 11:28
"Come unto me, all ye that labour and are heavy laden, and I will give you rest."

John 6:37
"All that the Father giveth me shall come to me; and him that cometh to me I will in no wise cast out."

2 Corinthians 5:17
"Therefore if any man be in Christ, he is a new creature: old things are passed away; behold, all things are become new."

John 10:28-29
"And I give unto them eternal life; and they shall never perish, neither shall any man pluck them out of my hand. My Father, which gave them me, is greater than all; and no man is able to pluck them out of my Father's hand."

Romans 8:38-39
"For I am persuaded, that neither death, nor life, nor angels, nor principalities, nor powers, nor things present, nor things to come, nor height, nor depth, nor any other creature, shall be able to separate us from the love of God, which is in Christ Jesus our Lord."

Colossians 1:13-14
(God) Who hath delivered us from the power of darkness, and hath translated us into the kingdom of his dear Son. In whom we have redemption through his blood, even the forgiveness of sins.

1 John 4:4
"Ye are of God, little children, and have overcome them (Satan and his demons): because greater is he that is in you (the Holy Spirit), than he that is in the world (Satan)."

Psalm 23:4

Yea, though I walk through the valley of the shadow of death, I will fear no evil: for thou art with me; thy rod and thy staff they comfort me.

Psalm 91:15

He shall call upon me, and I will answer him: I will be with him in trouble; I will deliver him, and honour him.

Psalm 34:4

I sought the Lord, and he heard me, and delivered me from all my fears.

1 Peter 1:3-4

He has caused us to be born again to a living hope through the resurrection of Jesus Christ from the dead, to an inheritance that is imperishable, undefiled, and unfading, kept in heaven for you…

Non-biblical quotes:

Nothing diminishes anxiety faster than action! – Anonymous

In the darkest of nights cling to the assurance that God loves you, that He always has advice for you, a path that you can tread and a solution to your problem - and you will experience that which you believe. God never disappoints anyone who places his trust in Him. - Basilea Schlink

The Holy Ghost is a comforter and a guide. But it is also a cleansing agent. That is why service in the kingdom is so crucial to enduring. When we are called to serve, we can pray for the Holy Ghost to be our companion with assurance it will come. - Henry B. Eyring

Our assurance is anchored in the love and grace of God expressed in the glorious exchange: our sin for His righteousness. - Tullian Tchividjian

Through reading the scriptures, we can gain the assurance of the Spirit that that which we read has come of God for the enlightenment, blessing, and joy of his children. - Gordon B. Hinckley

Earth has no sorrow that Heaven cannot heal. - Thomas Moore

The whole point of Heaven is to relieve us of the suffering, pain, death and tears brought into the world by the evil of humanity. That is why God says that in Heaven there will be no more sorrow, pain, death or crying. - David Brandt Berg.

References:

[1]*http://www.notapushymum.com/subpage13.html*

[2]https://www.newscientist.com/article/dn14250-microwave-ray-gun-controls-crowds-with-noise/

[3]*http://www.dailymail.co.uk/femail/article-2203593/My-midlife-meltdown-MARIAN-KEYES-tells-terrifying-story-detailing-reality-breakdown.html*

[4]Abridged from: The Epidemic of Mental Illness: Why? Marcia Angell June 2011 *http://www.nybooks.com/articles/2011/06/23/epidemic-mental-illness-why/*

[5]https://www.drugs.com/sfx/prozac-side-effects.html:

[6]*http://nationalpsychologist.com/2014/09/mass-shooters-received-only-limited-treatment/102638.html*

[7]http://www.mirror.co.uk/news/uk-news/selling-nhs-profit-full-list-4646154

[8]https://naturallyhealthynews.info/investigation-mps-and-sage-heavily-invested-in-vaccine-industry/

[9]https://wellnessandequality.com/2016/06/20/how-much-money-do-pediatricians-really-make-from-vaccines/

[10]http://abcnews.go.com/Politics/rand-paul-vaccines-lead-mental-disorders/story?id=28675890

[11]http://www.naturalnews.com/047072_MMR_vaccine_autism_government_coverup.html

[12]http://www.telegraph.co.uk/lifestyle/wellbeing/10076221/Malcolm-Brabant-I-suffered-psychosis-after-a-routine-injection.html

[13]http://www.independent.co.uk/life-style/health-and-families/health-news/lariam-hundreds-of-british-soldiers-suffering-from-mental-illness-after-being-given-anti-malarial-10179792.html

[14] http://vaccineriskawareness.com/pfizer-covid-19-vaccination-pdf-leaflet/

[15] https://www.amazon.co.uk/LSD-problem-child-Albert-Hofmann/dp/0199639418#reader_0199639418

[16] Original quote from Wired Magazine article from 2006. Link no longer available https://www.wired.com/2006/01/lsd-the-geeks-wonder-drug/

[17] https://blogs.scientificamerican.com/cross-check/tripping-in-lsds-birthplace-a-story-for-e2809cbicycle-daye2809d/

[18] http://www.alternet.org/drugs/dreaded-bad-trip-lsd-researchers-are-starting-understand-what-causes-them

[19] https://blogs.scientificamerican.com/cross-check/dmt-is-in-your-head-but-it-may-be-too-weird-for-the-psychedelic-renaissance/

[20] https://www.ncbi.nlm.nih.gov/pmc/articles/PMC4756795/

[21] http://www.naturalnews.com/049367_aborted_babies_flavor_chemicals_food_corporations.html

[22] http://www.bruceonpolitics.com/2017/07/14/secret-society-runs-great-britain/

[23] http://www.dailymail.co.uk/news/article-3320458/BBC-radio-presenter-sacked-calling-Christian-campaigner-bigoted-saying-homosexuality-sin.html

[24] https://www.womenarehuman.com/drag-queen-storytime-under-the-spotlight/

[25] https://www.theguardian.com/sport/2020/dec/07/study-suggests-ioc-adjustment-period-for-trans-women-may-be-too-short

[26] http://lgbt.foundation/About-us/media/facts-and-figures/#mental

[27] http://www.josephnicolosi.com/an-open-secret-the-truth-about/

[28] https://biblicalfoundations.weebly.com/allah-in-history.

[29] Sir Winston Spencer Churchill (The River War, first edition, Vol. II, pages 248-50 (London: Longmans, Green & Co., 1899).

30http://www.crossroad.to/articles2/2012/James/freemasonry-queen.htm

31http://www.dailymail.co.uk/news/article-4276336/MS-13-gang-members-accused-Satanic-rape-murder.html#ixzz4jJiPN863

32http://www.houstonpress.com/news/santa-muerte-patron-saint-of-the-drug-war-6595544

33http://www.illuminati-news.com/art-and-mc/index2.htm

34Abridged from:
http://www.goodnewsaboutgod.com/studies/spiritual/home_study/alien_hoax.htm

35*Neuropsychological Bases of God Beliefs*, Michael A. Persinger, Ph.D.

36https://www.webmd.com/infertility-and-reproduction/news/20080919/cell-phone-use-linked-male-infertility

37https://doi.org/10.1016/j.jchemneu.2015.08.001

38https://www.scmp.com/video/world/3129903/china-us-scientists-create-worlds-first-human-monkey-chimera-embryo-amid

39https://www.theguardian.com/science/2016/aug/18/fake-human-sacrifice-filmed-at-cern-with-pranking-scientists-suspected

40https://news.rice.edu/2019/12/18/quantum-dot-tattoos-hold-vaccination-record/

41https://www.susanblackmore.uk/wp-content/uploads/2017/05/Abduction-by-Aliens-or-Sleep-Paralysis.pdf

42http://www.alienresistance.org/ufo-alien-deception/alienabductions-stop-in-the-name-jesus-christ/

43https://cases.open.ubc.ca/monsanto-and-terminator-seeds/

44https://www.facebook.com/shelleylubben and Shelley Lubben, Truth Behind the Fantasy of Porn

Printed in Great Britain
by Amazon

39340874R00155